ANNA
SEWELL
*The Woman
Who Wrote*
BLACK
BEAUTY

Your very loving Sister
Anna Sewell

ANNA SEWELL

*The Woman
Who Wrote*

BLACK BEAUTY

Susan Chitty

TEMPUS

About the Author

Having read history at Somerville College, Oxford and starting a career in journalism, Susan Chitty's first book *The Diary of a Fashion Model*, originally appeared in serial form in *Punch*. She has since written several other books, including *That Singular Person Called Lear*, the biography of Edward Lear (also published by Tempus) and *My Life and Horses*. She lives in West Sussex with her husband, the writer Thomas Hinde.

For Andrew and Cordelia
Without whom this book would not have been begun
and for Miranda
In spite of whom it was completed

First published 1971 by Hodder and Stoughton
This edition first published 2007

Tempus Publishing Limited
The Mill, Brimscombe Port,
Stroud, Gloucestershire, GL5 2QG
www.tempus-publishing.com

British Library Cataloguing in Publication Data.
A catalogue record for this book is available from the British Library.

ISBN 978 07524 4282 2

Typesetting and origination by Tempus Publishing Limited
Printed and bound in Great Britain

CONTENTS

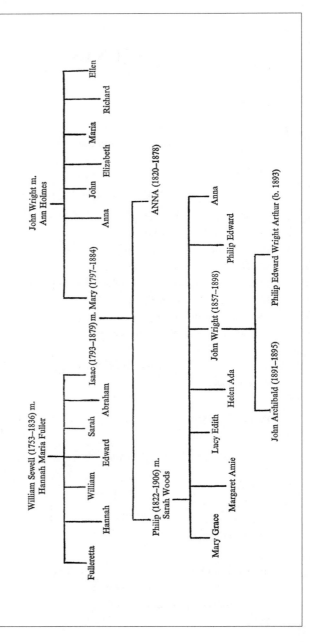

FAMILY TREE OF ANNA SEWELL

PREFACE

I wrote this book because a full-length life of Anna Sewell had never been written. *Black Beauty* was probably the most successful animal story ever written. To date it is estimated to have sold over thirty million copies and is said to be the sixth bestseller in the English language. Yet the name of its author does not even appear in the *Dictionary of National Biography* and many of the biographical notes introducing editions of her book are wildly inaccurate.

My qualifications for undertaking the task were based chiefly on a great love of the book. As a child I had read it regularly and can still raise a tear for poor Ginger. I did not claim to be a professional historian, though reading history at Oxford had given me at least a knowledge of the rudiments of the discipline. I did have some practical knowledge of horses.

The more I discovered about this lifelong invalid who wrote her only book in her fifties, sold it outright for twenty pounds and never lived to know of its colossal success, the more worthwhile it seemed to me to chronicle her life and seek out her inspiration. In parallel to this I tried to verify my rather vague impression that the book had been the greatest single influence in promoting the humane treatment of horses – and in particular the abolition of the bearing-rein, both in England and America. My researches took me to such different and sometimes remote places as the offices of Massachusetts humane societies and the East End slums.

Readers of my book may complain that it is as much a biography of Anna's mother, Mary Sewell, as it is of Anna herself. I do not deny the charge. The lives of the two women were so closely quilted together that it is impossible to tell the story of one without including that of the other. Mary Sewell was an authoress with a strong personality and Anna, because she never married, never escaped from her domination. Her mother survived her by six years.

I may also be accused of having failed to fully diagnose the mysterious illness that dogged Anna Sewell most of her life. This is not for lack of trying. The ignorance of the medical profession a hundred years ago was considerable and there remains no specific account of Anna's symptoms on which a modern medical expert could base a diagnosis. I was assisted to the tentative conclusions I have reached about the causes of her ill-health by Dr John Parsons of the Medical Research Council and I am deeply grateful to him for his help.

The list of others who have advised me would fill several pages. I can mention only a few here. They are Margaret J. Baker (author of the children's biography *Anna Sewell and Black Beauty*), Yvonne Franklin (who did research in Norfolk for me), Edward H. Milligan (librarian of the Friends' House Library), Peter Edwards (who lent me invaluable books on his relations the Sewells), Judith Williams, Dr C.E. Briscoe, Margaret Lucy Barne, Michael Metford Sewell, Anna Charlotte Sewell, Fr. Brocard Sewell, Major A.J. Crewdson and Dr J. Reiss (all connections of the Sewell family), my father, Rudolph Glossop F.G.S. (who commented on the geological works of Anne Wright for me), my mother Antonia White, and my husband Thomas Hinde who both commented on the manuscript.

I would also like to thank the following: A.B. Catling, H.B. Carter, John Waynflete Carter, Mr and Mrs David Clarkson, A.A. Dent, E.D. Folkes, A.A.C. Hedges (Great Yarmouth Borough Librarian and Curator), Philip Hepworth (Norwich City Librarian), T.W.J. Hurley (headmaster of the Red House School), John Jarrold, Phyllis Jones, C.J. Long (Hackney Borough Librarian), Miss Lee Warner, Canon A.F. Marsham, Len Mauley (Assistant P.R.O., Hackney Town Hall), Arthur W. Moss (author of *The Valiant Crusade*), Daisy Newman, S.C. Newton (East Sussex County Archivist), T. Richardson (P.R.O. of the R.S.P.C.A.), A.C. Shilling, A.J. Shirren, Will Warren, Mr and Mrs Mark Wathen and Mrs. Geoffrey Williamson.

Susan Chitty
West Hoathly, 1971

ILLUSTRATIONS

Key to acknowledgments

1 The Society of Friends Library

2 Thomas Hinde

3 The Yarmouth Mercury

4 The History of Yarrolds 1823–1923, Norwich, 1924

5 Peter Edwardes

PART I

MARY
SEWELL

MARY SEWELL

Anna Sewell was born at Yarmouth in 1820. Her parents, Isaac and
Mary, were both of Norfolk Quaker stock and her grandfather,
William Sewell, was a leading citizen in Yarmouth in his day. He
owned a large grocer's shop in the market place, and the opinion of Quaker Sewell had much weight in the town. He and his
wife, Hannah Maria, dominated the Friends' Meeting House. The
couple held the offices of preacher, elder and overseer at different
times and frequently all at once. William Sewell's origins, however,
were humble. His father Abraham Sewel (it was William who added
the second 'l') was described as a 'common carrier of Swaffham
and Wereham'. (Swaffham is a town thirty miles west of Norwich,
and Wereham is a neighbouring village.) Abraham's father was Isaac
and Isaac's father was another Abraham born in Yarmouth around
1640. This first Abraham is the earliest direct ancestor of Anna to be
traced. It is possible that he was a son of William Sewel who was
a freeman of Yarmouth in 1639. In Norwich, Quaker Sewels were
imprisoned for their faith between 1656 and 1660.

William and Hannah Maria had six other children besides Anna's
father Isaac. Their names were Hannah Maria, Fulleretta, Sarah,
William, Abraham and Edward. Isaac, born in 1794, was the youngest. Little is known of his childhood. It seems probable that he and
his brothers and sisters were educated by a tutor, some 'faithful
Friend' no doubt, for his parents would have insisted on a 'suitable
and guarded education' for their children. They were trained in strict
business habits and were set to work in the shop as soon as they
were old enough. This did not, however, cause them to become
'mere shop men and women'. On the contrary, Quaker Sewell was

not as narrow-minded in intellectual matters as might have been expected. He was very watchful over his sons, 'promoting in every way their intellectual studies'. He even founded a society called the Demosthenians which gathered at his house. At meetings, his sons and the other young men who worked in his shop read their essays to the young ladies. Later the young ladies formed a society of their own, called the Agenorians and read their essays to the young men.

We are better informed about the childhood of Anna's mother because, at the age of eighty-four, she wrote her *Reminiscences* for the benefit of her grandchildren. Mary Sewell was born in 1797, also one of a family of seven. Her father was John Wright of Felthorpe Farm. The Wrights had been Friends 'since the time of the Commonwealth when George Fox was a preacher'. John Wright's father had been a man of some education. As a boy he received tuition from a clergy-man at Coltishall and as a young man he completed his education in Holland, for at that time there was a lively trade between the two countries. He was respected as an arbitrator in his village but, in spite of marrying twice, he had no children. When his second wife died he resolved to remain a widower but was strongly persuaded to the contrary by Cousin Wright, a childless relative who promised that if John should have children and die he would be a father to them. Cousin Wright lived to rue his promise, for Mary's grandfather proceeded to marry and father six children (two boys and four girls) and then die. Cousin Wright was faithful to his promise, however, and often had the girls to stay at his house, where they were made thoroughly miserable by his jealous wife and mother-in-law.

Cousin Wright is a rather mysterious figure. He was a wealthy banker and, although he was a Quaker, he lived in some splendour in his mansion at Esher. He drove a coach and four up to the City, and his black horses were so fine that it is said that they were put to the Lord Mayor's coach on ceremonial occasions. The banking house in which he was a partner was Smith, Wright and Gray, a considerable bank at that time. On one occasion there was a general run upon the banks in the City. The head clerk of their bank had a hogshead rolled into the Exchange and, mounting it, proclaimed that anyone who wished to settle his account with Smith, Wright and Gray could be immediately paid. This restored confidence and the bank was not affected. Over a thousand private banks were less fortunate between

1793 and 1818, including of course, the one which held Miss Matty of Cranford's account.

The school to which Cousin Wright ultimately sent Mary's father, John, and her uncle, Richard, was Ackworth, the famous Quaker school in Yorkshire. They must have been among the first pupils at Ackworth, which was established around 1780, in the buildings of an abandoned hospital for the benefit of children 'whose parents were not in affluence'. A contemporary lithograph shows the school buildings as exceptionally elegant, the original hospital being attached by colonnades to the girls' and boys' wings which flanked it. Life within, however, was far from elegant and the discipline, even in those days of rugged schooling, was prison-like. Mary Sewell wrote of 'stone stair, stone floors – nothing to comfort the desires of the flesh in dress, food or affection'. Sarah Stickney Ellis, herself a pupil at the school, enlarged on the way of life there in *Friends at their own Fireside*. The uniform for boys consisted of 'a long grey coat and leathern lower garments'. Wooden trenchers were supplied for 'food, moist and dry; and on two days of the week it was very moist indeed. This … had to be taken up as might be with a narrow knife and often a strangely distorted fork of two prongs. Twice during the meal a tin can was passed down the table. On its first journey it contained water and on its second exceedingly small beer.'

According to Mary Sewell,

> Children were taken into this school very young, as early, I think, as seven or eight, and did not leave till they could be apprenticed at fourteen or fifteen. There was no regular holiday all this time, so that unless the parents or friends could afford to visit the children they might almost forget even their appearance.

Disease and death entered the school, not surprisingly, almost as soon as it was established. The minute books of the period include such entries as 'there died of smallpox three boys in the natural way'. A school rule specified that parents should pay a guinea for each child that took the disease and an extra guinea for funeral expenses in case of death. By way of recompense for these discomforts, the children were instructed in reading, writing and arithmetic, and given the run of a library stocked mostly with Quaker biographies.

But let Mary continue the story of her father's schooldays.

Poor John and Richard found themselves in chains. Richard, especially, was always in disgrace, from his unbounded spirits, his exuberant
wit, and ingenuity – always a leader of malcontents and adventurers.
The boys at Ackworth had to mend their own stockings – to my uncle
a most repulsive occupation. In order to extract a little fun out of
it, he on one occasion quilted a ball into the calf of the leg, and wore
it, attracting attention to it, as if it were a part of his leg.

The awful superior of the school was named Don Bavon (Mary
Sewell spelt the name thus) and when a grave misdemeanour had
been committed, the delinquent was summoned before the green
cloth on a long table, at the head of which sat Don Bavon. I never
heard in what the awe of his presence consisted, but there must have
been something either in his bearing or his judgements which caused
the green cloth to be mentioned with very solemn countenance. One
day my father was summoned into his presence for a very heinous
offence. He had caught a fly, and had daintily attached a piece of
down to its wing and sent it off on its rambles during school-time,
which of course excited amusement. The offence was noted with all
solemnity in the notebook of the school, having caused considerable
disorder. On another occasion my father was summoned before Don
Bavon, and was informed that his mother was dead, and that he should
communicate the information to his brother, Richard. My father,
wishing to do this gently, probably used the master's word and said,
'Richard, we have lost our mother.' 'Well,' said my uncle, 'I suppose
they will find her again.' Nothing more passed; probably he had no
explanation to give, and my uncle did not, till a long time afterward,
realise what had really happened.

When the boys left school, Richard was apprenticed to a buckle-
maker and John sent to learn farming with John Holmes of Tivetshall,
in Norfolk. It was here that he met his future wife, Ann Holmes.
John Holmes was a Quaker of the old school.

A tall, gaunt man, with what would have been a handsome countenance had the expression been more genial. He was very tall and
strong-built, with black eyes, strong eyebrows and good features; his

complexion was dark, and his hair was all combed back from his forehead. He wore a very broad-brimmed black beaver hat, looped up with three silk loops – not sharply cocked – no hat of the present day can compare with it in dignity and costliness; it gave a reverent aspect, well suited to those who took their place in the preaching gallery. His coat, waistcoat with deep pockets, and breeches buckled at the knees with silver buckles, were all one colour – very dark brown. His shoes had large buckles, and he wore a white cravat.

John Holmes had a violent temper and there were often rows with his six stalwart sons. Mary's father used to say of his household, 'that was a rough house' and told her a story to illustrate the point.

At harvest time John Holmes was supervising the storing of the wheat in his barn where it would await threshing during the winter. In order to pile the wheat up firmly to the top of the barn, a horse was kept upon it which a boy rode about to keep all level. This was called 'riding the goaf'. When it was piled up as high as was convenient, the horse had to be let down which was not so easily accomplished. The horse proved rather averse to the manoeuvre and the sons were arranging matters at the top of the goaf while the father grew impatient at the bottom, and at last gave peremptory orders to let it off, which was complied with, and the horse fell and broke its neck. It will throw some little light upon the scene to know that, on the part of the sons, there was no decided lamentation.

Mrs Holmes was an altogether gentler person, always referred to affectionately as the 'dear cretur' by her two daughters. Under her large white apron was a place of refuge for her little grandchildren when there were storms outside. But her life was not an easy one. All the washing, brewing, baking, cooking and needlework were done at home and the dairy work took up a large part of her day. On market day she would ride pillion to Norwich market and 'sit the market' as it was called.

To her daughter Ann Holmes, labouring in the dairy, the still-room and the kitchen from early morning until late at night, the educated young man who had come to learn farming appeared a veritable 'gentle squire'. She was fifteen at the time and 'comely ... and pleasant to look upon; her face was square, her eyes brown, and her hair black'. Intellectually she was no match for John Wright and Mary always felt it was pity rather than love that first drew her father to her mother. Nevertheless, the marriage, which took place five years later in the presence of 'Cousin Wright and a goodly company of Gurneys and others', proved a happy one. 'My mother,' wrote Mary Sewell, 'was remarkable for sound judgement, kind feeling, and common sense; she did not damp my father's greater enthusiasm, but probably she moderated it; and if he did not find her a strictly intellectual companion, he found her an excellent helpmeet, a good manager, industrious, neat and very orderly.'

Yet it was for her father that Mary Sewell's admiration reached its peak.

> Many a little family has for itself its hero or heroine. I want to try to immortalise my father in the memory of his descendants. He lives in my heart and memory as a hero who, if education and circumstances had favoured him, would have been a leading man in almost any place. He was refined in every thought, word and action; vulgarity and meanness could not approach him; he was an ardent patriot, and as a husband, father, master and neighbour he could not be surpassed. From my childhood to old age I can never remember anything that in the slightest degree impairs my admiration, veneration and deep love. I always feel that my words cannot represent the full glow in which I ever see him stand.

John and Ann Wright lived in Buxton, a village six miles north of Norwich, when they were first married, and there were born their first two children, Anna and John. Cousin Wright was duly invited to the christening of the heir and Ann Wright brought everything into requisition to entertain him suitably. It was something at a farm-house to have a carriage and four drive up to the door. Her efforts were rewarded for, as Cousin Wright leant over the cradle, he said, 'Nancy, that boy is my heir, and thee will ride in thy carriage.' Shortly afterwards the banker established the couple on one of his farms at Sutton in Suffolk, and it was here that Mary was born in 1797. The family were back within a few miles of Buxton, on Cousin Wright's farm at Felthorpe, before she was two, and it was at Felthorpe Farm that Mary spent her childhood and that her younger brothers and sisters, Elizabeth, Maria and Richard were born.

The farm was a large one (800 acres) but the land poor. Half of it was heath and woodland, and the remainder a poor sandy soil that had been reclaimed from heath. The trees were mostly oak and Scotch fir. Cousin Wright was the first man in Norfolk to plant these firs with a view to timber. At first this was called by the gentry 'Wright's Folly', but the folly in a few years was accounted wisdom, and the Royal Society presented him with a handsome gold medal.

Mary's father, John Wright, did his best to render this land fertile with a large flock of sheep, the nightly folding of which in field after field was profitable for the poor, dry land and saved the necessity of bringing manure by wagon from Norwich. He was a progressive farmer and influenced by his famous neighbour, Thomas Coke of Holkham. Holkham Hall was twenty-five miles north-west of Felthorpe, near the coast, and he visited it once a year for the famous sheep-shearing when agricultural experts gathered from all over Europe, sometimes six-hundred together, to admire new inventions and improvements. According to Mary, 'many a farmer returned home with his head full of new ideas' from these gatherings, and it was no doubt from Thomas Coke (later Lord Leicester) that John Wright had the idea of introducing Merino sheep on to his farm. At that time they were known as 'Spanish fine-woolled sheep' and were almost a royal monopoly. George III had started his flock in 1787 with two rams and four ewes smuggled out of Spain and Coke bought his first merinos in 1804. John Wright no doubt purchased his four Spanish rams at this period, proposing, like Coke, to cross them with Southdown ewes.

It was a daring step to take. Of the forty private importers of the sheep between 1800 and 1811, one-third were titled and all better equipped financially to take such risks. The majority of British farmers had no opinion of the 'outlandish' little Spanish sheep. They mistrusted the 'immense horns, the throat like a Southern Hound and the shambling walk of the legs that cross'. In the long run they proved right. The climate did not suit the sheep and it was eventually Australian purses, and not British ones, that grew long by raising them. John Wright proved himself enterprising but perhaps also somewhat rash in attempting the experiment.

Another of John Wright's innovations was one of the earliest thresh-ing machines. Until he acquired it, all the grain had been beaten from the ear by means of flails on the barn floor. Monotonous the task may have been, but it provided work at a time of the year when there was little to be had and the men looked on the new contrivance with no favour, 'prognosticating, of course, no good – as they do now at any change'. The first threshing machines were fixtures close to the barn doors. They consisted of a great wheel sup-ported in the centre by a pillar. Round the pillar at the bottom was a seat in which a man sat to drive the horses that walked round and round under the wheel. John Wright was unlucky with his threshing machine and his men's forebodings were soon justified.

Early one Saturday morning the girl ran up to my father to say that a boy in the stable had had his leg broken by the kicking of a horse. A horse was immediately put into a cart with plenty of straw, and the boy was taken to Norwich Hospital, my father riding there on horseback to secure his admittance. Before he got home again, my mother had sent off another man to meet him to tell him that one of the men who was feeding the machines had had his hand nearly cut off – of course we were all in great consternation, as the man stood bleeding in the kitchen nearly fainting. When he arrived at the hospital it was found impossible to save his hand, and he, of course, became a cripple, for life, unable to earn his living by farm labour. This was not the end of it – nor the worst. I cannot remember how long it was after this accident that on Saturday when my father was in Norwich, that the Thrashing machine was at work and a woman was driving the horses. She should have been in the barn binding up. sheaves, but she was nervous about the mice in the straw, and had had a dream that she was hurt at the mill, and she asked the driver of the horses to change places and let her drive. This was done. Again I forget what caused one of the horses to kick. The poor nervous woman jumped into the seat for fear of the horse and in some way threw herself on to the top of the wheel which, coming to the part where the wheels worked into each other, she was crushed. Tidings immediately flew into the house to my mother; and we all ran to the barn. The woman laid upon some straw. A dimness comes over my mind, but I know she was taken to her home and that evening she

died. This was the warrant for the thrashing machine to stop, and my
father yielded to it.

Mary often recounted incidents of life on the farm in later life,
particularly ones involving her father's horses, of which he was
extremely proud. On one occasion, when the sheep were starving
because of deep snow, he invented 'an implement which I cannot
describe. To this he fastened several horses abreast who by dragging
this implement removed the snow from the vegetation. The sheep,
following after, were thus saved. My father often told us how the
horses went plunging through bush and brake.'

She was fond of animals herself and had a lamb of her own which
she earned in the following manner.

> One cold spring, in the lambing-time, my father came into the
> kitchen with a newly-born lamb in his arms, as near dead as it well
> could be. He was just going off with my mother to the monthly
> meeting at Norwich. He called me quickly, saying, 'Here, Mary, if
> thee can make this lamb live, thee shall have it for thy own.' By the
> time they returned a joyful resurrection had taken place. I had been
> sitting all the morning with the lamb laid on flannel before a good
> fire. I kept rubbing it and giving it a little milk as it could take it, and
> before they came home it could stagger about the kitchen. My father
> was as good as his word – it was my lamb.

But the great event of the year, even better than sheep-shearing,
was harvesting.

> Harvest-time – to us children at least – was a season of joy. The
> harvest men were all boarded in the house, and the coppers full of
> dumplings, the boilers full of beef, were a sight to see. If the men were
> working near the house, a horn was blown, and they came trooping
> home, washed at the pump, and then took their seats at the long table.
> There was always a leader chosen among them called a captain, who
> sat at the top and kept order. When they were working farther from
> the house, which we preferred, a horse was put into a light cart, and
> the eatables were placed in tins, the meat in one, puddings in another,
> and vegetables in a third, with baskets full of bread, and kegs and stone

bottles of beer. When the cart appeared in the field, the scythes and sickles were laid down, and a place was chosen for the repast under a tree or hedge as might be. We children were often allowed to go with the cart. The fine rounds of beef and long puddings make me almost hungry now to think how good they looked. Everything was well cooked in my mother's house, and the harvest-cakes, of which every man had one in the afternoon, with a horn of beer, were better than I have ever been able to make since. Of course, they had the dew of youth upon them.

When all the fields were cleared, the harvest supper was the crowning achievement. The last waggon full of corn was adorned with branches of trees and drawn into the yard; then all the labourers went home and dressed themselves in their best, to come, with their wives, to the harvest supper. There were two long tables in the kitchen, which were plentifully covered with roast and boiled meat, plum-puddings, and home-brewed beer. After all this was finished, the captain would come to the parlourdoor to ask my father's presence in the kitchen, where my father's and Madam Wright's health was drunk, and I do not know what more. Any one who had a voice was called upon for a song, and the evening ended with taking the tables and boards off the tressles and having a dance, of which I remember the comic effect, as we children peeped behind the blinds of the glass door which separated the kitchen from the keeping room. [The keeping room was used as the children's schoolroom.]

Mary Sewell always felt that some of the ties that bound master and servant as fellow creatures snapped when the men took to boarding themselves and all their wages were paid in money.

Felthorpe Farm itself (now renamed Church Farm, Felthorpe) was a large house. The windows were gothic in style. On the ground floor was the hall, the best parlour, the study, the kitchen, the schoolroom, the wash-house and the dairy. There were five bedrooms besides the servants' rooms and the two attics. In front of the house was a semicircular lawn, a gravel road extended round it, passing the door, and each end was terminated by a white gate so that you could drive in at one gate to the door and drive out at the other. On the right, as you faced the house, was a shrubbery, and on the left an orchard.

Life on the farm at Felthorpe was simple, for, in Mary Sewell's words, 'there remained much of the puritan strictness in the families of Friends at that time.' No doubt there was solid comfort in the farmhouse, but chandeliers, carpets and expensive china and glass would have been out of place. Even sofas were regarded by Quakers as 'undesirable' and only three prints were to be seen on their walls. These represented William Penn making his treaty with the Indians, a plan of a slave ship and the buildings of Ackworth School. In the homes of really strict Quakers like the Holmes of Tivetshall even these would have been considered idolatrous.

The reading of almost any book other than devotional works and the Bible was forbidden. Novels were regarded as 'engines of Satan' and Mary was firmly forbidden them. Plays also were frowned upon and if the works of Shakespeare were to be found at all at Felthorpe they would have been under close guard. In her novel *Friends at their own Fireside* Mrs Ellis told how three fictional spinsters 'locked up their Shakespeare in a glass case lined with green silk. No servant ever saw them opening this glass case except for purposes of dusting … nor, indeed, were they very free to admit visitors into this room.'

Other arts beside literature and painting came under the axe. According to Mary Sewell, 'a musical instrument was never seen in any Quaker's house.' It was considered that 'the sedentary nature of the employment' rendered females unfit for child-bearing and induced hysteria. As a result music acquired for her an almost mystical charm. 'We delighted in music, as I believe all Quaker girls do to whom it is forbidden.' A visit to a Mr Harsant and his wife, neighbours in the next parish, 'was enchantment to us', for Mr Harsant possessed not only a violin but also a barrel-organ and a musical snuff-box.

Quaker families like the Wrights spoke a language of their own, using the biblical second person singular. George Fox introduced the custom with a view to reducing 'the rich and mighty of those times from a plural magnitude'. He also defended the usage on grammatical grounds, but in fact 'thee' was often used as the subject of a sentence where 'thou' would have been correct and phrases like 'thee is welcome' were far more common than the more grammatical 'thou art welcome'. All 'titles of the world' were dropped, including Mr and Mrs, so that Mary's parents would have been addressed as John Wright and Ann Wright even by strangers. The names of the months and days were exchanged for numbers 'because they had been ascribed by way of honour ... to the supposed gods and goddesses of the idolatrous Romans and the heathen Anglo-Saxons'. Even Christmas was abolished because of its 'vulgar, Popish name', and Quakers were forbidden the 'illumination of the windows of their houses, upon what are called rejoicing nights'.

In their demeanour as well as their language and their clothes Quaker girls were different from others. Mary and her sisters were expected to maintain a nun-like composure in keeping with their nun-like dresses. The heroine of Mrs Ellis's novel had 'entire mastery over every look, word and movement. Her face was still and white as marble, her eyes ever cast down and she went about her domestic duties making no more sound than a ghost.' Shaking hands and even nodding were discouraged. Quakers were not expected to have violent opinions or make downright statements. The strongest expression they were permitted was 'undesirable', and it was undesirable to say 'I am sure'. Indeed, if there was a choice between speech and silence, silence was preferred. In later life Mary often used the favourite Quaker saying, 'In multitude of words there wanteth not sin.' It must be admitted, however, that in this respect she seldom practised what she preached.

As a result of all these prohibitions Quaker children lived a life cut off from 'the World's people' who were their neighbours.

> All was conjecture respecting the private habits, even of families residing within a very short distance; and in still higher degree all was wonder, and often misconception, with regard to the religious observances of such families ... To have heard music, but especially to have seen dancing, was at that time as extra ordinary an item of individual experience, as it is now to have witnessed a battle, or a coronation.[*]

Mary was an intensely religious person all her life and, at the age of four, she had something that she always afterwards regarded as a direct revelation of God. It was on a calm, still summer evening; she was a little child, standing on a broad, flat stone which made the step

---

[*] Ellis, Sarah Stickney, *Friends at their own Fireside.*

to her father's front door. The sky above was full of the sunset glow, and a great tree on the grass plot stood out solemnly against it. 'And it seemed as if all the beauty and the stillness flowed into my little heart and filled it,' she said, 'and I felt God there.'

On First Days, as the Quakers call Sundays, young Mary made more conventional contact with the Almighty at the Friends' Meeting House at Lammas, the village next door.

Nor was her intellectual development neglected. Her mother was always sensible of her own want of education and anxious that her children should not labour under the same disadvantage. Furthermore, she was determined that, as far as lay in her power, her daughters should have as good an education as her sons. Indeed, Quakers in general believed in the equality of women within their society and gave them an equal share in its government. In the opinion of Clarkson, the author of *Quaker Portraiture* (1806), the women were often better educated than the men 'as the women are not taken from their books at an early age and put into trade'. Mary and her younger sister Elizabeth, a lively child, were at first driven in a low chaise by 'the boy' to Mrs Outlaw's, at the farther end of the village. Hers was one of the old dame schools, and she was 'quite primitive'. Later a more sophisticated instructress was imported in the form of

a bright young governess … a fine creature, all life and intelligence … and our school became a pleasure. She was specially clever in teaching history, and giving it the charm of reality. She would read Roman and Grecian history to us, and then talk about it; then she would make an abstract of what we had read, which we learned by heart and repeated, not like parrots, for I know I had a living appreciation of both characters and events. The coldest day in winter I would sit muffled up in a quiet place to learn the history lesson. She introduced us to a much more stirring kind of poetry than we had known before. In the afternoon whilst we worked she would draw from her own store of imagination and produce little romances. Once a week a French master came from Norwich; also a drawing-master, who taught many families in the county. He was a pleasant, friendly man. He would bait his horse in my father's stable, take tea with us, and then go on to some one else. There is no knowing what we might have turned out had this governess remained to carry us along the way of knowledge in such high heart … She entirely fulfilled my father's idea of a teacher for children, and great was his sorrow, in watching her successor, Miss Wardell, to see that, instead of climbing, we slid down the hill.

After a year of Miss Wardell, the place of governess was taken by Mary's sister Anna, freshly returned from a year at a Friends' finishing school at Tottenham and four years her senior. Little progress was made under her tuition either, for she was silent and abstracted and setting her younger sisters tasks amused her no more than it did them.

The distant thunder of the Napoleonic war formed a constant and exciting background to Mary's childhood, for Felthorpe was only eight miles from the east coast where, in 1805, Bonaparte was expected hourly. John Wright himself was 'drawn for a soldier', but his Quaker principles would not allow him to bear arms. These same principles, however, were not so strong as to prevent him hiring a substitute although this also was strictly forbidden in the Quaker book of rules known as *Minutes and Advices*, 'even if suffering be the lot that doth result from such obedience to divine requiring'.

John Wright's pacifism also allowed him to take an active interest in the war.

Being a farmer, he had horses and waggons at his disposal, and he undertook, should it be necessary, to convey the women and children to a place of safety when the landing place of the enemy was known. As this was uncertain, he was obliged always to keep in readiness. My sister Elizabeth and I entered very energetically into this preparation for removing … You may imagine how I was stirred one Saturday when he came home from Norwich, and coming to me, unrolled a paper parcel and displayed a long piece of scarlet bunting to make a flag which was to be hoisted on the church tower at the moment when Buonaparte and his conquering army had landed on our coast. 'Here, Mary my dear,' he said, 'thee must make this flag to put on the steeple to let the people know that the Frenchmen have come.' An officer appointed Admiral-to-the-Fleet, or Commander-in-Chief to the army, could hardly have felt himself of more importance than I then did, and indeed it seems difficult now to believe that I did not do something for the relief of our country at that time.

Around 1809, when Mary was twelve, the 'happy childhood life' at Felthorpe came to an end. John Wright's reasons for selling the farm are not clear. Mary Sewell thought it was because 'the cessation of the war removed the obstruction to commerce, and the price of corn became as low as it had been high'. This reason appears less convincing when we consider that the war had yet five years to run. It seems more likely that John Wright's 'speculative, enthusiastic and hopeful' spirit caused him to fall an easy prey to a Yarmouth shipowner who visited him several times and persuaded him to go into shipping. Many years later Mary Sewell recalled the day on which the farming stock at Felthorpe was sold. 'It was on the day of the auction I first saw my dear father's face look anxious, almost agonised. I remember now how that look struck to my heart when he saw his beautiful farm horses selling for far below their value. The old perennial sunshine ceased that day … Worldly prosperity never visited him again.'

Nevertheless the new life started auspiciously enough. Mary and Elizabeth drove the eight miles to Yarmouth with their parents in the family chaise drawn by Sportsman, John Wright's favourite driving horse, and soon overtook the wagon carrying their furniture. They moved into the comfortable mansion which had been built for them at Southtown complete with a laundry, wash-house and dairy. 'There were several Friends' families in Yarmouth. They were all in trade, and thoroughly respectable. There were a large number of young people, with whom we soon became acquainted. They were a pleasant, sociable community.' It was at the Quaker Meeting House at Yarmouth that Mary first met her future husband, Isaac Sewell. It was his mother, Hannah Maria, however, who made a deeper impression on her at the time.

> William Sewell's wife was an Elder, and kept her eye jealously upon us, lest we should lead the other young Friends out of the way of plainness of speech, behaviour, and apparel. My dear mother had herself rather a taste for dress, though she kept strictly within the limit of the law; but her children she liked to see prettily dressed, and with this unfortunate proclivity she ordered for our winter dresses, at a fashionable dressmaker's in Norwich, cloth pelisses of a very pretty sage green colour, with capes. These capes were trimmed with swansdown,

which made them not only very pretty, but very striking, when worn by four girls. When we took our seats at the top of the Meeting-house, all eyes were upon us, especially the eyes of the dear Elder whose silent cogitations were very painful and perplexed. When we went again in the afternoon, she passed us without speaking. This was very eloquent, but more soon followed. On the next morning she came to our house and asked for an opportunity of speaking alone with my mother, when she so seriously set forth the danger of leading other young girls into temptation of dress, that my dear mother was overcome with the fear of our becoming a stumbling-block in the way of others and, much to our disgust and disappointment, she sent back the pretty pelisses to have the swausdown taken off and a trifling cord put round them thus depriving them of all their glory.

When Mary was fourteen she was sent for a year to the finishing school at Tottenham that her sister Anna had attended.

> The method of teaching was the same at most other schools at that time – just learning lessons and repeating them word for word. All this, lodged in the memory, was considered as volumes of knowledge for future use. I believe a great deal of it was dead seed. The only thing I have to show for this year is the piece of embroidery in wool which, when I came home, was duly hung up. My education being now considered finished (we should now consider not begun), I set myself to carry it on after my own taste.

Mary's great delight was in poetry and for two years she read little besides. Her favourite poets were Southey, Moore and Byron. But especially Byron. During her girlhood, his good looks, his private life and his poetry were making him the darling and the despair of English society. The divorce from Lady Byron did not take place until Mary was nineteen, but tales of his scandalous life at Cambridge were current and the fruits of his adventures in Spain and the Levant Mary devoured greedily in the form of the first two cantos of *Childe Harold* and *The Oriental Tales*. Among these latter melodramas of blood and lust in bygone Turkey she preferred *The Bride of Abydos*, *The Giaour* and *The Corsair*, all of which she knew by heart and repeated to herself during First Day Meetings (*The Giaour* is 1,334 lines long).

The Quaker prohibitions against novels and plays do not seem to have extended to poetry, but one wonders what her future mother-in-law Elder Hannah Maria, would have thought had she known that the following lines were running through the white-capped head so meekly bowed before her.

> For he through Sin's long labyrinth had run,
> Nor made atonement when he did amiss;
> Had sigh'd to many though he loved but one,
> And that loved one, alas could ne'er be his.
> Ah, happy she to 'scape from him whose kiss
> Had been pollution unto aught so chaste;
> Who soon had left her charms for vulgar bliss,
> And spoiled her goodly lands to gild his waste,
> Nor calm domestic peace had ever deign'd to taste.

There were other books that Mary and Elizabeth read and 'half studied' together, and, with drawing and attending the various meetings of the Agenorian Society, their time passed pleasantly enough.

> We every now and then got a novel from the circulating library, but this being forbidden fruit, we devoured it in our bedroom before we got into bed, sometimes sobbing with Miss Radcliffe's *History of the Scottish Chiefs or Thadlus of Warsaw*, sometimes shuddering with the *Mysteries of Udolpho*. Our little room, being far away from the others, admitted of secret practices.

Perhaps Mrs Wright had less time than usual to supervise her daughters at this time. Quite unexpectedly, and to her considerable vexation, she produced a fifth daughter, Ellen, when her youngest son, Richard, was already ten and Mary was sixteen. 'This was a great trial to my dear mother. It fell out of season,' wrote Mary. 'But as the years went by she did not regret the addition.'

A year after the birth of Ellen the French war ended. The celebrations at Yarmouth for the victory at Waterloo were remembered by Mary to the end of her life. The town was illuminated from one end to the other and eight-thousand people were plied with beef, beer and plum-pudding at tables along the quay. The name of Isaac's father, William, is prominent in the list of subscribers (he donated a generous five pounds) but that of Mary's father, John Wright, is missing. William Sewell was also a member of the general committee which organised the entertainment with an efficiency that Marquis Wellington himself might have envied. Four stewards, supplied with peeled white wands for the maintenance of order, were appointed to each table and here the Wright family put in an appearance. Both Mary's father and her older brother (also named John Wright) were stewards. So also were her future husband and his father. No doubt for so important an occasion William Sewell overlooked his objection to toasts for it was his duty as president of a table to propose no less than fourteen for a variety of objects ranging from the well-being of the Prince Regent to the annihilation of all tyrants and a good fishing.

Before the dinner commenced Neptune ('personified by the well-known Joseph Penny') arrived by barge and processed through the town with fifty damsels in white and bands playing. Bonaparte in chains with a pistol held to his head followed the procession in a sledge pulled by sailors and Cossacks. The vast company sat down to eat promptly at two with spirits undamped by a shower of rain which fell while grace was being said. At three o'clock donkey races on the Denes were announced, a cunning device on the part of William Sewell and his fellow committee members 'to induce the great multitude (many of whom were necessarily of the lowest order of society) ... to quit their seats in proper time after the dinner.' When darkness fell the great day ended with the setting alight of the 'Funeral Pile of the Buonapartean Dynasty'. The pile was forty feet high and was surmounted by an effigy of the arch-demon himself, the head of which was filled with gunpowder.[*]

Mary, being a well-brought-up young woman, was only allowed to observe these junketings from afar. No doubt she contributed to the 'splendid display of female beauty' at one of the windows along the quay. She was probably at the mayor's house overlooking table twenty-four where her father was a steward, although she might have preferred a view of table forty-nine to which her brother and

---

[*] *A Narrative of the Grand Festival at Great Yarmouth,* 1814.

Isaac had both contrived to be appointed. Isaac had already begun to pay court to her and it was in the summer of the great victory that, as Mary put it, he proposed to be taken into her good books. She was not so minded, however, and he went to London for two or three years to learn the textile business at the City warehouse of a Manchester mill.

Soon after Mary had refused Isaac, her brother John was accepted by Anne Harford. Mary could never exhaust her fund of praise for this woman, and two lengthy eulogies of her appear within pages of each other in her *Reminiscences*. Anne had been brought up by a widowed mother and although she and her sisters never had any regular school education, they so 'diligently availed themselves of every opportunity and circumstance of advantage, that they were always considered women of cultivated minds'. Mary was convinced that if Anne 'had enjoyed the education given to women at the present day (1880) she would have been distinguished in more than one field of art or science'.

Anne was not a great beauty, but she had

> a very animated and intelligent countenance. She had fine grey eyes, with black eyelashes, eyebrows and hair. She was tall, and when becomingly dressed had a picturesque appearance. Her manners were charming. In the near neighbourhood a party was scarcely complete without her ... she was the central attraction in every little company, although altogether unconscious of it herself; her aim was always to interest and bring out the talents of others.

John Wright took this paragon to live at Dudwick House, Buxton. He was now a landed gentleman, for Cousin Wright had died and left him all his property. For some reason not given in any of the family records, his father, the older John Wright, had been passed over in the will. Perhaps the banker did not have faith in John Wright senior's business abilities. Be that as it may, the promise made to Ann by Cousin Wright that she would ride in a carriage one day was not kept, and it was her daughter-in-law who was to have a pair of fine horses to draw her about the county.

Mary's mother, the older Mrs John Wright, was soon to suffer worse privations than the lack of a carriage and pair. Her husband's affairs had never prospered since he went into partnership with his younger brother, Richard, to start the first river steam-packet in England. Anna's Great-uncle Richard, like Cousin Wright, is a rather mysterious figure in Mary Sewell's chronicle. She once remarked that each generation of the Wright family produced a black sheep and it was obvious that she accounted him one. Since the days at Ackworth when he had darned a ball into his stocking, he had refused to conform. When apprenticed to the buckle-maker at Birmingham, he developed some very advanced ideas. 'The infidel works of Voltaire and Tom Paine were then being greedily read among the artisans of Birmingham, and my Uncle Richard, who was never second in anything, swallowed this poison with zest, and it unhappily influenced his fine nature till near the end of his life.' Uncle Richard also had a ready wit which led to the parting of the ways with the buckle-maker. His master had just finished eating a piece of cheese that was very full of mites and exclaimed, 'There! I have slain more than ever Samson did.' 'And with the same weapon,' was his apprentice's rejoinder.

Somewhere about 1811 or 1812 he persuaded his elder brother to buy a captured French privateer for thirty-five pounds. She was a fifty-two-foot open boat carrying three lug sails and it was Richard's intention to fit her with some form of internal combustion engine, using hydrogen for fuel. He failed in this attempt and the back ship was sent to the Humber under sail for conversion into a steamer, no doubt at John Wright's expense. The *Experiment*, as the ship was appropriately named, was insured for the sea portion of her voyage back to Yarmouth on condition that her paddles were unshipped and that the engine was not worked. When she was driven ashore in a gale, however, Richard Wright rigged the paddles and got up steam, taking her out to sea under power as the tide refloated her and then continued his passage to Yarmouth under sail. He lost his right to insurance, but saved the boat.

The *Experiment* began to ply as a ferry between Yarmouth and Norwich on the River Yare in 1813. She was the first steamer on the east coast and, with her paddles 'something in the shape of a barn shovel', as a local newspaper described them, was as much an object of curiosity as the Merino sheep had been at Felthorpe. At this stage Richard Wright lost interest in the enterprise and 'went off to something else'. John Wright took over the management of the ship, and soon replaced her with two new ones, the *Telegraph* and the *Courier*. He did not prosper financially, however, because of the dishonesty of his partner who secured the posts of captain in both ships for his nephews and then conspired with them to send in bills for repairs that had never been carried out. Worse reverses were to follow. On the morning of Good Friday, 1817, the *Telegraph* attempted to race a rival packet, newly placed on the river, to Yarmouth. Palmer gives an account of what ensued in his *Perlustration of Great Yarmouth*.

The fires had been made up for the purpose, it was said, of forcing her ahead of the other vessel. The engine was a high pressure one; the safety valve was closed; and the consequence was that the boiler, which was of cast iron, burst. The vessel had not gone twenty yards from the Foundry bridge at Norwich, when the explosion took place and she was rent from stem to stern. There were twenty-two passengers on board, of whom thirteen were killed.

Mary Sewell was in Norwich at the time of the accident.

I was staying at a Friend's house in Norwich where the eldest daughter who was a friend of mine was about to slip off early one morning to be married to a young man to whom she was attached, but whom the relatives could not sanction because he was not a Quaker, which involved her being dismissed from the Society. I was invited at this time to cover the flight and take the place of teamaker at breakfast and keep up conversation, etc.

That Good Friday morning was bright with sunshine, and we had been dancing on the lawn and were very merry – when her brother came up to me and said the packet was blown up, a number of persons were killed and the people were crowding the streets so thickly 'that a ball might be rolled upon their heads'.

All that day I went or sent from place to place to seek my dear father but night came and I had not found him. My mother was at Tivetshall with little Ellen on a visit. A Friend went there to tell her of the calamity and bring her to Norwich. I met her at his house and the next morning we went to the Foundry to Thomas Aggs' house to meet my poor father – that we will pass over. As he had passed the day before, he had seen 13 dead bodies laid side by side in the Foundry garden close by the river's side where the explosion took place. My mother and I kept together till the evening when I went with her into the cabin of the other packet which slowly steamed off drawing the wrecked packet behind it. Each side of the river was lined with a speechless crowd; the air was perfectly still. There was the solemnity of death, and silence that might indeed be felt.

The *Telegraph* had not been adequately insured, and John Wright spent the remainder of his fortune on compensating the relatives of the victims. He also had the steam engine removed from his other ship, and in its place he put a platform eighteen feet in diameter round which walked four horses turning an upright shaft, from which power was transmitted to the paddle-shaft.

Mary's life as a leisured young lady ended abruptly at this point and she and her sisters Anna and Elizabeth had to seek situations as governesses which involved 'a great descent in the social scale'. Elizabeth obtained a post with Isaac Sewell's older sister, Fulleretta thereby drawing Mary's family even closer to that of her unwanted suitor; Anna went to a Friend's family in Essex and Mary was taken on as assistant at a school run by two sisters near by.

I had undertaken to teach writing and ciphering to all the school, besides hearing all the usual lessons, and a quantity of mending of stockings, etc. I was not afraid of anything but the ciphering that was my weak point. [*] My dear father engaged one of the tutors in a school in Yarmouth to come and initiate me before breakfast, but I was as much afraid of the man as I was of the figures, so it did not pay. But I got on, and nobody found me out; and I was a very pretty writer then, and could make good quill pens, and as I had to make and mend about forty every writing day, I had some practice. The mistress and her sister both liked me, and were very kind, and after a while I felt pretty much at home – as much as you can when the servants call you familiarly by your name as if you were one of them. I had always been used to be called 'Miss'.

---

[*] Mary once admitted that she could only add and subtract by making patterns on the roof of her mouth with the tip of her tongue.

When the three girls returned for the Christmas holidays, it was not to the luxurious mansion in Southtown but to a small farm house. Their father's property had been entirely lost and he had become his son's tenant on the home farm at Buxton. Mary Sewell never ceased to wonder at the success of this unusual arrangement, with 'the parents in the cottage in comparative poverty and the son and daughter in the large house, with all its fitting appointments'. She maintained that 'no jars or jealousies ever arose' and that the sound of the son's steps was ever music to the old people's ears.

Nevertheless, even Mary the optimist admitted that the first few years were not easy.

> I can never sufficiently admire the patient submission with which my mother again took to the irksome drudgery of a small farm house, after the ease and comfort she had enjoyed at Southtown, with her two competent servants; now she had only one, very inefficient. The many and various trials of the first few years can only be realised by those upon whom they especially fell. My father turned to the management of his little farm with the earnest, quiet energy of his character, and never complained.

There were others on the farm at Buxton for whom life was not easy. Maria, who had been sixteen at the time of her father's financial collapse, was obliged to stay at home and look after her parents. Her youngest sister Ellen was at that time a child of four and her mother was suffering from fits of depression distressing to all the members of the family. 'At the time of life when young girls are careless and light-hearted she came under the cloud of loneliness and sadness.'

Mary also had her problems, as she confided to her grandchildren in her *Reminiscences*. 'The great trial, to me, at this epoch, was that your dear grandfather came forward again with his proposition.' Isaac, having patiently served his three-year apprenticeship in the City, had taken the opportunity of the Christmas holidays to renew his proposal of marriage. He was now a partner in a small draper's shop in Yarmouth and considered himself in a position to support a wife. 'I was obliged to consent to see him,' wrote Mary, 'but my heart had never been entangled, and was not at all ready to put on chains.' A correspondence however was decided upon when she returned to the school.

The next half year passed away in my teaching occupations, which became much more pleasant to me, also in the increased enjoyment I had in the society of the Mistress's sister, who was her helper in the school. She was well read in Shakespeare, which had been a sealed book to me, and she soon made me an admirer of it. In my leisure time I still continued committing Byron's poems to memory. They were very effectual against the monotony of school drudgery, and I kept up with your grandfather a very uninteresting correspondence which led nowhere.

The holidays came again, but the way did not seem to clear up. There was no spark upon the tinder. I was enthusiastic and sentimental, and my poetical reading as well as my nature had filled me with the idea that a very rare atmosphere was needed for wedded life. I was very much perplexed in my mind. The Friends on both sides approved and wished the connection, and they could not see anything to hinder it. The next half year, however, brought another arbiter into the matter. The great affection of the mistress's sister for me and the pleasure we had in each others company vexed the mistress. She was jealous and uneasy, and I plainly saw that I was destroying the two sisters' happiness.

I must give up the situation. What was I then to do? Situations were difficult to be met with. I could not go home to be a burden on my dear father. This decided me that I must marry, and as I had a vivid imagination, I made beautiful pictures of a home of my own where my father, mother and sisters would come, and I thought I might be able to be some help, and so I wrought myself up to saying yes, and I did not repent whilst I kept my castles in view. When there came a fog, things dragged heavily, but they did drag on till they came to the Wedding day.

The couple were married in the little Meeting House at Lammas. The wedding dinner was at the house of Mary's brother John and the honeymoon consisted of a week by the sea at Cromer. The eight-mile journey was made by a chaise drawn by a good horse, and Mary's sister Elizabeth was the third member of the party.

So loveless a marriage may appear shocking to us, but such arrangements were common enough among Quakers at that time. Elizabeth Fry, the famous Quaker prison reformer, was married in very much the same way to her stolid unimaginative banker husband. It was the duty of a young woman's parents to select a suitable husband for her and the qualities they were commanded to seek were 'religious inclinations, suitable disposition, temper, sobriety of manners and diligence in business'.[*]

The young couple went to live in a tree-shaded eighteenth-century terrace house at 25 Church Plain, at the far end of Yarmouth Market Place from the shop owned by Isaac's father, William Sewell. The house still stands, although it is under threat of demolition, and bears a plaque to commemorate its former inhabitants. It is squeezed between St Nicholas, the largest parish church in England, on one side and the seventeenth-century almshouses for 'decayed fisher-men' on the other. A fake Tudor front was added in 1932 but the interior remains unchanged. It consists of one room downstairs, with the bedroom where Anna was born above and an attic above that. The kitchen is somewhat inconveniently placed beyond a yard at the back and there is a servant's bedroom above it.

Although the house was so small, Mary said 'it was large enough to be happy in; able to take in a friend, and to enter on my first experience of housekeeping.' She was surrounded by relatives for, besides Isaac's parents, his brother Abraham and his 'sweet and lovely' wife Dorothy Stickney were living in Yarmouth and Mary's sister Elizabeth was still teaching the children of Isaac's sister Fulleretta. Nor was Mary idle. 'Before many months had passed! I found plenty of needlework to do in preparing baby linen. There were no sewing machines in those days and the Friends, at any rate, did not go to ready made linen shops.' She may have had some misgivings about the coming birth for only two years previously the nation had been plunged into unprecedented mourning by the death of Princess Charlotte in childbirth. When her time came, however, there were no mishaps. On 30 March Anna was born to be, in her mother's words, 'an unclouded blessing – for fifty eight years the perennial joy of my life'.

---

[*] *Minutes and Advices.*

PART II

ANNA
SEWELL

38 CAMOMILE STREET,
LONDON 1820–22

The perennial joy of Mary's life did not bring worldly prosperity with her. Within days of Anna's birth it was discovered that Isaac's shop could not support two families and that he, as the younger partner, must go elsewhere. 'The world was all before us,' wrote Mary, 'but it was very difficult to choose a place of rest.' Eventually Isaac's brother William, who was considered a man of affairs, found a small house in Camomile Street, leading off Bishopsgate, and suggested that Isaac should convert it into a shop specialising in Quaker attire.

Camomile Street still exists. It is a small street on the east side of Bishopsgate, just south of Liverpool Street Station and close enough to Spitalfields Market to smell of strawberries on a summer's night. The Sewells would hardly recognise it now, for the two blocks that it occupies are almost entirely taken up with office buildings. Only a few of the old terrace houses still stand. They face each other at the Bishopsgate end of the street. Number 38A is of soot-blackened brick with one square window on each of its four floors. So narrow is the façade that the shop window is hardly wider than the shop door and, when I visited it one Tuesday at midday, an array of lipsticks and soaps indicated that it is now owned by a chemist. As the shop was closed, I was unable to see inside. The owner of a larger chemist's shop opposite was unable to tell me at what time it would open.

Mary and her baby moved into Camomile Street after a six-month stay with her parents at Buxton, during which Isaac had been supervising the rather expensive conversion. She had misgiving about leaving the close-knit Circle of friends and relations at Yarmouth, and these proved far from groundless. 'I was taking my first lesson in fog, dirt, noise and distraction. Till then I had lived in the country and

loved it with the ardent love of childhood and youth. I was a most
rebellious scholar. I loathed and hated the place, and I was nearly a
stranger in it.' She was appalled by the London fog, which she later
described in the opening verses of her ballad, *Mother's Last Words*:

> The yellow fog lay thick and dim
>   O'er London city, far and wide;
> It filled the spacious parks and squares,
>   Where noble lords and ladies ride.
>
> It filled the streets, the shops were dark,
>   The gas was burning through the day;
> The Monument was blotted out,
>   And lost in gloom the river lay.
>
> But thicker still, and darker far,
>   The noisome smoke-cloud firmly fell
> Amongst the narrow courts and lanes,
>   Where toiling people poorly dwell.

She was even more appalled by the misery of the dwellers in 'the
narrow courts and lanes'. Her neighbours in Shoreditch were agricultural labourers who had moved into London as the result of the
Industrial Revolution. They lived crowded together in conditions of
unbelievable filth. Many of their houses were without water or drains
and those who lived close enough to the Thames used it for both
purposes. Young and a stranger though she was, Mary started to visit
these people. One of the women she interested herself in, the wife of
a docker, died of cholera, leaving a number of children destitute. It
was the fate of such children that later provided her with the subject
for some of the ballads for which she was to become famous.

Mary did not have to leave the house to see the misery about her.
There was a gin shop opposite (this was before the time of gin pal-
aces). It still stands, transformed into a respectable public house, the
Mail Coach, behind a mock Tudor façade. In those days it was a

   dirty, disgusting looking place, and often resounded with oaths, songs
   and quarrels. On the edge of the pavement before the door, sat an

apple woman with her little stall; a tall, haggard, white-faced woman
she was, with black straggling hair, and a careworn countenance.
In all seasons of the year there she sat – in the summer with her little
bunches of cherries tied to sticks, and her small heaps of strawberries,
gooseberries and currants piled up on leaves. In the autumn, her stall
was covered with pears, apples and plums; in winter, with apples, nuts,
oranges and slices of cocoanut. Hot or cold, wet or dry, there she was,
often sitting in the rain, with her battered umbrella partially sheltering
her and the fruit. Sometimes I have seen two or three children come to
her, evidently her own; one of them, a baby, was brought in the arms
of a little, lank, light-haired girl about eight years old. She would take
the infant, kiss it, and give it suck; if it cried violently, she would go
into the gin shop with it, and presently bring it out pacified.

Mary's own baby was more fortunate. There was no money for
a nurse and Mary largely cared for Anna herself, with the help of a
general servant. Evidently the child thrived and some verses included
in a ballad called *The Drunkard's Wife* almost certainly apply to Anna
as a two-year-old.

> Her prattling tongue, her pretty ways,
>   Were always my delight;
> And she grew up so strong and well,
>   And was so quick and bright.
>
> And yet she had a tender heart,
>   The least reproof could move;
> And, oh! she looked so earnestly,
>   Till certain of my love.
>
> And when she flung her little arms
>   Close fondling round my neck,
> My foolish heart broke down with joy,
>   Sweet tears I could not check.

In spite of her joy in her child, Mary's own life was far from happy
at this time, and although she never resorted to gin, she admits she
'often had recourse to a strong cup of coffee'. Isaac's shop was not

a success. It seems that his brother William, in recommending it, had overlooked the fact that there was a much larger establishment dealing in Quaker clothing within a very short distance. The street was a quiet one, the shop unknown, 'with no ability to look attractive'. Very few customers came and Isaac soon dismissed the assistant he had brought with him from Yarmouth and hired a boy. In the evening, when the shutters were up, Mary used to come down and help clear up the shop and during the day she sewed garments to sell in it. 'I made some little fancy things to put in the window. I forget if they were sold. A lady called one day and asked if I knew of a needlewoman who could make some nightclothes for her. I said "yes" and if she would send them to me I would get them done for her, and was glad to do them myself without telling.'

Soon the work began to tell even on her abundant energies. She was expecting another child and the house was an inconvenient one, being all stairs. Furthermore, she was worried about Anna who lived mostly in the underground kitchen with 'a dark print roundabout slip' on not to show the dirt. 'I thought it would be impossible for me to bring up my little girl among black houses and dirty streets, with never a flower for her little hand to gather, nor a bird's song for her to hear. I used to sit and look over the roofs and the bits of blue sky, and cry like a child. Great London was to me like a huge cage with iron bars.' Certainly Camomile Street was a far cry from Felthorpe Farm and there were no pet lambs for Anna to play with. There was, however, a cab rank opposite where hackney-coaches, as cabs were then called, stood waiting when unemployed. Mary must often have taken Anna out with an apple core to feed the horses there and it may well have been from this that Anna's love of horses developed. This love can occur in children at a very early age. I myself have an eighteen-month-old daughter who will give me no peace in the mornings until she has been taken to the field at the end of the garden to feed 'the 'orses'.

Business went from bad to worse in the little shop. Eventually no customers came at all and a family council was called. It was the custom in Quaker families for decisions to be taken jointly and the Sewells were 'an exceptionally affectionate family, free and open with each other in their concerns. When one of them made a change, there was a dinner and a bottle of good wine.' Anna's Uncle William was again called in and again his advice was taken for, as Mary remarked bitterly, experience had not yet taught her to ignore it. William recommended a partnership in a large and long-established shop in Hackney and Isaac took Mary and Anna to live in the house that went with it. His partner, however, who had put up most of the capital, proved reckless and unsound and the business soon broke up. At this juncture Anna's brother Philip was born. He was two years younger than his sister and arrived at a moment when his father's affairs were in an even blacker state than they had been when Anna was born, for Isaac was now declared bankrupt. Mary's health broke down and her doctor ordered her to leave London. The home in which she had hoped to receive her parents and sisters was now a couple of furnished rooms in Hackney. All her furniture had to be auctioned to pay Isaac's debts. She accepted this last misfortune courageously enough although she admitted to grieving a little over some of her wedding presents 'specially the tea urn my dear mother had given me'. Eventually Isaac became a traveller in Nottingham lace and was able to rent a small house in the part of Hackney then know as Dalston. It was in this house that Anna spent her childhood.

2

12 PARK ROAD,
DALSTON 1822–32

Park Road, Dalston, still stands although it has been renamed
Parkholme Road. It is typical of those streets of red-brick terrace
houses which reproduced themselves again and again in the nineteenth century to accommodate the clerks, commercial travellers and
small shopkeepers of Victorian London. It is in the heart of Pooter
land where the Sunday joint would still be turning up on Wednesday
and one general servant would be kept to wash, scrub and cook for
seventeen hours a day on sixteen pounds a year. Yet in 1822 it was not
entirely unattractive. It was still on the outer edge of the red-brick
tide which, before the end of the century, was to engulf it and sweep
far beyond it to Stoke Newington, Tottenham and even as far north as
Enfield. It could still be described as a 'countrylike suburb'* although
the fields adjoining it may well have been littered with scaffolding
from which would soon rise the next identical street.

Number 12 no longer stands but probably like its neighbours it
was a stucco terrace house with a semi-basement kitchen, a back and
a front room on the ground and first floors and attic bedrooms. It was
furnished with only what furniture John Wright had bought back
for his sister at the auction. 'It will easily be supposed,' wrote Mary
Sewell in her *Reminiscences*, 'that strict economy had to be practised at
Dalston.' Mary, however, contrived to make a virtue of this necessity.
'There is no hardship,' she wrote, 'in plain, simple food and clothing.
Trouble often comes when these are superabundant, but as long as
there is enough without carking care, there is freedom; and I believe

---

* Bayly, E. B., Preface to *Poems and Ballads of Mrs. Sewell*.

that is the best atmosphere for a child's mind and body.' Food was
certainly not superabundant. Mary considered that the majority of
the children of the period were overfed. She wrote:

> If the common diet of our children were more like that of the noble
> youths of the captivity of Babylon, I believe they would not only be
> fatter, fairer and more robust in their bodies, but better-tempered,
> kinder-hearted and clearer-headed. If there be one thing more than
> another directly calculated to make happy childhood miserable and
> selfish, it is to allow them an unrestrained, over-full, rich and stimulat-
> ing diet. Look at the joyous child who jumps down from his simple
> breakfast of bread-and-milk, and runs away, ready for anything. Look
> at another child, who drags himself off his seat, after partaking largely
> of coffee, hot rolls, ham or potted meat, looking back to the table
> again with lingering eyes. [*]

Dinners, as well as breakfasts, she considered were frequently excessive. 'Very few children require a meat dinner seven days in the week;
most of them would be better with farinaceous food and vegetables
for one or two days at least.' The farinaceous food she recommended
above all others was 'porridge thick and hot'. In a ballad called
The Miller's Wife, she told how this thrifty woman fed her children.

> She did not stuff their little mouths
> With cakes and lumps of meat;
> She said that porridge was the thing
> That children ought to eat.
>
> And they were fed on porridge too,
> And firmly stood to that;
> And certainly the children grew
> Exceeding fair and fat.

Nor were the children waited on by a hierarchy of maids. 'I had only
one little servant,' wrote Mary 'and we washed at home.' As soon as

---

[*] Sewell, Mary, *Thy Poor Brother.*

they were old enough, Anna and Philip were encouraged to share with their mother 'in little household occupations'.

Anna was a pretty child with a fresh complexion, dark curly hair and a broad determined jaw. She was intelligent and highly strung. Her mother called her Nanny. Philip, also, was a handsome, clever child and on this promising material Mary set to work as an educator. She had strong views about the responsibilities of a mother. 'Train up a child in the way he should go and he will not depart from it,' was a passage from scripture she never tired of quoting. 'The education of the home is more powerful than that of the school or the pulpit,' she used to say. Indeed, so strong was the influence of her home that it created remarkable practical Christians not only of her children but of her grandchildren. Two of Philip's children, Edward and Margaret, who died in 1937, are still remembered in Norfolk for their many good works in prisons, schools and the community as a whole. (Margaret was a woman of great intelligence as well as goodness and was the first of the Sewell women to be given a proper education. She was one of the early students at Newnham and later became Warden of the University Settlement at Southwark. Her three sisters were lifelong crusaders against vivisection.)

But Mary had to be more than a mother, for Isaac's salary would not stretch to schools or governesses. Indeed, there was not even money for books until she wrote a simple one herself, entitled *Walks with Mama*, and from it earned three pounds. This sum she described as 'a little fortune to me then', and out of it she bought Edgeworth's *Practical Education*, 'the book I value above all others as a help'.

Practical Education was in fact the work of two authors, Richard Lovell Edgeworth and Maria, the second of his twenty-two children, better known to the world as the author of the Irish novel, *Castle Rackrent*. The Edgeworths were disciples of Rousseau and believed that independence and self-reliance were the qualities most to be encouraged in children. They did not go as far as Rousseau, who had suggested that his imaginary pupil, Emile, should invent a microscope before using one, but they considered that children ought to be allowed to discover the truths of the natural world for themselves. In moral matters, also, they should experience the results of disobedience, even if these were painful to the point of being dangerous. While pursuing these experiments young people should be accompanied, rather than led, by a preceptor who would step in with words of explanation or admonition at the right moment

It was in the role of preceptor that Mary at last found an outlet for her pedagogic energies. If fate had denied her the opportunity to be a headmistress (and she would have made an excellent one), she would be an all-knowing tutor to her children, discovering with them the mysteries of science and pointing the way to moral perfection as they picked themselves up from yet another tumble on the stony path. A friend once compared her face to that of Lord Lyndhurst: 'As we look at his bust now, and compare her photograph with it, we see the same massive mouldings of brow and temple – unmistakable signs of great capacity – and the same firm outlines of cheek and chin – equally unmistakable signs of tenacity of purpose.'[*] Mixed with the gentleness of the mother in her there was a streak of the forcefulness of the Chancellor. Even many years later as a grandmother her earnestness made her less attractive than her husband to small children. Mrs Bayly her biographer writes:

> Grandfather was the hero of the day to them, far more adept in pleasing very little ones at play than the earnest grandmother. It would not have come into her mind to put little bits of cheese on their biscuits and call them 'horses with riders', or to do a host of other playful things by which the dear grandfather was fondly remembered … Her instinct for being side by side with her companions and drawing them to her own level, did not quite meet the requirements of the baby stage.[**]

Isaac, however, was seldom at home. 'He had to leave at eight o'clock in the morning and seldom returned till eight in the evening. Sunday was a very happy time when we were all together.' Throughout Anna's life, Isaac remains a shadowy, background figure, glimpsed at rare intervals when Mary moves aside. On several occasions Mary

---

[*] Lord Lyndhurst (1772–1863) was a famous lawyer and Conservative statesman. His father was the American painter, Copley. The bust mentioned was presumably that executed in 1841, now at Trinity College, Cambridge.

[**] Mrs Bayly, *The Life and Letters of Mrs. Sewell,* Nisbet, 1889.

emphasised that he was a very unselfish man. One quality he had that she largely lacked; a sense of humour. A story current in the Sewell family about a bird known as the Ridgmont raven probably originated with him. It seems that this bird, which could talk, made the following parting comment on being carried away by an eagle: 'What's the matther wi' Ralf?'* Perhaps not one of wit's greatest inventions, but Mary Sewell would never have told such a story.

Nor could Anna and her brother take occasional refuge in the company of a 'vulgar indulgent nursery maid' or cook. For Mary, like the Edgeworths, considered that servants should be excluded from the nursery as far as possible. 'If children,' said the Edgeworths, 'pass one hour in a day with servants, it will be in vain to attempt their education.' Even the babe in arms must be preserved from the vicious and ignorant nurse who 'stops it from crying … that she may relieve herself … from the painful weakness of compassion'. An educated member of the family should always be with it. 'The candle would not then be thrust into the infant's eyes to make it take notice of the light through the mist of tears, the eternal bunch of keys would not dance and jingle at every peevish summons, nor would the roaring of passion be overpowered by insulting songs.' Ingenious methods were suggested by the Edgeworths for ensuring that, as the child grew older, he never had an opportunity to speak to those who made his bed and cooked his meals. Keeping the 'little servant' from Anna and her brother must have taxed the ingenuity of Mary Sewell. But in principle Mary was with the Edgeworths.

> If children are continually with servants when not with their mother, every little thing is done for them, all their little quarrels are set right for them, and they are never, as it were, acting on their own foundation and receiving the natural reward of their conduct. There are appeals and interferences which prevent a child from seeing cause and effect simply, and also from gaining an independent mastery in many little matters suited to their abilities. For instance, if you wish to be alone or to go out, I would not give the children over to others, but leave them together, with what ought to be

---

* *Home Life and Letters of Mrs. Ellis* by her nieces.

sufficient amusement. It is their interest then to make themselves agreeable to each other and also to call forth all their ingenuity for their own amusement. 'Don't do this,' and 'Give your brother that,' and 'I'll tell your ma,' – all these ill-working speeches are done with. However excellent a servant may be, she can never stand to a child in the place of unquestioned rule and authority, and that invaluable virtue of simple, unquestioning obedience in a child's mind is necessarily impaired.

A large bare room was set aside as a nursery for the children at Number 12, probably the front room on the first floor. There was no carpet on the floor that they could spoil and the table and chairs were of plain wood. In this room the infant Anna's moral training began, for Mary considered that the metal of a child's character must be formed early. She recommended that not an hour of the two-year-old's day should be unaccounted for. She wrote in a letter of advice to a friend:

At stated times the child should be set up at the table to amuse itself quietly, without any assistance except being furnished with its amusements for the time, and these should generally be the same. Children should not be accustomed to too much variety; they do not need it, and it is a waste of our resources. A child will amuse itself for a very long time in stringing beads, putting different kinds of seeds or beads into different divisions of a box, drawing, cutting, etc. There should be a degree of perfectness, and even something approaching to business habits, encouraged and expected, even in these little amusements, to give worth and interest to them. Perfect play is the anticipation of perfect work. It is surprising how soon a little child will accommodate itself to, and expect a routine, if it be invincibly regular. When the clock strikes, let the child be laid down in his bed, or set up at the table. When it strikes again, let him get up. It is irregularity and uncertainty that fret a child and put his obedience to the test and bring the will of the parent and child into collision.

It is doubtful whether the bare wooden floor of Anna's playroom was unduly littered with toys, for, even if her mother could have afforded them, the Edgeworths would not have approved. Of what use, they cried, were the gaudy and ingenious confections of the toyshop? 'When the wooden woman has churned her hour in her empty churn; when the stiff-backed man has hammered or sawed till his arms are broken, or till his employer's are tired; when the gilt lamb has ba-aed, the obstinate pig squeaked, and the provoking cuckoo cried cuckoo, till no one in the house can endure the noise; what remains to be done?' How much more suitable, they said, were pieces of wood of different sizes, with which they may build, balls, pulleys, wheels, strings and strong little carts, in which they may carry weeds. Even dolls were regarded dubiously except in 'as far as they are the means of inspiring girls with a taste for neatness in dress, and with a desire to make those things for themselves for which women are usually dependent on milliners. A watchful eye should be kept on the child who plays with them to mark the first symptoms of a love of finery and fashion.' As for dolls' tea-parties, they were sternly forbidden. 'A little girl, presiding at her baby teatable, is pleased with the notion that she is like her mamma; and, before she can have any idea, of the real pleasure of conversation and society, she is confirmed in the persuasion that tattling and visiting are some of the most enviable privileges of grown people.'

Story-books also were severely censored and only those whose narrative was well mixed with instruction or admonition was permitted. Maria Edgeworth supplied the demand she created in two stout volumes of stories entitled *The Parent's Assistant*, and *Early Lessons*, and these must surely have been read to Anna from a very early age. In her preface to *The Parent's Assistant*, Maria firmly stated that 'all poetical allusions' had been avoided in the stories and 'at the same time care has been taken to avoid inflaming the imagination, or exciting a restless spirit of adventure, by exhibiting false views of life, and raising hopes which, in the ordinary course of things, cannot be realised'.

Maria Edgeworth's tales were of two kinds, the educational and the moral. Many in the *Harry and Lucy* series were typical of the former. A brother and sister go for walks with their parents not to take the air but to take instruction. They learn about ships, hammocks, the making of bricks, the shoeing of horses and the manufacture of horn spoons and tortoiseshell combs. The adventures of 'the obedient little boy' called Frank in the series of that name are equally tedious. Frank goes for walks with his mamma but is also able to gain instruction from objects as familiar as the gate-leg table in the family drawing room.

> One evening, when his father and mother were drinking tea, he was sitting under the tea-table; and he took hold of one of the legs of the table ... which he found that he could move very easily. His mother said to him, 'Frank, what are you doing?' And he answered, 'Mamma, I am playing with the leg of the table.' And his mother said, 'What do you mean by saying that you are playing with the leg of the table?' And Frank said, 'I mean that I am pulling it towards me, mamma.' And his mother said, 'Let it alone, my dear.' And Frank took his hands away from the leg of the table and he let it alone.

A lengthy explanation of the functioning of a gate-leg table followed.

In the moral tales bad deeds were punished and good ones, just as inevitably, rewarded. Thus Rosamund, who squandered her money on the chemist's jar full of purple liquid must wear her old shoes until her feet hurt, but Tom, who gave his to a chimney-sweep, was saved by him when his horse throws him into the water; Jem who 'jumped up at five and went singing, to work each day' earned the money to save his mother's pony, but Lazy Lawrence 'formed a sudden close intimacy with the stable-boy (a very bad boy)' took to thieving and was lucky to escape Botany Bay.

Fortunately for Anna these moral tales were not without plot and suspense for which Miss Edgeworth apologised. 'To prevent the precepts of morality from tiring the ear and the mind,' she explained, 'it was necessary to make the stories in which they are introduced in some measure dramatic.' The characters, too, have life, particularly the bad ones like Lady Diana Sweepstake, Mrs Teresa Tattle and Miss Barbara Case, the lawyer's daughter. And this in spite of Maria Edgeworth's avowed intention to avoid 'the common fault of making the most mischievous characters appear the most *active* and ingenious'.

Miss Barbara Case is the child villain of *Simple Susan*, a story which still appears from time to time in libraries of children's classics and deserves to be remembered if only for the fact that it reduced

Sir Walter Scott to tears (admittedly a task not too difficult to per-
form). Susan represented in her neat little person all that Mary Sewell
wanted Anna to be. She was the sweet-tempered, modest, industrious
daughter of poor but honest Farmer Price. Cruel attorney Case and
his daughter Barbara (who read 'dirty novels' in secret) plotted to
deprive her of her beloved pet lamb and serve it up as mutton to Sir
Arthur Somers, the squire. They failed because of the intervention of
Sir Arthur himself. And the moral was, among others, that 'those who
never attempt to appear what they are, not ... never are in danger
of being laughed at'.

As a moralist Mary Sewell was, if anything, even sterner than the
Edgeworths. In her opinion there was no such thing as a 'necessary
infirmity'. Faults must be rooted out, and those who were guilty of
transgression must be made to suffer for their own good. Mrs Bayly
remarked that it was 'rather striking that one so full of intense sympathy
with the erring and fallen could be so merciless, not only to cruelty and
oppression, but to easy slippery faults – laziness, bad work, wastefulness,
and every, sort of giddy way'. A young friend of Mrs Sewell wrote, 'I
remember Mrs Sewell's pulling me up sharply for advocating forgive-
ness of a personal injury which involved cruelty to an animal. "Forgive
him!" she cried. "I'd have roused the town against him"'.

Mary Sewell instilled the idea of kindness to animals into her
children from an early age. She had been an animal lover since the
days when she brought the dying lamb back to life on her father's
farm at Felthorpe and although most of her life, was devoted to
alleviating human rather than animal suffering, she would never let
a case of cruelty pass without intervention. She would have preferred
her intervention to be gentle, but it seldom was. To quote a friend,
'She was very conscious of her own tendency to speak sometimes
more strongly than she intended, whether in criticism or rebuke, and
had a kind of despairing admiration for those who could keep the
iron hand in a velvet glove.'

A 'tender consideration for ... the creatures of God' was an important article of the Quaker code. The sixth query,* directed against

---

* Roughly a dozen queries were read out at Quaker Meetings at regular intervals.
  They embodied the chief rules by which Quakers lived.

'vain sports' included a prohibition of hunting and all 'distressing of dumb beasts for amusement'. 'Quakers,' wrote Clarkson in his *Quaker Portraiture*, 'must so calculate their powers and their years as to shield them from excessive labour. They must so anticipate their feelings as to prohibit them from pains. They must so estimate their instinct, and make an allowance for their want of understanding, as not to attach to their petty mischiefs the necessity of an unbecoming revenge.'

The Edgeworthian virtues of honesty, industry, thrift and courage were among those that Mary wished to foster in Anna. Physical courage she put particular emphasis on, perhaps because it was one of the few virtues she considered she lacked.

> Many a night have I laid trembling in my bed, fearing that an old beggar man, who occasionally came to my father's house, would come down the chimney, and take me away to cut up into matches; indeed, I am not quite sure that an indefinite fear of old John Sprags does not creep over me now sometimes when I am going about the house in the dark.

When Anna and Philip were still very little children she accustomed them to playing in the dark. 'Many a game of hide and seek I had with them in a room bordered by a dressing room and two closets, and admitting of all kinds of surprises.'

If Mary lacked physical courage she did not lack honesty. Phrases like 'Liars make crooked ways for themselves', 'Truth goes furthest in the end' and 'There are no by-ways to the Kingdom of Heaven', were always on her lips. A couplet from *Our Father's Care* ran:

> Remember that God keeps you always in sight
> And sees through the dark just as well as the light.

Thrift came in many forms. Anna was taught to be careful with money. Her mother tells us the child kept 'an accurate account of expenses'. She also would have been taught to take care of her clothes. Oldness in them she was to regard as a quality, not a defect. 'The aversion to *old* things should, if possible be prevented in children,' said the Edgeworths.

We should not express contempt for *old* things, but we should treat them with increased respect, and exult in their having arrived, under our protection, to such creditable age. 'I have had such a hat so long therefore it does not signify what becomes of it!' is the speech of a *promising* little spendthrift. 'I have taken care of my hat, it has lasted so long; and I hope I shall make it last longer,' is the exultation of a young economist.[*]

As soon as she was old enough to hold a needle Anna was supplied, as the Edgeworths suggested, with 'an independent stock of all the little things which are in daily use; housewives and pocket-books well stored with useful implements'. Mary Sewell intended to make of Anna 'a great hand with the needle and probably held before her the example of Simple Susan who excelled at plain work. Plain work meant dressmaking, shirt-making and mending, and was considered virtuous. Fancy work meant crochet and embroidery, and led inevitably to the Devil. Abigail, the foolish servant in Mary Sewell's book *Patience Hart* indulged in fancy work and ended up with 'no clothes and no character and nothing but the wages of sin to exist upon'. It is true that eventually Mary herself took to embroidering flower pieces on satin, but this was after Anna was dead, when she herself was too old for more useful occupations.

So strongly did Mary Sewell feel about the good effects of plain sewing that she composed an entire verse drama for children on the theme, entitled *The Children of Summerbrook*. Summerbrook was an imaginary village. The heroine was Mary Day, a village girl considered by Mary Sewell's biographer to be based on Anna as a child. She and her brother George (supposed to be Philip) cared for their ailing mother while their father, 'a noble British tar', was at sea. Needless to say, Mary Day 'could neatly hem and sew'. Not only did she sew, but at school she helped others, like little Nelly, to sew too. Nelly could neither thread her needle nor get the knots out of her thread, but Mary smoothed her way for her. At this stage in the story the villainess, Lucy Bell, appeared. Lucy Bell thought of nothing but fine clothes and fancy work and scorned Mary Day as a 'little prim, old-fashioned thing'.

[*] Edgeworth, *Practical Education*.

> I do delight in fancy work,
> > I hate to hem and sew.
> If I could choose I would not set
> > Another stitch, I know.

Lucy Bell's love of finery soon led her into mischief. Mr Charmin had remodelled the village shop and among the 'flowers and fringes, parasols and lace' in the new plate–glass window, Lucy Bell spied a wreath of artificial roses, the very thing to complete her outfit for the school treat at Squire Tyerman's. To buy it she stole a shilling from Mary Day, but divine retribution soon overtook her. A thunderstorm at Squire Tyerman's ruined her finery and on the way home she was so overcome with guilt that she confessed the theft of the shilling to Mary Day, who was sheltering her under her umbrella. From that day began the reformation of Lucy Bell. Never again did she indulge in fancy work. Instead she sewed a shirt to earn the money to repay Mary Day.

> She had to go to school each day,
> > And make the shirt you know,
> So all her play time she gave up,
> > That she might sit and sew.

Every day, with the aid of sermons from Mary Day, she grew more and more virtuous. By the end of the drama nothing would still her needle. When she saw a tear in little Nelly's dress on the way to school she pursued the child with a needle.

> But I have got my needle here,
> > I'll mend it in a trice;
> And then she ran it quickly up –
> > Do look! So neat and nice.

Hand in hand with the virtue of thrift went that of self-denial, for the more we do without ourselves, the more we will have to give to those in greater need. Anna and Philip were expected to help supply some of the wants Mary found in the wretched homes she visited. In *Thy Poor Brother*, a book she published as a guide to distract visitors, she describes a mother returning from the hovel of a woman weak from lack of proper nourishment.

> She calls her own children round her, and draws this picture before them. She says, 'Here is an opportunity for you to be kind, my children. Which of you will give your meat dinner, once in the week, to this poor woman, that she may get strong again and be able to help her little children?' And almost before the words are spoken, they spring forward, one and all, and say, 'I will! I will!' for a well-trained child delights in pitiful kindness.

In another episode of the book we hear how the charitable mother resolved 'to keep her healthy young people out of the easy-chairs so that one could be sent as an itinerant invalid chair among her poor neighbours'. In a third the children are reminded of the parched throat of a fever-stricken man just as they are about to help themselves from a bowl of freshly picked June strawberries. At once they push the fruit aside and beg that it and all their fruit for several weeks be taken to the poor sufferer.

Mary's moral code, although stern, was not imposed by force. She preferred to suggest rather than to command and considered that the results of transgression were its best punishment. 'When he (the child) has done wrong let the natural consequences of wrongdoing fall upon him ... let them fall with their full weight, but let them be the only penalties.' And elsewhere (for Mrs Sewell considered that if a point was worth making it was worth making many times), 'Let punishment as much as possible be felt to be the natural consequence of misconduct. If a child soils himself unnecessarily, let him be excluded from the clean party.' Like the best of us, Mary Sewell did not always live up to her principles. Although Anna or Philip were never chastised they sometimes endured the lesser punishment (lesser, at any rate, in their mother's eyes) of 'the witholding of a kiss at night. That,' she said, 'was enough to send them to bed with tears and sobs.'

When Anna was about five, her mother set about the cultivation of her mind, and this seems to have been an altogether jollier proceeding than the training of her morals. For Mary was an excellent teacher in an age when good teachers were rare. There are only too many references in the literature of the time to the imposition of tasks as a method of education. Children were set long passages to learn by heart regardless of whether they understood their contents. Indeed, Mary herself was educated in this way. So was David Copperfield – a contemporary of Anna's, if only a fictional one. There is the memorable scene where he attempts to recite a lesson to the hateful Murdstones. Charles Kingsley, another contemporary of Anna's, himself suffered a nervous breakdown as a result of overwork as a boy, and introduced one of its victims in *The Water Babies*. The child had turned into a turnip, filled with water and unable to move. It called to Tom as he passed:

> 'Can you tell me anything at all about anything you like?'
>
> 'About what?' says Tom.
>
> 'About anything you like, for as fast as I learn things I forget them again.'
>
> And the more he listened the more he forgot, and the more the water ran out of him. Tom thought he was crying but it was only his poor brains running away, from being worked so hard.

Mary was true to Richard Edgeworth's principle that 'the knowledge that cannot be immediately applied to use, has no interest for children' and she threw herself with enthusiasm into the simple experiments in chemistry recommended by him. One suspects that she was as delighted (and surprised) as Anna and Philip when water coloured blue with radish skins turned red when lemon juice was added, thereby proving the presence of an *acid*. She no doubt marvelled as they did when the lump of chalk in the glass of vinegar demonstrated the principle of *effervescence*, or when the addition of water to camphire in solution caused the camphire to *precipitate*. Nor would her spirit have quailed before a complicated experiment to show the repulsion and attraction of oil and water, involving a cork, a needle, a plate and a tumbler. One only hopes she drew the line at introducing a still into the playroom and proceeding to demonstrate the principle of *distillation*.

Of the other subjects recommended in the Edgeworth book Mary makes no mention. We do not hear of Anna studying geography, geometry or classical literature, although Mary may have read

Plutarch's Lives to her in translation as her own governess had. As regards arithmetic, knowing what we do of Mary's proficiency in that subject, we may assume that she taught it only in its elementary stages. Of the subjects more commonly taught to girls at that time, French, German and music, we also hear nothing. French Mary almost certainly did not teach, for Philip, when he was eventually sent to Hackney Grammar School, learnt the Fables of La Fontaine by heart in order to persuade the French master to give him lessons. Drawing, on the other hand, she did encourage. Anna showed a marked artistic talent from a very early age and her mother gave her every encouragement. Her subjects were mostly flowers, animals and insects, for Mary considered the ability to draw these an advantage in a girl who would presumably one day be a mother. Among her papers was found a practical sketch of its use.

A little boy – we will say about four years old – runs from the garden to his mother.

'Oh! mother, do come and look at this beautiful thing on the rose tree. I want to know what it is.'

'I am busy now, Charles. Tell me what it is like. What colour is it?'

'Oh, I think it is red.'

'Oh, I suppose it is a ladybird.'

'Oh no, it is a great deal bigger than a ladybird.'

'Well, perhaps it is a tiger moth, that has two red wings. Look, like this,' and the mother slightly sketches the tiger moth on the slate.

'Oh no, it is not at all like that.'

The mother eventually discovers that the insect is chestnut-coloured, oval shaped and has six legs.

'And what sort of head has this wonderful creature?'

'Oh mother! Its head is like the branches of a tree.'

The mother immediately attaches a small branch of a tree to the body, with several twigs; not forgetting a few leaves.

'Is it like this?'

'Oh no, it has no leaves.'

She rubs out the leaves. 'Like this, then?'

The child looks at it intently. 'It has not so many little twigs.'

'Perhaps you had better go again and see how many twigs there are on the branch.'

'It has two branches, and only one little twig on each.'

The mother then carefully sketches the stag-beetle.

The introduction of the stag beetle into Anna's education brings us to the subject that Mary preferred to teach above all others, natural history. 'It is such a delightful task that I really almost envy a mother who has it for her work and duty.' This enthusiasm Anna shared. Indeed, natural history vied with drawing as Anna's major childhood interest.

The fauna and flora of Park Road being somewhat limited, nature excursions were made into the countryside north of London. As Mary walked about the fields and lanes of Essex with Anna and Philip, she must have seen herself in the role of the mother in such stories as *Harry and Lucy*. Indeed, the children in the illustrations for any of Maria Edgeworth's stories could well have been Anna and Philip, although Anna would not have worn the wide-brimmed straw hat favoured by Rosamund for her study of the robin, and Mary was too good a naturalist to identify, as Frank's mother did, bluebells and conkers on the same walk.

The two children set out on these nature walks each furnished with a little basket ready to bring home treasure for examination, and the shelves of the playroom were soon loaded with objects of interest, properly labelled and arranged, no doubt, as the Edgeworths would have expected. 'It would be almost ridiculous,' wrote their mother, 'to mention the number of sciences into which they took the first steps. Sometimes their father would bring them home a shell; by degrees they had a nice little collection, and would occasionally visit the British Museum to learn their names.'

Live specimens were also brought back from these expeditions. Plants dug up in the woods were transferred to the corner of the garden that Mary almost certainly allocated to the children, for she was a keen gardener. Animals found a home in the playroom and Anna and Philip were early accustomed to their care. Insects also were kept, for both children would handle beetles, spiders, earwigs, etc., with pleasure, and were much amused if anyone was afraid of them. But any bug that found its way into the playroom at Park Road need have no fear of the poison bottle. Moths and butterflies were 'kept under a glass for a short period' while Anna painted them and then released. 'We never compassed death to make a collection,' wrote Mary Sewell. 'We made one trial – that was sufficient.' Elsewhere she wrote, 'The accounts of naturalists' murderous tours have been very revolting to my mind; but the plea of scientific discovery turns black to white.'

The collecting of birds' eggs was discouraged for the same reason. Mary was too sensitive to the sufferings of the bereaved hen to permit it. Indeed, she wrote a poem on the subject called *The Chaffinch's Nest*. The collecting of materials to *make* birds' nests she did approve, and we have her description of an idyllic afternoon thus employed by Anna and Philip.

> What little things will make fairy days of enjoyment for children! Take two intelligent little children who have been accustomed to prove all things as far as they can, and give them a chaffinch's nest and a summer afternoon to collect materials similar to those of which it is composed, and then try their skill in making one … imagine the delight of that search for wool, moss, hair, grass, etc. Fancy the many thoughts that will occur to them as to where these things are to be found; fancy the eager eyes questioning every nook, collecting enough to make twenty nests if it could but be matted together; fancy the joy over a hair or feather, a tuft of wool gathered from a thorn bush, and the little sprigs of velvet moss. Life may have many joys afterwards, but that long summer afternoon will stand out radiant amongst them. And then the nest-making – the ineffectual attempts, the bungling performance, and then the lesson upon the exquisite faculty of instinct preparing the way for a hundred thousand more. Natural history may always be made to lead happily and gracefully and tenderly to God.

'Lead happily and gracefully and tenderly to God.' This last statement brings us to the crux of Mary Sewell's theory of education and to the parting of the ways with the Edgeworths. Their book, as she rightly said, had 'nothing to do with the religious formation of character', and it was for the religious formation of character that Mary cared above all else. The enthusiastic study of nature had an ulterior motive. That motive Mary Day later explained to Lucy Bell in verse, in *The Children of Summerbrook*.

> Whilst you and I are often wrong
> > And many a blunder make,
> A little spider weaves a web
> > Without the least mistake.
>
> My mother says that we may learn
> > From e'en the smallest thing,
> That all God's creatures everywhere
> > A useful lesson bring.

Mary considered it her duty to create of Anna 'a beautiful natural temple which the Blessed Master may irradiate ... at whatever time He may please to enter'. And, like Cromwell and his Iron-sides, Mary was convinced that God was on her side in her task. She once even went so far as to describe herself as a 'heaven-taught mother' and to express the wish that there were more like herself. Her edicts were backed up with quotations from the Bible.

> Whenever I wanted to correct anything wrong, I tried to put every-
> thing I said upon some foundation truth from the Bible. Then when
> I spoke to my children about what God wished them to do, or not
> to do, they knew that the God who was telling them to do all things
> 'without murmurings and disputings' was the same who had taught
> the little bee to hum and painted the flowers in such lovely colours.

No doubt at night Mrs Sewell heard the children's prayers as did the governess in *Patience Hart*.

> When they had finished the little regular prayer they always make,
> she asked them if they had not had anything that day to be particularly
> thankful for; and if they could not remember, she used to tell them
> of some pleasure they had enjoyed, or some kindness that had been
> shown to them; and then she used to ask them if there was no fault
> they had to confess, and ask God to forgive them; and so she used
> to help them on.

No doubt foremost among the sins Anna was prompted to confess were any cases of disobedience to the mother at whose knee she knelt.

It is not easy to imagine how the Edgeworths would have reacted to such sentiments, but the Quakers would certainly have approved. Two years before Anna's birth, a minute was agreed at the yearly meeting on this very subject. It ran: 'Dear Friends, who fill the important station of parents, never forget that … your labours will only be effectual as they are carried on and blessed by the power of the Spirit of Christ.' Two years after Anna's birth the elders recorded a further minute. 'Those who neglect to bend the tender minds of their children to parental authority and connive at their early tendencies to hurtful gratifications are, more or less, making way for the enemy and the destroyer.'

Anna was brought up as a strict Quaker. She was probably dressed in the plain Quaker manner and taught to regard colour and complication in her dress as a short cut to perdition. She may even have learnt a couplet written for the benefit of Friends' children in 1745:

> The rich man, gaily cloth'd, is now in Hell
> And dogs did eat attired Jezebel.

Mary Sewell makes no mention of being 'eldered', as her mother had been for excessive gaiety in her daughters' clothes. She had not the money for such indiscretions and, having run a shop dealing in Quaker apparel, she was familiar with its niceties. Anna would have worn long gowns, for Mary did not approve of short skirts for children when they came into fashion. She put her opinions into the mouth of Patience Hart who 'thought it was hardly decent for young ladies to show their legs so much'.* Her gowns would also

---

* It must be added here that the 'almost naked knees' would have been well covered by 'handsome trowsers' and indeed the shortness of the skirt was only intended to display the elaborate working of these. Needless to say, naughty Lucy Bell, the villainess of *The Children of Summerbrook,* approved of such frivolities:

> My mother says the frock wont come
> Quite down to Patty's knee,
> And so the work and little tucks
> Will all be shown, you see.

have been in sober colours. Their necklines would have been low and their sleeves full like those of the two younger girls in the 1830 portrait of Elizabeth Fry's children. Like them she would have omitted the modest handkerchief folded across the breast of the older girl in the centre of the picture. She would also have been spared the 'stiff muslin citadel' of the Quaker cap tied with strings under the chin. Mrs Sewell was against dressing children in such a manner as to restrict their freedom of movement. In *Patience Hart* she castigated a nursemaid who forbade her charges to play on the beach for fear of spoiling their clothes and pitied children who were 'dressed in the height, of fashion, not like children at all'. But on Sundays there would be no avoiding the Quaker bonnet. According to Mary Sewell, 'By this time the Friends' bonnet was almost universal. Here and there might be seen a straw cottage, but it was not considered genteel.' Genteel the Friends' bonnet may have been, but comfortable never. The crown was soft but the brim was stiff and formed a funnel round the wearer's face which thus became invisible in profile. Amelia Gummere, who died at the beginning of this century, could remember wearing one and described the 'crashing kiss' when two such bonnets met. The little girl in a painting entitled 'The Meeting House in Jordan's'* has wisely discarded hers in order to sleep. She could well be taken for Anna if her dress were not of a slightly later period.

Quaker meetings were an ordeal for a child. Not all adults find it easy to sit without moving head or limbs for one hour, let alone two. A seasoned Quaker will tell you that there is an art in relaxing to a point where awareness of the outside world ceases and complete immobility ensues. To those who have not acquired the art, awareness of the hardness of the bench becomes all absorbing after forty-five minutes and attention is centred not on things of the spirit but on how to move a cramped arm or leg without causing a disturbance. A child is liable to reach this stage after five minutes. 'I sometimes feel so extremely impatient for Meeting to break up that I cannot, if you would give me the world, sit still. Oh, how I long to get a broom and *bang* all the old Quakers who look so triumphant and

---

* Painted by J. Walter West.

so disagreable.' These words were written by Elizabeth Fry's sister Richenda thirty years earlier.

There were of course distractions. For the first ten minutes the arrival of late-comers could be observed and Anna would have a good view of the females among these composing themselves for worship. (The sexes sat separately.) This was the age of the shawl, a product of the East India trade, and there was an art in sitting down in one without crushing the point that hung down at the back. Amelia Gummere described it thus:

> An observant attender of Quaker meetings must have noticed the manner in which the plain Quakeress takes her seat, as with a hand behind her, palm outward, she gives an indescribable little 'flip' to the corner of her shawl, to avoid wrinkles in the tail! The air with which that 'flip' is given by a quick-motioned young woman, is levity itself.[*]

When 'waiting in silence upon the Lord' had begun there was less to watch. There were, of course, the faces of the elders who sat opposite the congregation. These were so immobile that a fictional small boy used to imagine that their owners had actually died. Then there were noises to listen to. In the silence of a Quaker meeting the rustle of a silk dress became thunderous and heavy breathing in the row behind was like the roaring of a pair of bellows. Mary Sewell as a girl had diverted herself by reciting Byron. History does not record how Anna made the time pass but certainly it passed too slowly. Her mother writes that 'She never liked silent meetings; she chafed against them as purposeless.' She would have been as relieved as Richenda when, after two hours of immobility, two female friends, as if prompted by a signal from on high, would take off their gloves, shake hands and walk slowly out, followed by the rest of the congregation.

The Sewells had attended the Gracechurch Street Meeting House ever since they left Yarmouth, bringing with them the required certificate 'of their sober and orderly conversation'. Gracechurch Street was considered the most important of the six London monthly meetings because it included the City within its limits. The most

[*] Gummere, Amelia Mott, *Quaker Costume.*

famous Meeting House to stand on the site was burnt down the
year after Anna was born. Known as the Quakers' 'New theatre in
Gracechurch Street', it had been specially constructed to house the
Yearly Meetings of all the Friends.

The rebuilt Meeting House was slightly less grand, the Yearly
Meetings having by this time migrated to Devonshire House near
by. Its members, however, as in Fox's day, continued to be 'the richest
trading-men in London'. They included the great banking families
such as the Barclays and the Gurneys, although their ranks had been
thinned by the defections during the Napoleonic wars of the Lloyds
and the Hanburys, who had supported the formation of volunteer
defence corps. Enough remained to make First Day Meetings the
occasion for much social visiting. One of the houses most noted
for its hospitality was Mildred Court, the home of Elizabeth Fry,
who had been a Gurney before she married. Mrs Fry ceased to be
a member of the Gracechurch Street meeting when she moved to
her country seat in 1809, but, as Mary Sewell recalled, she continued
to reside at Mildred Court and keep open house there during the
period of the yearly meeting until her husband's bank failed in 1830,
and Anna must almost certainly have heard her preach. She would
often have been told by her mother of Elizabeth Fry's first visit to
the women's yard at Newgate prison when the guards stood by and
waited to see her clothes torn from her body by a mass of women
reduced to the level of wild beasts.

Elizabeth Fry was not alone among the prominent members of
the Gracechurch Street meeting to move out to the country, or at
any rate the suburbs. Like the Sewells, many of the wealthy Friends
'solicitous for the health of their families took homes in the suburbs
where yet green fields were to be found'.[*] Unlike then they made the
First Day journey in their carriages which 'were to be seen waiting
in long rows (both in Gracechurch Street and Lombard Street)'. For
the Sewells and others in their position the problem of transport must
have been a serious one, for the public stage-coaches seldom plied on
a Sunday and the day of the omnibus was yet to come. Their problem
was solved by the establishment of the Stoke Newington Meeting

---

[*] Beck and Ball, *London Meeting Houses.*

House in 1829 'on account of so many members of the former meeting having moved to this locality'. The Stoke Newington Meeting was only a Meeting for worship and was under the Gracechurch Monthly Meeting for purposes of administration.

The new Meeting House, which Anna began to attend when she was nine, stood just off Church Street, Stoke Newington, and was demolished only a few years ago. It was severe in taste, but much admired for its proportions. William Alderson, the architect who designed it, later won a prize for planning a lunatic asylum.

The most distinguished member of the Stoke Newington Meeting was William Allen, the famous chemist and philanthropist, whose grave can still be seen in the burial ground of the present Meeting House. He was a partner, with Robert Owen and Jeremy Bentham, in the model factory at New Lanark Mills and was introduced to the Tsar of Russia as 'a model Quaker'.

Perhaps of more interest to Anna at the Stoke Newington Meeting House were the young ladies from Fleetwood House to whom William Allen taught chemistry. Fleetwood House was the Quaker boarding school that he had helped to found. It stood near the Meeting House in Church Street and its wealthy pupils (the fees were fifty pounds a year with washing extra) arrived at meeting on foot in identical bonnets supplied by the milliner in Bishopsgate whose competition had contributed to the ruin of Anna's parents. Before the Stoke Newington Meeting House was built, the young ladies were transported to meeting in horse-drawn vehicles, where the poet Pease delighted

> To see them arriving at Gracechurch Street Meeting
> All snugly packed up, twenty-five in a van

The child being educated at home must have envied them each other's companionship.

When morning meeting was over, the dreary stretches of the Victorian Sunday lay ahead. Even children might be expected to attend a second meeting in the afternoon. If they were not, the only diversion permitted was the reading of the Gospel or pious books by Friends. In the evening there were family prayers, a life-long habit with Isaac and Mary Sewell. The 'little servant' would be in attendance and Isaac read a chapter from the Bible. A silence followed which might or might not be filled with an extemporised prayer from the master or mistress of the house. Family devotions took place on weekday evenings as well and Isaac probably insisted on grace before meals. Here again a set prayer was not the custom among Quakers. 'When they are all seated at table, they sit in solemn silence and in a thoughtful position for some time. If the master of the family ... should feel any religious impression on his mind ... he gives utterance.'*

Anna and Philip did not submit to this stern discipline entirely without protest. Mary called them 'nice toward little children' when she was over eighty, and could not speak too highly of their 'very happy dispositions and fine tempers'. 'Toward' Anna may have seemed through the mists of time, but a faded note found by Mrs Bayly among Mary Sewell's papers tell a different story. It was headed 'Anna Sewell's Birthday.'

12 Park Road, 30th of 3rd month, 1829

Anna Sewell has this day completed her ninth year, and is in many respects a delight and comfort to her mother, who, that she may be able to test her progress from year to year, wishes now to write a short account of her attainments in her learning, and of the qualities of her mind, etc. [There follows entire approbation of her truth and candour and her progress in some branches of learning. But the mother goes on to speak of Anna's want of perseverance.] Much disposed to idle over lessons and work. She needs to get the habit of a cheerful surrender of her own will – to give up entirely telling tales of her brother. She begins to be useful to her mother, but is not tidy. In *everything* her mother hopes she will be improved by another year.

Of Philip, she wrote:

More persevering in play than in work: he has an awkward habit of repeating what other people say; can neither sit nor stand still; takes no pains to speak distinctly. Altogether he is a nice little boy, and his

* Clarkson, *A Portrait of Quakerism* 1805

mother hopes by this day twelvemonth he will have lost all his bad habits and increased his good ones.

Mrs Bayly reports that she 'looked on to the next year's papers with some curiosity to see if the mother's wishes were realised. Instead of improvement, the faults and failings recorded are more numerous than before.'

This picture of Anna's moral development at the age of nine is the more valuable because it is the earliest we have of her. Mary had been careful to enumerate her faults, but she only mentioned one of her virtues, honesty. Mercilessly honest Anna certainly was and remained so all her life. Mary complained many years later. 'If I ask Nanny to arrange the fruit she will always turn the worst side out.' But honesty was not Anna's only virtue, as her mother testified elsewhere. 'She had a great deal of courage and independence of character, never burdened with any kind of fear.' While living at Dalston she had a 'painful accident'. She dislocated her elbow, which was some time in recovering its strength and usefulness. 'I bore it well,' was her comment to an aunt. The accident itself is significant in the light of future events and so is the manner in which she endured it. The Edgeworths would have approved of her fortitude. Indeed, one wonders if her comment was not an echo of one of Frank's. That young gentleman, having been permitted to burn himself with sealing wax for his own good, declared, 'It hurts me very much mamma! ... But I will not cry – I will bear it well.'

'You do bear it well,' said his father. 'Shake hands with me, with the hand that is not burnt.'[*]

Her courage extended to the protection of ill-treated animals. Cruelty or oppression of any kind roused all her indignation. Men who shot birds for pleasure she called Boobies. Mary describes a confrontation with a Booby who had 'shot a blackbird, which fell into our front garden. The man came to the gate to get possession of it. Anna rushed to the door. With an obsequious smile, the man said, "If you please, Miss, will you let me take my bird?" "No," she said. "Thee cruel man, thee shant have it at all."' A startling speech for a little Quaker girl who had been taught to preface every suggestion with the phrase 'Hadn't thee better'.

---

[*] Edgeworth, Maria, *Early Lessons*.

It was also at the age of nine (probably just after the birthday report was written) that Anna gave very real proof of her unselfishness. Mary tells the story.

> At the time we lived in Dalston the potato famine occurred in Ireland. We had been planning for some time for a visit to the seaside, and I had been carefully economising so as to have sufficient money to meet the expense. Our plans and conversation centred on this trip. With rather a fainting heart I pictured to them the sufferings of the Irish, and how much money was wanted to buy food for them. I told them I had no money to spare except the money I had laid by for our trip. Would they be willing to give that up and send the money to the Irish people? They both at once said they would. I told them to think about it during the day, and if at night they were of the same mind, the money should be sent. At night they were quite determined that the money should be appropriated to the starving Irish. Eventually they gained more than they had given up, my husband's kind brother William proposed to send us all to the sea at Sandgate for some weeks, at his own expense.

Here was a Maria Edgeworth story come to life. It found Anna firmly cast in the role of the good child reaping her inevitable reward.

The holiday at Sandgate was one of many happy ones that Anna spent away from Dalston, for her childhood did not consist solely of study, plain sewing and self-denial. Sandgate was a resort after Mary Sewell's heart. Although only one and a half miles west of Folkestone, in those days it had not been submerged by its larger neighbour. The beach was sandy and sheltered, the South Downs were at hand, picturesquely surmounted by Henry VIII's castle, and there was a pleasant marine walk connecting it with Hythe. Above all, it was quiet. Mary Sewell felt, as did her friend Sarah Stickney Ellis, that children should 'see the great ocean as it really is, broad, bold and deep, without the fringe of fashion on its shores'. 'How often,' wrote Mrs Ellis, ' … are children taken in the summer to fashionable watering places … to wear their best clothes, walk out in tight shoes, and hear their mammas and aunts descant on the elegance of the Duchess of D's equipage!' Mrs Sewell put the complaints of such children into the mouths of Gerald, Rose and Edith in *Patience Hart*. 'Oh! Patience,' said Miss Edith, 'we did want you so at Brighton to make ponds in the sand.'' And I wanted you to get stones for me to throw into the sea.' 'And I wanted you to help me to look for the sea weed and the little shells.' 'I suppose you enjoyed yourselves very much?' 'No, not very much,' said Miss Rose. 'We had nobody to play with us and Judith would not let us dig with the spades mamma bought us, because she said we made ourselves wet.'

The Sewell children were also fortunate to be spared sea-bathing, a newly fashionable pursuit. Judging from the account Master Gerald gave of it to Patience, Mary Sewell considered it a form of cruelty. 'I hate that nasty old woman with that blue gown on. She said I was a pretty little gentleman and then she put me into the water all over my head, and the water was so nasty, Patience; I never will go again, I never will.'

Mary Sewell considered that a holiday should be the occasion for useful increase of knowledge, however, and much natural history was learnt at Sandgate. Uncle William's only child Lucy, a girl of thirteen, was of the party and the young naturalists made many excursions in search of specimens. The plundering of rock pools which Philip Henry Gosse, the father of Edmund Gosse, initiated by his charmingly illustrated books on shore life had not yet become fashionable and the children probably confined their attention to sea shells. While on a visit to Folkestone, they saw the famous Blue Clay fossils. Gerard Edward Smith, a botanist, was staying there at the time, and 'helped much to foster their love of flowers, which ever went on increasing'.

We can imagine Lucy, Anna and Philip, as Kingsley described his own children thirty years later, 'drinking in health from every breeze and instruction in every step, running ever and anon with proud delight to add their little treasure to see their father's stock'. For them, no doubt, as for the Kingsley children, there were 'happy evenings spent over the microscope and the vase, in examining, arranging, preserving, and noting down in the diary the wonders and labours of the happy busy day'.

The holiday at Sandgate may have been Anna's only long seaside holiday. Certainly it is the only one of which there is a record. But she had many country holidays. Most of her summers were spent on her grandfather's farm at Buxton in Norfolk. Mary's parents took a great interest in her and Philip, for they were for many years their only grandchildren. Every Christmas there was a hamper of farm

produce from Buxton. Mary Sewell recalls that the arrival of this
hamper was one of the big events of the year at 12 Park Road.

> Children were not overwhelmed with presents at that time, as they
> now often are. The unpacking as well as the packing was all heartfelt.
> The children stood around and, as every labelled article came, it was
> received with joyful acclamations. Grandmother sent ducks and sau-
> sages and mince-pies, and grandfather, apples, pears and walnuts, and
> things on which were written, 'For my dear boy', or 'For my little
> maid'; something from each aunt then at Buxton, and letters – not
> much in money cost, but oh, how much in deep love!

Part of the excitement of a stay at Buxton was the journey. Anna
almost certainly travelled in the same stage-coach as that in which
David Copperfield made his famous journey from Yarmouth to
London; the coach whose London starting-point was an inn in
Whitechapel, 'I forget whether it was the "Blue Bull' or the "Blue
Boar"; but I know it was Blue Something, and that its likeness was
painted up on the back of the coach.' Like Copperfield she must
have travelled all night, for the journey took seventeen hours; she
must have seen the four fresh horses for the first stage hitched to
the coach as it stood in the yard; she must have endured the good-
natured banter of her fellow passengers at the coaching inn where
they stopped for supper, she must have spent an uncomfortable night
wedged between sleeping adults and passed through villages where
early-rising boys got up behind and swung for a little way.

At Yarmouth, Anna and Philip always stayed a few days. No doubt
they explored the vast desolate wastes and beaches whose flatness
had caused the young Copperfield to suppose himself at one of the
poles. Yarmouth was not a resort in those days. It was a busy port
and the centre of the bloater industry. Old Peggotty had been proud
to call herself a Yarmouth Bloater. The steep narrow streets, known
as rows, smelt of 'fish, and pitch and oakum, and tar'; there were
sailors everywhere and 'carts jingling up and down over the stones'.
Anna stayed with her Sewell relations. Her grandparents, William
and Hannah Maria Sewell, had moved to London at the same time
as her parents and the grocer's shop in the market place was now
run by Isaac's brothers Abraham and Edward. The shop, at 28 Market

Place, still stands. It is now a Hennekey's bar surrounded by twentieth-century chain stores. It retains its fine eighteenth-century brick façade. Sewell Row (now renamed Row 46) still flanks it on the left-hand side, blessedly silent because, being less than two yards wide, no traffic can enter. The shop would have been a fascinating place for a child for there were often 'quaint Dutch sailors' there yarning about their voyages. Young Anna was probably not encouraged to loiter there but she must have enjoyed the company of Edward's six children who lived above it.

Edward Sewell was a man of some standing in Yarmouth, being Councillor for North Ward in 1836 and again in 1845. We know little of him apart from the fact that, according to Sarah Stickney Ellis, who had him to stay, he was 'neat in his ways'. He married a cousin of Mary Sewell, Martha Holmes, and one of his daughters, another Mary Sewell, was born the same year as Anna and grew up to be a woman of some charm and character. She never married, and eventually moved to Hitchin where she helped bring up her brother's large and somewhat neglected family. Her diaries, chiefly filled with domestic details, still exist.

Abraham's six children lived near by, in the area of Yarmouth known as the North End. Abraham also was a councillor and a man of deep religious convictions as can be seen from the letter he wrote to his son Joseph Stickney, in later years, persuading him to remain a Quaker. He believed, however, that Christianity did not mean cutting oneself off from all human interests. Neither was he above a little human vanity, for it was he who first used a seal bearing the crest of the Sewells[*] who were lords of the manor of Great Henney, near Bures in the Colchester area. This branch of the Sewell family produced two distinguished men in the eighteenth century, George Sewell, the writer, and Sir Thomas Sewell, Master of the Rolls. The family died out with Sir Thomas and there is no proof that Abraham had any connection with it.

Abraham's wife, 'sweet and lovely' Dorothy Stickney Sewell, was also a remarkably person. She was the sister of Sarah Stickney Ellis and came from Holderness in Yorkshire, where her father had been a

[*] See Appendix II.

progressive farmer with a keen interest in scientific matters. He and his wife had mixed largely with non-Quakers until their early deaths, and among their children 'individuality had been allowed free play'. Dorothy introduced a broader outlook and less conventional stand-ard into her home. She was the close confidant of her son, Joseph.

Joseph Stickney Sewell, the second of her three boys, was destined to achieve fame as a missionary in Madagascar. He was a year older than Anna, somewhat 'dreamy and self-absorbed' as a boy, with a tendency to morbid self-analysis ... too full of his own plans to share as fully in his brothers' and sisters' interests as he might have done. He both adored and envied his elder brother, William, the charmer of the family, who died before he was thirty. William was gifted with 'natural courtesy and gentleness of manner and a broad sympathy'. Joseph, being sensitive and shy, 'considered it impossible to acquire such graces by cultivation and rather gloried in being downright and abrupt in manner'. It is therefore doubtful whether Anna or Joseph were close friends in spite of the closeness of their ages. When he was nine, whatever relationship the two cousins may have had was promptly ended by his being sent to Ackworth, where, it will be remembered, holidays were against the rules.

The decision to send a sensitive, mother-loving boy to this institu-tion is slightly surprising. Dorothy can have had no illusions about life at the school. She had almost certainly spent her own orphaned childhood there. Sarah Stickney Ellis was educated there and drew a grisly picture of the place. She even invented a small inmate called Arthur who died from too much fagging.

Ackworth now is, of course, a very different place from what it was in Joseph's day and even Joseph enjoyed advantages that had been denied to Grandfather Wright. There was a wooden floor now in the Meeting House and backs had been added to the seats there. Wooden trenchers had been abolished, so had shared beds and the communal wash-bowl. The former method of heating (one fire to each room, however large), had been supplemented by steam pipes and the famous flagstone path, where brothers could enjoy 'the gra-cious and ennobling conversation of sisters from the opposite wing', had been laid.

Punishments, on the other hand, had become if anything more savage. Rooms had been built for solitary confinement and furnished

in prison style. Disease and death also continued to stalk the ill
drained buildings. Smallpox, the ravager of Grandfather Wright's
generation, had been controlled by vaccination, but scarlet fever
had come to its place. In Joseph's last year at school three boys
died of it. He himself contracted the disease but regarded it as the
happiest event of his school life, for his mother came to nurse him
in the school sanitorium. He often admitted that he did not know
how he was going to live through the first three years of exile from
his family.

Joseph's younger brother Edward was also a thoughtful boy and
in later life wrote some pious poetry and two books on doctrinal
subjects. Of William's three sisters, with whom Anna is most likely
to have associated, we have only the names.

It is probable that Isaac's sister, Fulleretta, and her husband, Joseph
Hunter, were still living in Yarmouth with the six children (again
three boys and three girls) to whom Anna's aunt, Elizabeth Wright,
was governess. If they were, they brought the number of Norfolk
cousins up to eighteen.

After a few days at Yarmouth Anna and Philip usually took ship for
Norwich. Steamships were still plying on the River Yare in spite of
Grandfather Wright's disastrous experience. At the dock at Norwich
a dog-cart or a gig was no doubt waiting to carry the children to
Buxton. It is possible, however, that they did the last six miles of the
journey by carrier's cart. Willing Barkises were the only purveyors
of cheap local transport at this time.

Buxton, as we have already said, lay to the north on the Aylsham
road. It was surrounded by the famous landscape that inspired the
Norwich school of painters; that landscape where the sky, as somebody said, seems to come down to your feet and a solitary tree on the
horizon stands out with an almost unearthly significance. Dudwick
House, the home of Uncle and Aunt Wright, lay half a mile to the
west of the flint village church. The picturesque thatched lodge at its
gates can still be seen, opposite the Black Lion, Buxton, and the lodge-
keeper's sister still remembers running to be first to open the gate for
the carriage and earn sixpence. The drive that winds through the trees
of the park has not changed since Anna's day, but Dudwick House
itself, a fine red-brick eighteenth-century building, was replaced by the
present Dudwick Hall in 1939. The situation of the house, however,

is the same and the sweep of gravel driveway in front and the lawn behind are as they always were. Farther up the drive are the original stable blocks, one on either side. The larger one, still known locally (if not accurately) as Black Beauty's stables, is built of mellowed red brick round a courtyard and is entered through handsome pillars with stone balls on top. To the outside corner is attached a coachman's cottage with gothic windows overlooking a walled kitchen garden and the deer park, no doubt the home of John Wright's coachman.

It was, however, at the home farm at the end of the back drive that Anna stayed as a child, for it was here that, ten years previously, Uncle Wright had installed her grandparents and her aunts. It is a square flint-built house standing back from the road with a garden in front. Before it was added to, it consisted of a room on either side of the front door with a kitchen and dairy at the back (the stone-slab shelves in the dairy can still be seen). Upstairs there were probably no more than four bedrooms. A pair of interconnecting ones with low sloping ceilings are used by the present farmer's wife as a store-room. It was in these that Anna and Philip no doubt slept. One suspects that when Mary spoke of 'the little crushed company' that moved in after the steamship disaster, she meant physically crushed as well as mentally.

Mary Sewell's sister Aunt Maria, now twenty-eight, was still living at home. By this time she must have given up all hope of marriage and settled down to the life of the dutiful daughter. Many years later she was to write three novels and although they were by no means masterpieces they suggested that she was a woman of some sensitivity and imagination. Aunt Ellen was still in her teens and able to supply a commodity otherwise lacking at Buxton, youth. Uncle and Aunt Wright at the big house were childless. Indeed, Anna was the only one of Mary's six brothers and sisters to have children. Somewhat late in life she had become the second wife of 'that good man' Joseph Crewdson of Manchester, a widower with six children. Her own son, Theodore, was not born until 1835.

In Mary Sewell's words, Grandfather Wright was

the central attraction to all the grandchildren. When he was sitting, they were by his side. There was never any noise or boisterous play, but any one who watched could see that the conversation was full of deep interest. My father knew the heart of a child; his own nature was full of hope and experiment – that high temperature in which intelligent children delight to dwell.

Buxton in those days must have been a paradise for children. There Anna tasted for herself the joys of harvest-time that had so often been described to her by her mother. She must have seen her grandfather's Suffolk Punches led out of the brick-built yard on a summer morning and harnessed to the wagons in the barn that still stands behind the house. In fine weather she must have seen them haul in the last load by moonlight.

But it was up at the big house that she made her first close acquaintance with horses. Uncle Wright kept the stable block at the back of the house well filled and it was on his horses that Anna learnt to ride. Fortunately, riding was at this time considered a desirable accomplishment in a young lady. Becky Sharp's graceful mastery of the kicker endeared her, as much as her singing and playing, to Rawdon Crawley in *Vanity Fair*. More important, from Mrs Sewell's point of view, it was said to be healthy and character-forming. Sarah Stickney Ellis was, a few years later, to devote a page to its commendation in *The Mothers of England*, a book on education much approved by Mrs Sewell.

> Horse-exercise affords one of the most exhilarating and delightful amusements of the country. Let them learn to ride without fear, to accommodate themselves to the different movements of their pony, so as not to be thrown up into the air, to drop down again like a dead weight, and let them learn, too, what to do on the instant when a horse starts, rears, or strikes off into a gallop; and they will then have learned beside the art of riding, a great deal that will be serviceable to them in after life.
>
> But they should learn in addition to the art of riding, the nature and habits of the horse. So noble, sagacious and beautiful an animal is well worthy of their study. They should be instructed in its muscular construction and especially the wonderful adaptation of its feet and legs to the purposes in which it is rendered so serviceable to man; and they should also learn the action and the use of the bridle with all the other trappings and accountrements of a horse …
> On a clear fresh morning in the country, while riding by the side of a kind and intelligent father, everything told to a child about the lively

little animal which carries it along so cheerfully, pricking its ears at every movement in the hawthorn hedge, keeping pace with its more majestic companion, and determined not to be outdone, either in a light gallop over the rebounding turf, or a leap over the little brook which crosses the way – everything told to a child about a crea-ture so intensely interesting as its own pony is sure to be listened to and remembered.

Such arguments no doubt convinced Mrs Sewell that the expense of a riding-habit was justified.

Anna's instructor was probably her uncle's groom and her mount the pony that drew her aunt's chaise. Later she rode Balaam, a well-mannered horse with a good mouth who was accustomed to the side-saddle. Balaam was an old favourite who had been in the stables for many years Uncle Wright, being a Quaker, did not hunt and was not over-concerned with show. It is probable, therefore, that Anna's mount drew the family carriage when required. He would have been an animal of thoroughbred type standing about 15.2 hands high.

There are many pleasant rides within a six-mile radius of Buxton, and although Anna's outings were probably more sedate than those of a close neighbour, Elizabeth Fry, who, twenty years earlier, had held up the mail coach with the aid of her six sisters all wearing red cloaks, she nevertheless enjoyed a greater measure of freedom on these excursions than at any other time in her life.

One of her favourite rides was across the fields to see neighbours at Rippon Hall, half a mile away. In the 1830s Rippon Hall was no more than a substantial brick farmhouse with fine Tudor chimneys and extensive farm buildings. Since then a Victorian wing has been added, but the route that Anna used to take on her pony, through the plantation of ancient yews and oaks that fringe the park and alongside the walled kitchen garden, has not changed. The horses of Christopher Birkbeck, the present owner, still graze in the park.

Another favourite ride, no doubt, was to her mother's old home at Felthorpe, only five miles to the south-east, and for long gallops there was Buxton Heath, still a wild area of heather and gorse where rare gentians can be found.

The Quaker Meeting House at Lammas where Anna's parents had been married was less than a mile away and the route to it was a picturesque one. To reach it Anna would have ridden down the front drive of Dudwick House, past the church and the newly built village school that still bears a plaque in memory of Cousin Wright who endowed it, and over the River Bure. On the bridge, by the old water-mill, she must surely have paused to watch the river meander through water-meadows and admire the view of Lammas Church crouching among trees beyond. No doubt she attended First Day Meetings in the eighteenth-century Meeting House, although even at that time the Quaker population of the district was dwindling so fast that her pious grandmother often attended the weekday meeting there in complete solitude.

The Meeting House still stands although it has come down some-what in the world. Ten years ago it was being used as a chapel by the Wesleyan Reform Union. Now two of its windows have been blocked and it serves as a store for a neighbouring farm. It is sol-idly built of red brick with a well-pitched roof and should stand for some years yet. Behind it, the burial ground, now a small enclosure of rough grass planted with handsome yew trees, is flanked by the garden walls of a newly built villa. In Anna's day it was a 'seques-tered spot, surrounded by trees and high hawthorn hedges, where the birds are never disturbed'. A patient searcher will find some simple tombstones buried in the long grass. One of these bears the following inscription:

> In affectionate remembrance
> of Anna Sewell
> daughter of Isaac and
> Mary Sewell who died
> at Catton, April 25th 1878
> Aged 58 years.

Near by are the graves of Isaac and Mary Sewell and both the John Wrights with their wives, also marked by tombstones in defiance of the Quaker disapproval of the 'vain custom of erecting monu-ments over the dead bodies of Friends'. The four graves are seldom disturbed now. Occasionally an admirer of Anna tugs the rough grass from round her stone, attempts to read the almost illegible inscription and takes a photograph. In 1965 the grave was 'discovered' and the

whole burial ground cleared by the school children of Buxton. There
were a few letters to the *Eastern Daily Press* and then the grass grew up
again as tall as before. The land has now been bought by a resident of
Lammas who refuses to discuss her plans for it.

At Buxton Anna did not only learn to ride horses. She also learnt to
drive them. Her aunt was probably her instructress, for Aunt Wright,
although she had grown pale and something of an invalid since her
marriage, drove a pony and chaise in all weathers. This was unusual. A
woman of her standing would normally have ridden in a carriage. She
also drove without a groom which was even more unusual, preferring
to get down and open the gates for herself.

Aunt Wright was a woman of wider interests than her husband,
who was a country gentleman and chiefly concerned with the
running of his estates. Both husband and wife were liberal and self-
denying, but whereas John Wright had little imagination and, even
in his adoring sister Mary's opinion 'sometimes failed to see all the
bearings that a subject might properly admit of', Anne Wright had
no such shortcomings. She had a passion for natural history and a
great gift for communicating this passion to the young. 'Mrs. Wright's
stories' were famous. According to Mary Sewell, 'she enchanted
children instructing them with the utmost simplicity. She could
interest a company of children anywhere; her interest and affection
flowed out to them so intensely that she never felt the burden of self-
consciousness, and the plentiful store of her imagination always seemed
within reach.' During one of her long illnesses when 'debarred from the
enlivening company of her young friends' she started a correspondence
with them about natural history. This correspondence she was urged
by her friends to publish and it appeared in 1850 under the title of *The
Observing Eye*. The book had a considerable success. Queen Victoria
read it and pronounced it suitable for use in the royal nursery. The critics praised it as 'elevating to the infant heart', and one went so far as to
quote her description of the gills of a fish in full. She followed it up eight
years later with *What is a Bird?*, a series of twenty-six lectures originally
delivered to the boys at the Red House School, a reformatory founded
by her husband. Her aim was to discourage bird-nesting, which she
disliked as much as did her sister-in-law. Indeed, the only birds that were
ever molested on the estate at Buxton were the blackbirds and sparrows
Philip was allowed, rather surprisingly, to shoot as 'garden robbers'.

Another of Aunt Wright's pursuits was geology, 'that sublime field of modern science', newly fashionable among several of her neighbours. Adam Sedgwick, the Woodwardian Professor of Geology, was Prebendary of Norwich at this time. According to Augustus Hare, 'he threw a mantle of love over everyone', which may account for the local ladies' enthusiasm for fossils. Another keen amateur in the area was Anna Gurney, a little old lady who was paralysed at an early age. 'She lived in a beautiful little cottage at Northrepps full of fossils and other treasures near the sea-coast.'* The two women must almost certainly have been acquainted, for both were Quakers and Northrepps was within calling distance of Buxton. Anne Wright was later to lecture on geology to the boys at the Red House School reformatory and to publish these lectures too in the form of a textbook. This book was very much what one might expect from a devout and intelligent amateur, of the period, for although Charles Lyell, in 1830, had published the first volume of his great work *The Principles of Geology*, she preferred the explanation of the earth's history given by the Catastrophic School. The lads at the reformatory must have thrilled to her description of the destruction of the carboniferous trees. 'The shaken limestone strata reeling to and fro, were either tossed up into the mountains or sunk into the depths of the ocean, and as the waters swept over the descending lands, their roaring waves, laden with mud and sand, bore away extensive forests.'

Anne Wright was a woman of deep piety and read the Good Book daily. She even published a commentary on Leviticus explaining Jewish sacrificial rites to children. She had taste for general reading also, 'but none for languages nor for romance, to which her heart always appeared a stranger. The profitable was her aim, and to please others for their good to edification was her delight.' She would never have been guilty, like Mary Sewell, of repeating the lusher passages of the *Oriental Tales* to herself during a First Day Meeting. She did, however, have a taste for art, and no doubt encouraged her niece to paint. She herself had executed some landscapes which were admired in their day but which have not survived. As she looked

---

* Hare, Augustus, *Autobiography*.

back upon some of her earlier attempts, when travelling in Jersey and
Switzerland, she 'would express a passing regret that she possessed a
talent that she might have cultivated if other employments had not
superseded it'.

These other employments were chiefly of a charitable nature, for
Aunt Wright took her duties as lady of the manor seriously, and after
her death a sixteen-page pamphlet was published describing her
'philanthropic efforts'. There were few village deathbeds at which
she did not pronounce 'the truths that make wise unto Salvation'
and these same truths she also instilled into the minds of villagers at
the beginning of life's journey. She even rewrote the catechism for
the benefit of the children at the village school. Once a year these
children were entertained on the lawn in front of the house for
prize-giving, 'each little urchin emulous to win an approving smile
as their progress in learning was tested'.

Mary Sewell described one of these school treats 'in her verse cycle
The Children of Summerbrook, and it is probable that she and Anna had
been present at one. If so, they would certainly have helped with the
morning preparations, when

> Busy hands up at the Hall,
> 　Were cutting piles of cake
> And called on all, both great and small
> 　Some work to undertake.

After the prize-giving, in the early afternoon, amusements were
provided.

> Some games had kindly been contrived,
> 　The merry hours to pass;
> They played at ball, and races ran,
> 　Upon the level grass.

> Some children played at blind man's buff,
> 　Some swung upon a tree;
> Until 'twas time to say the grace,
> 　And then sit down to tea.

> Twas wonderful to see the lumps
>   The little ones would take;
> And what an appetite they had
>   For Squire Tyerman's cake.

Back in Dalston, Mary Sewell was as busily engaged in good works as her sister-in-law at Buxton, and no doubt benefited by her children's absence to put in extra hours in the district. Her enthusiasm for poor visiting, which had begun when she lived in Camomile Street, amounted to a passion as she grew older. Whenever she moved house (and the Sewells were to move frequently), she sought out the most desperate cases of local need, just as more worldly women seek out the best shops. When she wrote 'the harvest was never more plenteous than now' (meaning the harvest of the poor) there was a suggestion almost of satisfaction in her tone. In one of the last letters she ever wrote, at the age of eighty-seven, she expressed a wish that death might be 'postponable' while there was still so much good to be done on earth.

Admittedly she lived in the age of the great humanitarians: Wilberforce and Shaftesbury were her contemporaries. Furthermore, she was a Quaker and Quakers, like Elizabeth Fry and William Allen, played a leading part in the humanitarian movement: 'Visiting and cheering the habitations of human misery' was a duty laid upon Friends long before the occupation became fashionable. They had been campaigning against the 'unchristian traffic in negroes' since 1727 and were already demanding the abolition of the death penalty. She also had the example of her mother, Anne Wright, to follow. At Felthorpe Anne had been 'the lady of the village'; all the little kindnesses proceeded from 'Madam Wright'. When vaccination came in, Mary's younger sister and brother, Maria and Richard, were immunised and taken to a house where smallpox was raging to persuade the villagers of its efficacy. (In connection with this incident, Mary remarked in her *Reminiscences*, 'It is only fair to say that Richard had the smallpox very badly when he was a young man.') When beer was being brewed at the farmhouse, Mary and Elizabeth were sent round with jugs of it to the neighbours. At the age of seven or eight they performed their own first act of charity. A boy from a very poor family had been ordered to dig a hole in the orchard. Both girls dropped their weekly penny 'accidentally' into the hole and when he attempted to return them said, 'Oh no, it is of no consequence.'

Yet this promising start was not at once followed up. During the idle years as a poetical maiden at Yarmouth Mary does not appear to have been unduly concerned about the destitute widows of the local fishermen of whom there must have been plenty. She did not, like Elizabeth Fry at the same age, sally forth with hampers of food for the needy or start a school for poor 'schollers' in the attic. It was only after she was married that she started to visit the poor. No doubt this was understandable. In London she was presented at the same time with people whose wants were pressing and the means to supply some of these wants – a kitchen of her own. There may, however, have been less worthy reasons for her changed attitude. The role of Lady Bountiful was an aristocratic one and Mary had the humiliation of those years as a governess to live down. In her book on poor visiting, *Thy Poor Brother*, she always figures as The Lady. The Lady is a dignified figure, wise, merciful and always in control of the situation. Whatever her motives were for visiting the poor, Mary was undoubtedly loved by them. She deplored the type of visitor who entered a poor home, distributed tracts, scoldings and good advice in equal quantities and drove off in her carriage leaving the object of her charity more demoralised than ever. One of the first ballads she wrote, *The Working Woman's Appeal*, was on this subject. The speaker is a poor labourer's wife who is visited on washing-day by her former mistress, Mrs Goldiman, all in 'shotten silk of pink and green'.

> She only knew of cottages
>   That poets write about,
> Where work is pleasant exercise
>   Both in the house and out,
> And children all have curling hair
>   Like cherubim, no doubt.
>
> The worst revenge that I would take,
>   The only one I'd seek,
> Would be, that Mistress Goldiman
>   Should manage here a week;
> And after that experience
>   I'd like to hear her speak.

Mary Sewell's sympathy was always with the poor working woman. 'A poor woman with a large family to manage for, and few shillings to manage with, and who does it well and cheerfully, is, in my estimation, the wonder of the world.' She was always more inclined to set out on her visits armed with a scrubbing brush and soap than a pile of tracts. The help she gave was often of a very practical nature. On one occasion she called for the first time at a poor home and, getting no reply to her knock, followed the sounds of screams to an upstairs room where a distracted mother was pursuing some wandering leeches round a bedroom with a view to fixing them to a screaming three-year-old suffering from inflammation of the lungs. She at once came to the rescue, took the child on her lap and confined the errant leeches to the part by holding a footless wine glass over them.

Unlike Mrs Goldiman, she was slow to blame the 'poor toiling woman' for the bad management and confusion of their lives. She could imagine what it was like to bring up a family in one room without a copper to do the washing in.

> I know it needs the patience
>   That a martyr may require,
> To wash without a copper,
>   With a pot upon the fire;
> The chimney smoke all driving down,
>   And smuts as black as mire.[*]

She did not blame the mother who fed her family on cups of tea and hunks of baker's bread when there was no means of cooking beyond an open fire. Instead she wrote a poem about a woman who felt she could

> Cry her heart away before
>   An ironmonger's shop
> And wish a little cooking stove,
>   Would from the heavens drop.[**]

---

[*] Sewell, Mary, *The Working Woman's Appeal.*

[**] Sewell, Mary, *A Sad Story.*

While she was living at Dalston she continued to visit the poor women of Shoreditch whom she had got to know from Camomile Street. In *Thy Poor Brother* she described how she, in the person of The Lady, imagined herself into the place of one of these in particular, 'a poor sickly thing', with a house that was always in confusion and ragged dirty children who were the weary occupants of that comfortless room in the alley. She gives her imagination play, and finds herself intending to wash the clothes that look so dirty. She gathers together a few of the children's clothes (only a few of them can be spared as they have no change; the rest must be washed when they are in bed). She pulls off one of the sheets, but feels that she has not the strength to wash it, and, if she had, how can it be dried? There is no place to hang it up out-of-doors; and, with the children all about, how can it be dried in that little room? Besides, there is only a shovelful of coals left and who knows where the next are to come from? She will give up the washing today. She will clean the house instead – the floor is so very dirty but again difficulties meet her: there is neither broom, house-cloth or scrubbing-brush (scrubbing-brushes are so dear, quite beyond a poor woman's means to buy them); the handle too is off the bucket, and the water has to be brought from a distance. She would like to polish up that dull stove a bit, to make a neat fireside, but there has not been a penny to spare for black-lead for a long time, and the hair of the brush is worn down to the wood: it is of no use. Oh, how tired and discouraged she begins to feel! How she would like some nice little thing to eat, or, better than all, a cup of tea to refresh herself with! But since her husband has been out of work she has not had any; tea is so expensive, and they have no credit and there is only a little piece of bread in the house, and the children must have that.

Mary Sewell had the art of genuinely sympathising with people in distress and an ability to say the right thing that some of her admirers regarded as divinely inspired. An old woman once said to her, 'Ah, Mrs. Sewell, what a back you are to me.' 'Back,' added Mary Sewell in recounting the incident. 'Not bank.' She was never rich and despised 'bare gift charity'. To use a favourite expression of hers, she spared out of her want, not out of her abundance. The extent of her actual gifts was often no more than a small pudding or a regular allowance of sixpence a week, but she considered the sympathy she gave was

of greater value than any material gift. 'The great secret of help,' she
wrote, 'is encouragement.'

The slums of Shoreditch were not salubrious places. Yet she had
only to hear of a case of need and she would pack her basket with
provisions and seek it out. *The Drunkard's Wife* gives a picture of her
at work.

> Our servant Jane learnt in the town –
>   I cannot tell you how –
> That someone had been starved to death
>   In little Wapping Row.
>
> And so I stored my basket well,
>   And went out there to see,
> And found it was the truth indeed
>   A dreadful history.
>
> I pass'd through many dismal courts
>   Thro' lanes and alleys low,
> Before I found the wretched house
>   I sought in Wapping Row.
>
> High up a dark and winding stair,
>   From floor to floor I went
> And heard sometimes a woman swear
>   Or beaten child lament.
>
> Upon the topmost flight I found
>   A close and wretched room;
> Alas, that any human soul
>   Should call such place a home.
>
> No fire was burning in the grate,
>   The walls were damp and bare,
> The window panes were stuffed with rags,
>   No furniture was there.

> But in a corner dark and chill,
>   Some dirty straw was spread,
> And there a little ghastly child
>   Was lying still and dead.

Not only did Mary Sewell risk cholera in such places as these. She was also well aware of the danger of attack.

> One cannot tell what people dwell
>   In such abodes as these;
> The worst of thieves and murderers
>   Might shelter here with ease.[*]

No doubt Anna accompanied her mother on some of the less dangerous of these expeditions. Certainly, as we know, she was kept informed about them and often gave up her food to feed the poor. Yet it was never suggested to her that poverty could be abolished. Like many of her contemporaries, Mary Sewell deplored the misery of many working-class people, while at the same time she never blamed it on the greed of the rich or wished to change the system. The most she allowed herself was an occasional exclamation of wonder at the unequal way in which wealth was divided.

> It passes me to understand
>   Why things should go this way;
> Why some folks life is chained to work,
>   And some do nought but play –
> But 'tis a riddle I suppose,
>   Will all come clear one day.[**]

Her childhood had been spent under the shadow of the French Revolution and, to her, socialism in any form meant ungodliness and the guillotine. 'To raise the masses is not our business ... our work lies with a few of the atoms,' she once said. Not only did she disapprove

---

[*] Sewell, Mary, *A Sad Story.*

[**] Sewell, Mary, *The London Attic.*

of revolution. She was not even in favour of charitable societies. 'We do not want societies,' she wrote. 'We want individual kindness. I have no objection whatever to kind-hearted ladies having their working-parties and sending frocks, handkerchiefs and flannel petticoats to the black populations but let them first see to their poor neighbours.' It is true that she herself was associated with movements from time to time. At Dalston she campaigned for the abolition of the slave trade and went from door to door collecting money for a society that supplied sweeps with long-handled brushes as a substitute for little boys. Yet she much preferred 'private benevolence'. Workhouses, or Union houses as they were sometimes called, were the result of societies and she abhorred workhouses. 'My plan for supporting the respectable aged poor outside the Unions … is very easy,' she wrote. 'Let a few people contribute a few shillings a week to the parish guardians to distribute and all this misery will cease.'

Apart from such remedies she could only recommend resignation and trust in God, and this she did in large doses.

> Poor women! In this world of toil
>   Keep up your hearts with prayer;
> Still trust in God and do your best –
>   You never need despair. [*]

---

[*] Sewell, Mary, *The Miller's Wife.*

3

PALATINE COTTAGE, STOKE
NEWINGTON 1832–36

The Sewell family moved from 12 Park Road when Anna was twelve. Isaac was a restless man and delighted in places which afforded scope for alteration and improvement. In his walks round Hackney he had noticed an empty building which had been coach house and stable to a gentleman's residence called Palatine House. He decided that it was suitable for conversion into a cottage. Number 12 Park Road was becoming too small for his family and he felt that his income justified a larger establishment. (He was now employed in his brother William's business, the nature of which is unknown.) He bought the place with the aid of a loan from his bachelor uncle, Philip, a Norfolk miller.

Palatine House was a bow-fronted mansion in Stoke Newington Road. It was one of the first nine houses to be built on the Palatine Estate, named after some German Protestant refugees who settled there at the beginning of the eighteenth century to avoid persecution. At one time it had been the home of Charles Greenwood, a close friend of John Wesley and Wesley himself had often sought a 'quiet retreat' there.[*]

Palatine House itself still stands, the last of the Palatine houses to survive the massive demolition and rebuilding operations of the 1870s which converted the whole area into identical streets of red-brick terrace houses.[**] It is now known as 109 Stoke Newington Road and has come down sadly in the world. It is to be found

---

[*] Curnock, Nehemiah, ed., *Journal of John Wesley.*
[**] History of the Palatine Estate.

at the bottom of a steep alley littered with discarded lavatories and the vast metal weights used by house-breakers. Beyond it is Palatine Cottage in an even more advanced state of decay. Battalions of empty Coke bottles stand inside the cracked windows and the outlines of the small house are obscured by lean-tos and piles of old timber.

Anna was almost beside herself with delight when she was first taken to see the place. It stood in a large overgrown garden where there were old damask roses growing wild and acacia and tulip trees. A long strip of ornamental water, where goldfish still survived, divided the garden from four acres of meadowland where her parents proposed to keep cows. There was also an orchard and several out-houses. She watched the conversion of stalls, loose-boxes and haylofts into rooms with eager anticipation. In six months the structural work was done and she helped her mother paper the rooms and did much of the painting herself. Her mother afterwards commented, 'I now often wonder at the difficult things I trusted and encouraged my children to attempt.'

The three years at Palatine Cottage were probably the happiest in Anna's life. The arrival of the cows turned the place into a miniature farm and now she could imagine herself at Buxton all the year round. It was her father's idea to keep the cows. He hoped to increase his income by selling milk to the neighbours, many of whom were Friends. A man and his wife were employed to look after them and deliver the milk, but plenty of work remained. Mary churned and made the butter, Philip measured the milk in the morning and often milked a cow and Anna helped with the pigs, ducks, hens and rabbits. The bees were her special responsibility. There were several hives of them at the end of the garden and she studied their habits with wonder and affection. Her interest in insect life continued to grow during her teens.

Soon domestic work was added to the farm work. The cows were unremunerative, Isaac's salary did not increase and the general serv-ant had to be dismissed. Philip now included knife-sharpening and shoe-cleaning in his chores and Anna helped with the housework and cooking. Mary Sewell drew an idyllic picture of her family at this time, all working together at these simple tasks. 'There was no idea of degradation belonging to the work, but a great deal of animation, and time passed most pleasantly as we worked together.' The two children now began to resemble their fictional counterparts of Summerbrook more closely, although one doubts whether even now they quite reached the summit of perfection achieved by George and Mary Day. These two entirely ran the house for their mother when she was confined to bed for a period. Here are some verses on the subject of Mary Day's activities:

> Before the cock had called the hens
>   That roosted in the shed
> Young Mary Day had dressed herself
>   And shaken up her bed.
>
> She threw the window open wide,
>   To breathe the morning air,
> She washed her round and rosy cheeks,
>   And brushed her shining hair.
>
> Then briskly down the stairs she went,
>   And when the fire was made,
> She swept the room and dusted it,
>   And then the breakfast laid.
>
> And she took up a cup of tea,
>   And nicely buttered bread,
> To tempt her mother's appetite
>   As she lay ill in bed.

George was equally irreproachable. In the poem entitled *George the Gentleman*, we have the following account of his activities.

> George was the very prince of boys morn, noon, or night
> Whate'er he had to do, 'twas always right;
> No murmur, no excuses, no debate
> That 'twas too early, or it was too late;
> For when by George his mother's will was known,
> In little time his mother's will was done.

And as to Mary, that dear girl and he
Were just as happy as they well could be,
'Our little Polly' was the name she bore,
And when her brother heard her at the door,
He went like any Squire of the land,
And took the wet umbrella from her hand,
And changed her shoes and gently shook her dress
Till Mary laughed at George's carefulness
And too gave him such a kiss as sisters can
And said, 'Ah! George, you are a gentleman.'

A big change now took place in Anna's life. She went to school for the first time. Philip had already completed a successful year or two at Hackney Grammar School and was now at a Friends' School at Stoke Newington. But Anna had been educated entirely at home. The good angel behind this development was the black sheep of the family. His name was Uncle Richard and he was Mary's youngest brother. He was now in his late twenties and beginning to show a distressing resemblance to his own Uncle Richard, the originator of the steam-ferry scheme. He had taken some land at Enfield, presumably with a view to developing it, and had come to live with his sister. As a result Mary could no longer find time to 'help on dear Anna's education' and she was sent to 'a good day school' within a mile of the house. Mary did not specify that the school was run by Friends, and it is possible that it was not.

To Anna going to school meant an entry into a new life. Here at last was material for her lively intellectual curiosity to feed upon. Better still, here was the companionship of girls of her own age. She quickly made friends. Subjects like mathematics and French, that Mary had barely touched upon, were taught. Anna had a gift for languages and threw herself into their study with enthusiasm. But most exciting of all, here at last she received professional tuition in drawing and painting. Anna's art education up to the age of twelve had consisted of careful watercolour sketches of botanical specimens and insects. It is unlikely that art classes in a small school in the 1830s was of a very high order, but nevertheless they seem to have taken Anna beyond the mere copying of other artist's work. By the time she was fifteen she had been introduced to oils and was learning to paint landscapes from the original.

At this exciting period, when the future seemed so full of promise, Anna had an accident which was ultimately to change the course of her life. Returning from school one afternoon, she was caught in a heavy shower of rain and, having no umbrella, ran home. The carriage road sloped rather steeply to the garden gate, and as she reached it she fell and badly hurt her ankle. Mary, who heard her call and helped her indoors, did not recognise the gravity of the injury at the time. She used to refer to it as a very bad sprain. Yet the fact remains that from this time on Anna was seldom able to walk without difficulty. In her *Reminiscences* Mary implies that Anna's life as a semi-invalid commenced at this period. 'I can scarcely bear, even now,' she wrote 'to recall the beginning of this life of constant frustration … how often did my heart yearn over those apparently wasted faculties, how it bled to see the cramp of those crippling fetters sometimes upon one faculty, sometimes upon another, leaving her powerless to execute what she could so clearly see and do so well!' Yet one suspects that Mary was no more accurate in her account of her daughter's physical misfortunes than she had been in her account of her father's financial ones. Anna was taken out of school after the accident and sent away for a very long holiday, first to some close friends near Lancaster, and then to Buxton. Her Uncle Richard, who appears to have been suffering from some kind of breakdown, possibly mental, accompanied her. A letter she wrote home from Buxton gives a picture of her that is very different from Mary's.

23rd Day. 9th Month. 1835.

My dearest Mother,

I know willt be surprised to see another letter so soon. I am afraid the postage of my letters will almost ruin you but the last were to prevent uneasiness about us and this about Uncle Richard's clothes of which he is very much in need. He wants a coat and trousers and some shirts. I do not see why all his things should not be sent but he wants his clothes directly and he wishes if they are packed up that thou wouldst send them off by van as soon as possible. I willt thou also send my trousers for I want them now with the flannel shifts Aunt Ellen made. I began yesterday to make my stuff frock. We left Yarmouth on 3 day morning at 9. We kept down in the cabin all the time except a little while. On first day I awoke with an obstropolus cold and sore throat which so increased in the evening that I felt quite poorly and went to bed early and found it worse in the morning so that I had not much pleasure in Yarmouth. But what with wine, whey and treak posset it is better to-day. This morning I have been doing some French exercises and I rode to Rippon Hall on Bob. He is very rough to ride after Balaam. Aunt Ellen has pronounced in a very decided manner that my green peleese is to be kept as it is for me to ride out in. I hope thou willt write very particularly about all things by Aunt Wright. But pray do not congratulate me on my wise resolution about not going on with my oil paints for I have heartedly repented of it since I have been here and seen all the fine old oakes and elms with the bright colours of Autumn. At Bridgmont there were very few fine trees but here I have never seen anything so beautiful and I have not werewith to continue this beauty in miniature although I question whether it would be beauty then. But I could not have believed, if I had found it myself, how entirely just painting that view of Lancaster has altered the way in which I look at scenery. I am now always looking for something to make a picture of; what tints will harmonise together, what colors will do for this oak and ash and what for the distances. In fact I never enjoyed looking at the country so much before. It seems like another sense. I shall send my 3 attempts at oils soon with the carrier and I shall try and conjer up several letters if so be that I can create out of nothing anything worth the trouble of reading.

Now for the poor Bees. I think the dairy would be a good place for them in a few more weeks if they can be kept dry. Aunt Ellen feeds hers. I cannot yet think calmly on that sad affair with those dear little industrious Bees. Has thou any wax flowers pretty ones and yet such as thou hardly like to put in bunches because I am going to send some for M.I. to put in specimen glasses or small jars on the chiffonier. I think she would like them so and she has been very kind to me. There is but very little wax here and I believe nothing else so I should not like to use it all up but if thou hast not any pleasant little things by thee that thou canst spare willt thou send me some materials. I said the flowers because I do not believe I shall have time to make them. Aunt Ellen have laid me out such a power of work for the winter that I do not expect I shall have time for what I had laid out for myself which is no little.

Dost thou not find a great many I's in my letters? I afraid thou willt think they are quite Egotistical. Give my very dear love to my dear father and Philip. I am afraid father gets quite worn up. Uncle Richard seems pretty well. He walks out a good deal with Grandfather who is quite well, just as kind as ever; Grandmother and Aunt Ellen are very well they all send their dear love to thee, father and Philip. Grandfather is always talking about Philip and never ends without saying he's a nice lad, he *must* come next year. I was measured this morning and am 1 inch and ¼ higher than Philip. I believe I grew all this at Bridgmont and I gained 8 pounds in weight. Oh, it is a brave place. When I went away I felt as if I had left my home, a half mother, two sisters and a brother. I hope I have not seen the last of it. I should be very unhappy if I thought I had. Even with a lame foot it is a Paradise. Perhaps I was too happy there, but I never was so happy in any place in my life.

Willt thou send my recipe book and if thou chances to see anything of mine that I shall want. For when I write a letter I forget everything. I hope you will all write to me. Give my love to all the friends, at the school particularly. It is now post time and if I do not conclude, this will be too late. And believe me, my dearest mother, thy very loving daughter A.S. Did Philip receive those beetles I sent by R. Alger?

167 NORTH STREET,
BRIGHTON 1836–45

While Anna was at Buxton, Mary took a step that affected her daughter's life as deeply as it did her own. She resigned from the Society of Friends. The note, in faded brown ink, accepting the resignation after 'solid consideration' can still be read in the Minutes of the Gracechurch Street Meeting.

Mary's change of heart was due to the visit from Uncle and Aunt Wright mentioned in Anna's letter. The couple had intended to spend a few days at Palatine Cottage on their way home from a holiday in Jersey, but Aunt Wright's precarious health had given way and the 'few days' lengthened into seven weeks. Uncle Wright had recently been converted to the doctrine of Justification by Faith upon which, wrote Mary, 'he daily expatiated, rather to my annoyance; but I saw it had given him happiness which I was very conscious I did not possess. After they left us, I set myself to read the New Testament more critically than I had ever done before, … and I saw the truth of Christ's full atonement.'

The doctrine of Justification by Faith was evolved by John Wesley but it came also to be held by some Low Church or Evangelical Anglicans. Those who subscribed to it believed that man could not be saved by works, but only by a conviction of Christ's atonement. This conviction was something that happened suddenly, and was somewhat in the nature of a moment of revelation or conversion.

Mary was also strongly influenced at this time by a book just published by Isaac Crewdson of Manchester. It was called *A Beacon to the Society of Friends* and was read by many. Not only did it support the doctrine of Justification but it recommended in general the reading of the scriptures by Quakers who had relied too exclusively on the inner promptings of the Holy Spirit. He pointed out that, without the guidance of the Gospels, their 'supposedly inspired impressions' might be nothing more than 'the conviction of conscience, the illusion of imagination, or even the suggestion of Satan'. Needless to say, the book caused a furore, and as a result of it, many people besides Mary left the Society and joined the Beaconite Faction. Among them were Uncle Wright and all the Wright aunts at Buxton.

Through reading the gospels Mary also became convinced of the necessity for baptism and nothing less than total immersion would satisfy her ardent spirit. She confided in a famous Baptist preacher of the day, Benjamin Wills Newton, who was standing in for a local pastor, and he offered to baptise her at his chapel with Mrs Newton in attendance. All that remained was to ask Isaac's consent to a ceremony profoundly shocking to Quakers. Mary never forgot the night on which she asked for it. He was very late and she would not begin the subject till he had had his supper, and she felt it would be impossible to sit by him with this upon her mind unuttered. She left all ready and went up to her room, where she sat in the dark, listening for him. Ten o'clock passed. At last he came. She heard him go into the room where his supper was laid. Presently he came upstairs. It was dark, but he knew by the first sound of her voice that something had happened, and asked, 'What's the matter?'

She said, 'Let us kneel down together beside the bed and I will tell thee.' Recounting the interview in after years, she used to say, with streaming tears, 'His kindness to me I shall *never* forget.'

Elsewhere Mary praised Isaac's kindness and patience. 'Never bigoted or pronouncing harsh judgement on others, his spirit was truly catholic and charitable.' But although Isaac tolerated her views he did not share them. He remained a Quaker to the end of his days and he never allowed Mary to accompany him to the Friends' Meeting House again. She told her grandchildren, 'It was heart-breaking work not to be going with dear Grandfather to Meeting. I wished to have gone to the Friends' Meeting one part of the day and to Church or Chapel on the other, but he did not approve of this.' The relationship of husband and wife was not improved by this divergence of their religious views. Mary draws aside the curtain of Victorian reticence sufficiently to admit that 'not to be fully united in external practical religion is a matter if possible to be avoided in domestic life. I made many mistakes through ignorance, which I remember with pain.'

When Mary sent in her resignation to the Gracechurch Street Meeting she did not merely change her place of worship. She exiled herself from the way of life to which she had been born.

> To find myself suddenly cut adrift from so much that had been precious to me all my life was more painful than I can express. I was still one with Friends in almost all my views. Almost all my relatives as well as acquaintances were Friends, in whose opinion, for the most part, I had now sadly fallen ... and there was, as might be supposed, much misjudging. Some thought I wanted more liberty ... and I wished to be rid of the Quaker bonnet. So far from this, it was quite a trial for me to give it up, for I thought then, and think still, that the Friends' dress is the prettiest a woman can wear ... I never expect to see so pretty a sight again as the Women's Meeting at Devonshire House – perfectly unique. No colour was to be seen in it except the varying shades from white, silver grey, every gradation of dove-colour, drab, fawn, and brown, up to black, which usually was confined to the bonnet. The young Friends were far from being indifferent to their dress, and as they sat in quiet rows on the forms, with their sweet, pure faces and modest demeanour, it was a lovely sight to see. The Yearly Meeting was a grand time for meeting acquaintances from far and near: it was quite a gala time for the young men and women, and many parties were made up for visiting exhibitions of painting, and other London sights.

When Anna returned from Buxton she had to decide between remaining a Quaker and following her mother's example. It was always assumed that she chose the latter course but Mary never actually stated this. She wrote, 'Philip continued to go with his father, and dear Anna, being lame, could seldom go anywhere'; and elsewhere, 'Anna sometimes, when she was able, went with me.' In fact the minutes of the Meeting attended by Isaac Sewell list both Anna and Philip as members.[*] It is certain that Anna eventually left the Quakers, but it seems that it was a result of thinking the matter out for herself and not merely in imitation of her mother.

---

[*] Minutes for the Brighton Meeting, 1820–49.

Another change took place in Anna's life at this time. When she came home from Buxton it was not to the cottage in Stoke Newington but to a town house in Brighton, for in 1836 Isaac at last secured a well-paid job. He became the first manager of the Brighton branch of the London and County Joint Stock Bank. The bank eventually amalgamated with others to form the Westminster but in its day it was prosperous and successful. Isaac's position involved much responsibility. Many joint stock banks failed at this time as a result of reckless lending and Brighton was too big a town for a bank manager to be fully acquainted with the affairs of all his clients. It is remarkable that a man with Isaac's business record should have secured the position, for he had suffered yet another financial reverse since the bankruptcy of 1822. The scheme to make money out of selling milk at Stoke Newington had proved a failure. The man and woman who looked after the cows and delivered the milk pocketed the takings and vanished one day. A scheme to take in lodgers had been equally unsuccessful, for the American who rented a couple of rooms demanded the services of a maid and her wages absorbed the profits. Eventually Isaac had been obliged to let the house for twenty pounds a year and move his family into lodgings in nearby Shacklewell. Anna must have been deeply distressed at the loss of the farm. We know, from the Buxton letter, how deeply attached she had been to her bees, and it seems unlikely that she was insensible to the charms of the rabbits, the pigs and the chickens. It is possible that she remained at Buxton during this period and was spared the sorrow of parting.

In spite of all these misfortunes Isaac proved an efficient bank manager and held his position for many years. According to Mary:

he was considered a thorough man of business, was scrupulously upright and exact in everything, exceedingly industrious and perse-vering, and never saved himself trouble by throwing it upon others. He was most considerate to all he employed, and never made an enemy. He was so skilful in training young men in the conduct of bank business, that clerks intended for other banks were often sent to him first.

The bank was listed as standing at 167 North Street in the 1848 Brighton Directory. (Isaac Sewell, resident manager, hours 10–5.) The house, standing on the corner of Princes Place, has been replaced by the premises of the Alliance Building Society. Now, as then, the area is one of the busiest in Brighton. Opposite is Hanningtons, the largest department store in the town and behind are the gardens of the Prince Regent's Dome. It was here that Anna was to live for the next ten years.

Life in a busy and fashionable resort must have seemed strange after the comparative seclusion of Stoke Newington; The bank was surrounded by shops and only three doors down, at 170, stood the establishment of Robert Folthorp, bookseller, stationer and proprietor of the Royal Library and reading rooms, no doubt a favourite resort of Anna. Brighton was still in its heyday. The Prince Regent (George IV) had not been dead many years and the fashionable world was constantly popping down for an airing in one of the forty-six stage-coaches that plied daily from London. At the point where these coaches set down their passengers was always to be found Captain Eld, a well-known Brighton character, who must have been familiar to Anna if only through the columns of the local paper. Captain Eld (the original of the lugubrious Captain Miserrimus Doleful of *Handley Cross*) was described by Surtees as an unofficial master of ceremonies or *Arbiter Elegantiarum*. He pursued new arrivals to their hotels, presented them with his card and waited for them to subscribe one pound towards his maintenance by signing the red book at the public library. As Brighton was a very exclusive place, and as nobody would dream of entering its society unless their name was on the list of one of the lady patronesses, Captain Eld's cards were of little value and after his decease his place remained unfilled.

Private balls at Brighton were extremely gay and during the winter season (Brighton ceased to have a summer season when the cult of sea-bathing went out of fashion) there was always a pack of young officers and men of good family pursuing foxes by day and heiresses by night. Typical of these was Baron Goblenz, a friend of Surtees. On one occasion he was told that there was a young lady present worth ten thousand pounds. He assumed that it was ten thousand pounds a year, and when disillusioned on this point he concluded, 'Ah vell! It will be ten thousand pounds the first year at all events.'

It is not easy to imagine Anna and her mother against this background. They were hardly likely to be attracted by the two chief daylight occupations of the ladies of Brighton; shopping for things they did not intend to buy, and calling on people they knew to be out. Mary Sewell quickly applied herself to the business of poor-visiting. These were the Hungry Forties, the years when the misery of the working people was moving towards the explosion of the Chartist riots of 1848. The Chartists were active in Brighton and Mary Sewell, we may be sure, had little sympathy with them. She complained that the poor of Brighton were pauperised by too much charity which deprived them of self-respect. She cited a case of a man who offered her his baby rather than struggle to bring up the child himself. She concerned herself therefore more with the moral than the physical condition of her poor neighbours and became a frequent visitor at the ward in the Brighton workhouse known as the 'black hole' and chiefly inhabited by fallen women.

The description of her first visit to this ward has echoes of Elizabeth Fry's visit to the women prisoners at Newgate twenty-five years earlier, and no doubt unconsciously she saw herself following in the steps of her heroine. The ward was so bad that even the chaplain seldom visited it, and strongly advised her against the attempt.

He gave me alarming accounts of window smashing, of fighting and swearing in this ward, and the governor and matron fully corroborated his statements, and advised me not to adventure myself into it. But I was not discouraged.

I went quietly up the stairs, and walked into the middle of the room. It was a large, bare, barn-like looking place, with no furniture but two rows of beds. 'Dear friends,' I said, 'I have heard that many of you are in trouble and difficulty. I have come to see if I can help or comfort any of you. I have been advised not to come; it was thought you would not receive me well; but I did not believe that.' An old woman instantly interrupted me – 'Oh dear! my lady, we would not mislist you upon no account; we are very glad to see you.' 'Come, then,' I said, 'let us sit down and talk together; tell me your troubles and let me see if I can help you.' They made a cluster round me in the centre of the room, sitting on the beds, and many a perplexed and sorrowful story did I learn from them, requiring indeed a friendly helper.

I visited this place regularly once a week for a long time and by degrees became acquainted with the individual cases of trouble. Some poor girls were assisted to go to a penitentiary.

Although Anna never appears to have accompanied her mother on expeditions of this sort, she was affected by them, for on at least two occasions Mary brought deserving cases to share the family hearth. The Sewell's cook for a time was a former inmate of the 'black hole'. She was a destitute Irish widow whose last pennies had been spent on masses for the soul of her dead husband and she had no knowledge of cooking. Mary undertook to teach her the art and eventually placed her with a clergyman's family where not only did she prove a satisfactory servant but she even forsook her Popish ways and 'became a sincere Christian'.

Another sojourner in the Sewell kitchen may be mentioned here though her visit in fact probably occurred after the Sewells had left Brighton. The sufferer in question was a woman nervous by temperament, living in poor circumstances, with too many children to care for. She had already experienced one bout of madness and when Mary visited her she found her attempting ineffectually to keep her children from falling into the fire. 'Whilst she is thus ruling her children, the perspiration runs down her face, and her hands tremble so much that she can scarcely hold the infant; and truly, she looks as if her expectation of being crazy was not distant from its fulfilment.' Mary decided a period in her own peaceful home was the only way to save the woman's reason.

She described this holiday in detail in *Thy Poor Brother*.

She brought her youngest child with her, and both were comfortably installed in the kitchen, under the special care of kind and considerate servants. She had every personal comfort, with plenty of rest and nourishment. Her child was laid in the family cradle and was an object of general interest. She worked at her needle when she chose, read to herself, or was read to, or conversed with. She understood, for the first time in her life, the meaning of the word 'leisure'. She rode out, and enjoyed the country and the air; she walked in the garden, and gathered the flowers and, as she expressed it herself, felt as if she was in Paradise. At the end of a few weeks, she returned home, her health restored.

The visit 'caused quite a sensation among the residents in the immediate vicinity', and indeed so shocked the publishers of the American
edition of the book that they added a footnote assuring trans-Atlantic
readers that 'liberal provisions made for the relief of such sufferers in …
the U.S. would … preclude the necessity for such a step which would
be quite impracticable for most families.'

Anna's contribution to the lightening of the lot of the poor was
limited to teaching in Sunday School at this time. In the forties this
could imply a good deal more than giving purely religious instruction. The children of the poor worked long hours in factories at
this time and there was no universal education. Not only were they
ignorant of the Bible but of almost everything else as well. The only
instruction that many of them ever received in reading and ciphering was from young gentlewomen who taught them voluntarily
on Sundays. (Charlotte Yonge, the famous Victorian novelist, was
another keen worker in this field.) We can imagine Anna, a rather
serious young woman, confronting a room full of these unwashed
urchins. We know that she would have been sombrely dressed for
the occasion, not only because she retained the habits of a Quaker
all her life, but because her mother devoted a paragraph of *Thy Poor
Brother* to the subject. Woe, she said, to the gaudily attired young
woman who attempts to convey the 'scheme of redemption' to a
class of little girls for 'they will be admiring her artificial flowers,
be twisting an imaginary ribbon into tasteful bows like hers, or
be counting her flounces, her fringes, or her buttons; or they may be
wishing, like a little girl I have heard of, that they were "grown-up
women, to wear a dress like the ladies, to draggle"'.

Anna's life at Brighton, however, was not entirely taken up with
Sunday School teaching. She and Philip together enjoyed some of
the more sober entertainments that the city could offer and attended
lectures, classes and the sermons of famous preachers. She even visited the Royal Academy exhibition in 1844 with a party of friends.
Indeed, this appears to have been the most socially active period of
her life. She began to have friends of her own, although Mary quickly
claimed a share in them. She kept a diary from the age of twenty to
twenty-five and entries refer to walks and expeditions with others of
her age. A close friend of both Anna and Philip was Henry S. King who
worked for Smith, Elder and Co., the firm that published *Jane Eyre*.

He was a pious and intelligent young man and a great admirer of the famous Robertson of Brighton.

Strangely enough neither Anna nor Mary ever attended a service at Trinity chapel, Ship Street, where Robertson preached. It is true that he did not arrive in Brighton until two years after they had left but Mary, at any rate, continued to visit the poor of the city, and we, know that she greatly admired him. Frederick William Robertson was not only a brilliant preacher but a tireless worker in the cause of reconciling the estranged working class with the Church. His founding of the British Mechanic's Institute caused violent public controversy in the city.

Anna's interests continued, however, to be artistic rather than literary. Her niece, Margaret Sewell, possessed several of her 'oil and pencil drawings' and asserted that some, at least, of them were original. Others were copies. The painter whose work Anna particularly singled out to imitate was Landseer, for she was a child of her age. Among the paintings that Margaret Sewell inherited were copies of two animal pieces by the creator of *The Monarch of the Glen*. These, along with all Anna's paintings, have vanished. For an assessment of the quality of Anna's work we must rely on Margaret Sewell. She claimed that she was 'no mean artist' and that 'in the opinion of competent critics ... had she been trained she would have done notable work'.[*] However, comments of this sort were passed on the work of a good many Victorian young ladies.

Anna at this time acquired another of the accomplishments of the Victorian miss. She learned to play the piano. Also, according to Margaret Sewell, she sang well, having a 'voice that was very sweet and true though not strong'. While the family were living at Brighton Philip became engaged to Sarah Woods, a Quaker from Tottenham. She also was musical and one of Mary Sewell's happiest memories was Sarah and Anna at the piano together. When she was an old woman, after both girls were dead, she had a fancy to hear some of the tunes they used to play. She hired a piano without telling anyone why. 'But, oh, my stiff old fingers! I learned two tunes – could play them off – and just in the notes of "Excelsior" I could

---

hear my Nannie's voice. But I couldn't express what I wanted ...
and I sent the piano away.'

Anna was now at a stage in her life when one might have expected
her to take an interest in young men. Philip had his Sarah but we
hear no hint of a romance in Anna's life. No doubt her lameness was
a drawback but it could not have prevented her from having a normal
desire to attract. Perhaps she had hopes of the eminently suitable
Henry S. King, but if she had they were doomed to disappointment,
for he did not marry until twenty years later.

It was at this age that Anna began to suffer from what she called
'the darkness', a state of spiritual loneliness that amounted almost
to loss of faith. Her cry during this period, constantly reiterated in
the diary, was 'Oh, that I knew where to find Him.' The event that
appears to have precipitated this spiritual crisis was the arrival in
Brighton of a 'false prophet'. As a child her faith had been simple and
firm. She used to say, 'Mother's Bible was read to make everybody
happy and good.' In her late teens she began to explore the possibili-
ties of other churches while remaining a somewhat unenthusiastic
Quaker. (She seems to have frequently found her lameness a useful
excuse for not going to any church on Sunday, in spite of the fact
that Chapel Royal was on her doorstep and the Quaker Meeting
House not much farther away in The Lanes.) With the arrival of
the prophet in Brighton in 1840 everything changed. His name is
unknown but his teaching was evidently of an extreme nature. In the
words of Mrs Bayly, he 'professed to have received direct teaching
from Heaven, and to have fresh light to impart, especially concerning
the work of the Holy Spirit'.

Mary fell completely under his influence for a time, but Anna
was more cautious and held back. Mrs Bayly once remarked that
with them the roles of mother and daughter were reversed. 'I cannot
say that the daughter led, for the impulse to action came usually
from the mother, but the daughter pronounced judgement.' Although
Anna had not been deluded by the prophet, her faith was shaken by
her mother's disillusionment, and it was probably at this time that her
attendance at the picturesque Quaker Meeting House in Ship Street
finally ceased. Her diary suggests that she was profoundly unhappy.
She spoke of 'the irresistible charm of worldly things' and of her
sense of guilt at capitulating to this charm. 'Lord, break my bondage,'

she wrote, 'for I have not the strength to do it myself. I have not the strength to give up myself to Christ, nor the sense of being willing that that His perfect will should be fulfilled in me, lest it should mean entire crucifixion of self.' She attempted to find distractions. She attended a series of history classes. 'They are very interesting,' she wrote, 'but they do not satisfy the soul. I am very miserable.' She now began to follow her mother on her lifelong shuttle between dissenting chapels of different denominations and the Anglican Church. At different times in her life Mary, and no doubt Anna, frequented the chapels of Unitarians, Moravians, Plymouth Brethren, Baptists and Methodists and, at the end of forty years of searching, Mary admitted that if she joined a church again, it would be the Quakers. In their habits and attitudes both women remained Quakers, and Mary at least found the elaborate ritual of the Anglican Church hard to accept. She has left us a vivid description of her first impressions of a Church of England service.

> The Prayer Book was quite a puzzle, and the continual up and down was a great disturbance; the rapid transition from prayer to praise and confession was quite beyond the facility of my mind. One thing struck me as painfully irreverent. The children in the choir ... were in full view of the congregation. These children had to go through the whole of the service in an audible voice whilst a man with a long stick kept touching them up to their duty.

Yet it was in an Anglican church, in the New Year of 1845, that Anna eventually saw the light.

> At the beginning of this month we went on Sunday morning to Clarence Chapel. Mr. Warren preached from the text, 'Christ has redeemed us from the curse of the law, being made a curse for us.' It was a powerful sermon, and the Lord mercifully used it as the conveyance of his good Spirit, to bring again life and light to my dark soul. As I listened, I truly felt Christ precious. I believed, and was justified from all things. I was made to sing as in years long past. This is not, I trust, a transient revival. I do now trust in none but Jesus.

She felt she had experienced the kind of conversion demanded by the doctrine of Justification by Faith, the deep conviction of Christ's atonement which alone, independent of works, could bring salvation. She was still basking in the sunshine of the experience two months later, on her twenty-fifth birthday. 'March 20th. This is my birthday. Oh what a happy one compared to any I have had so long! I feel as if I had exchanged a rough, stormy sea for a calm, smooth river.'

There were, however, to be lapses from this state. A continuation of the same entry reads:

> Last Sunday was the first time I took my class in the afternoon. I did not get on very well, for in the morning I had given way to sin, and therefore did not get near to Christ, for I sinned wilfully, knowingly resisting the voice of the Spirit in my heart, and so the sting was left behind. The darkness returned for 2 or 3 days, then I was able to lay my sin at the feet of my Saviour, and leave it there. Today (Sunday) I had a very pleasant time with my children, and taught them from Daniel, third chapter.

All through her life 'the darkness' was to return from time to time. Mary used to refer to this state as visiting Doubting Castle.[*] 'Anna will keep a little dark room in that same old castle, where she sometimes goes and bemoans herself; and I scold her because the castle is let to a quite different sort of people.'

Another Anglican clergyman from whom Anna, and also Mary, derived much help was Charles Maitland who was perpetual curate at the chapel-of-ease at St James's (now amalgamated with St Mary's Brighton). The Rev. Maitland was not a man whom one might expect to attract a former Quaker, for he had been a regular soldier most of his life and had served as a lieutenant of artillery at Waterloo. He was, however, a remarkably saintly man, he expressed himself in plain language and watched carefully over these unofficial members of his somewhat staid flock.

---

[*] In *A Pilgrim's Progress,* Christian was imprisoned in Doubting Castle by the giant, Despair.

Philip also left the Quakers at this time, although possibly for different reasons. He had already begun to train in his father's bank when, at the age of eighteen, he developed an ambition to become a missionary and for this he decided it was necessary to take Orders. This decision no doubt was the result of Sarah Stickney's marriage to William Ellis. Ellis was an Anglican missionary, secretary of the London Missionary Society, and a man of some distinction. Although he had started life as a gardener, he had risen to win Southey's praise for *Polynesian Researches*, a book which made the public realise that all missionaries were not ignorant and narrow-minded. Philip had no doubt also been impressed by his newly published *History of Madagascar* which described the courage of the Christian natives under the persecution of Queen Ranavolona.

It is interesting to note that a first cousin of Philip and Anna, Joseph Stickney Sewell, had developed a similar ambition a year earlier. At the age of nineteen he had been deeply affected by the death of his mother, Dorothy, which occurred soon after the family moved to Malton in Yorkshire. (The takings from the shop in Yarmouth had proved inadequate for the support of two families.) He was dissatisfied with his life as the apprentice of a miller at Kirkstall and developed a passionate desire to be baptised and to become a missionary. He felt, like Philip, that being a Quaker stood between him and both ambitions. Joseph in fact did not become a missionary until many years later. Nor did he leave the Society of Friends. A battery of arguments from three Yarmouth elders and several theological salvos in epistolary form from his father persuaded him to remain inside the fold but he was never the most orthodox of Quakers. On the point of baptism he did, however, recant and eventually published a book entitled *Water Baptism, neither a Sacrament nor an Ordinance*.

Neither did Philip become a missionary. While preparing to enter Cambridge his health broke down and his doctor advised him to adopt an outdoor life. He decided to become a civil engineer and, after studying under two qualified men, took up his first appointment, surveying the possibility of draining the salt lagoons of the Camargue, about the time that his family left Brighton for Lancing.

5

LANCING, HAYWARDS HEATH AND CHICHESTER 1845–58

The Sewells moved about Sussex in a rather restless manner for the next ten years, spending some time each in Lancing, Haywards Heath and Chichester. The move to Lancing (at that time little more than a village by the sea) was no doubt occasioned by Mary Sewell's longing for the country. She always regarded Brighton as a place of dead stones and found even walks on the pier before breakfast communing with 'the restless beautiful sea' a poor substitute for the woods and fields of her childhood. Isaac continued to work at the bank and the move to rural Sussex was only made possible by the building of a railway line between Shoreham and Brighton.

These were the years of the railway mania that was to ruin so many in the middle forties. The proliferation of lines was to affect the Sewells in more ways than one, for Philip, when he returned from the South of France, was employed by a company who were proposing to link Carlisle and Settle by rail. (As the track was not in fact laid until 1867, we must assume that his duties were confined to prospecting.)

The house at Lancing was some miles from Shoreham station and it was at this time that the Sewells bought the pony and trap which was to play so important a part in Anna's life. It was her duty to drive her father to and from the station, and it was during these twice daily drives that she picked up her remarkable knowledge of driving. Margaret Sewell bears witness to the fact that Anna was 'a very good whip'. Like all good drivers she could convey her wishes to her horse with the minimum of fuss. Not only did she never in fact use the whip but she seldom even appeared to use the reins. Chiefly she relied on her voice. Mrs Bayly has left us a description of a journey to a station – which in fact took place some years later.

Anna was enveloped in a large mackintosh and the persistent rain obliged us to keep our umbrellas. She seemed simply to hold the reins in her hand, trusting to her voice to give all needed directions to her horse. She evidently believed in a horse having a moral nature, if we may judge by her mode of remonstrance. 'Now thee shouldn't walk up this hill – don't thee see how it rains? Now thee must go a little faster – thee would be sorry for us to be late at the station.'

As a result of this daily contact with horses Anna developed a deep intuitive sympathy with them. Mary Sewell described this in a letter to Mr Flower, the famous expert on harness, in reply to his congratulations on the publication of *Black Beauty*.

And so it came to pass, between her and her own horse, and horses in general, a mutual confidence and friendship sprang up, and she learned all their secrets. She learned much through her ear, in this way quickly detecting if anything is wrong with a horse's foot, and through her eye she knows at once if anything annoys them.

We may be sure that Anna's interest in her pony did not stop at the stable door, for any lover of horses knows that their performance is directly related to their condition. It would of course have been neither possible nor suitable for Anna to care for the pony herself and Sewells always employed a boy or a young man for this purpose. Anna, however, had grown used to the care of animals at Palatine Cottage, and there is little doubt that she supervised the activities of this young man as closely as Philip had supervised the measuring of the milk at Stoke Newington. She probably kept the key of the corn chest on her and went down to the stable to see the pony eat his oats morning and evening. In this way she could ensure that the straw in the stable was clean and that the water-bucket was full. She may also have paid a judicious visit at the hour of the morning grooming to make sure that the animal's coat was thoroughly cleaned and his hoofs picked out. On warm Sundays she would have been sure to give orders that he be turned into the paddock for the day.

The arrival of the pony and trap proved timely, for with the removal to Lancing occurred a marked deterioration in Anna's ability to walk. We have seen that in Brighton she was able to lead a moderately active life, go out with friends and visit picture galleries. By the time she had been at Lancing a year she seems to have been barely able to take more than a few steps at a time. An extract from her diary, written in the spring she moved to Lancing, shows her struggling against the onset of this more severe form of lameness.

> Mother went to Brighton and I stayed to attend to the planting of seeds in the garden; my feet were very weak, and I prayed that they might be strengthened sufficiently for me to attend to what was necessary. The Lord most graciously heard me, and gave me more strength than I have had for some time, so that I am able to see after the garden properly.

At a later date she wrote:

> I have felt it very sweet to receive this improvement in my feet (which continues) from the Hand of Jesus. I would not be without this dispensation, and pray Thee, Lord, to do with me what Thou seest best. I thank Thee for my lameness. I am sure it is sent in love though it be a trial. I should without it have too much pleasure in the flesh, and have forgotten Thee.

The improvement, however, did not continue, and at this point it seems appropriate to enquire what was the exact nature of the original injury to Anna's ankle. So severe a case of lameness was obviously not the result of a mere sprain, as Mary Sewell supposed. It seems more likely to have been caused by a dislocation. It will be recalled that, a few years before the accident, Anna had dislocated an elbow which had been slow to mend. Such severe dislocations are rare in normal children but they are common enough among undernourished ones. We are therefore led to the possible conclusion that Anna as a child may have been underfed. We remember all those meat dinners she was encouraged to give to the poor and those bowls of porridge 'thick and hot' that took their place. She was a sensitive child and may well have developed a sense of guilt about eating while others starved and so have been unwilling to consume even the meagre portions allowed her. It is significant that, when away from home at the age of fifteen, she put on eight pounds in a matter of weeks. And this was *after* the accident.

It was at Lancing also that Anna began to complain of more distressing symptoms; she had pains in her chest, a lack of strength in her back and, worst of all, a 'weakness' in her head. It was now that began the life of constant frustration that Mrs Sewell had ascribed to the period immediately after the accident. This life of frustration Mrs Bayly described vividly. 'Anna,' she wrote, 'could see at once how a picture should be composed, a fact or sentiment expressed, a garment cut out; how flowers should be arranged; what a committee should or should not do – but with all these mental resources, the frail body refused to do its part, and days and weeks had often to be spent in enforced idleness.' It was not only the frail body that refused to do its part. The frail head also was often unfit for work. Mrs Bayly continues, 'Her hungry nature longed for food of many kinds – political, social, philanthropic – all these departments teemed with interest for her; yet there were periods when to read a short paragraph in a newspaper, or the report of a Society, was for days together an impossibility.' Margaret Sewell also bore witness to this inability to concentrate. 'My aunt,' she wrote, 'could never read or write for more than a short time at a sitting.'

We are now confronted with the great mystery of Anna's life, the cause of her chronic illness. There does not appear to have been any hereditary justification for it. Both her parents survived into their eighties (Mary Sewell was eighty-seven when she died) and both came from families remarkable for their longevity. Mary's sister Elizabeth died at ninety-five while Isaac and his five brothers achieved an average age of seventy-nine, and this in spite of the defection of his unmarried sister Hannah Maria who succumbed suddenly to an apoplexy at Stoke Newington at the early age of seventy-three. Grandfather Sewell's generation was even more remarkable. Their average age of demise was 84¼. (These figures do not of course allow for 'the little ones with golden hair who sleep under the daisies'. Infant mortality was high in both families.)

Mary Sewell ascribed all Anna's maladies to the fall outside the garden gate at Palatine Cottage. She considered the doctors made many mistakes in their treatment of the ankle – and that some of the 'cures' were worse than the complaint. Anna was heavily bled soon after she wrote the Buxton letter and to this 'draining away of her life blood' Mary Sewell ascribed many of her subsequent weaknesses.

There is, however, no medical evidence to support this supposition. It seems more probable that Anna's disease had a psychological cause. There was some slight history of mental instability in her family. Her father, at the age of eighty, became subject to 'mental impressions of a very distressing character', and it will be recalled that, after the collapse of the family fortunes, her maternal grandmother went through a period of depression. It is significant that Anna's symptoms abated in middle age and that, even when she was suffering, she never looked ill. Genteel spinsters with unspecified maladies were no rarity in the Victorian era. The names of Elizabeth Barrett Browning, Emily Dickinson and Florence Nightingale spring immediately to mind. With them, as with Anna Sewell, we do not have to seek far to find psychological explanations for their indisposition. These women retired to their beds because they did not have enough to do, or rather, because the occupations that were considered suitable for them did not interest them.

The lot of the Victorian spinster of good family was far from enviable. A career of any sort was out of the question. The only occupation considered suitable was, to use Florence Nightingale's words, 'Faddling, twaddling and the endless tweedling of nosegays in jugs.' Elsewhere she wrote, 'Women do not consider themselves human beings at all. There is absolutely no God, no country, no duty to them ... except family ... I know of no tyranny like the petty grinding tyranny of a good English family.' Mary Sewell's friend, Sarah Stickney Ellis, also deplored the fate of the hundreds of young women who 'have comparatively nothing to do'. She wrote, 'It is truly astonishing that the prejudices of society should place a barrier betwixt them and those efforts by which their health of body and mind might be radically improved.'

Anna was not by nature idle. But she may not have been interested in the kind of activities that her mother considered suitable. At the age of fifteen her passion was painting. Yet the sum total of her production as a painter appears to have been but a handful of canvases, and the reason may well have been that Mary Sewell did not approve of painting. We learn, from the Buxton letter, that she considered oil paints an extravagance and applauded Anna's decision to stop using them. We know also from the letter how deeply Anna's puritanical upbringing had filled her with guilt about pleasure.

The diary quoted in the last chapter makes it clear that this sense of guilt about pleasure had increased with maturity. Confronted with a strong urge on the one side to express herself artistically and with a strong inhibition against it on the other, personified in her mother, what refuge had Anna had but the sickroom?

The blame for Anna's incapacity, it seems, must therefore be set fairly and squarely on the shoulders of busy, kind-hearted, holy Mary Sewell. She had established a massive ascendancy over her daughter in the schoolroom and, when the time came for her to let go, she did not let go. Her attachment to her daughter was abnormal. She constantly referred to her as 'The Jewel' or 'The Darling'. When Anna died she mourned her as she never did her husband. In a letter to a friend she wrote, 'Our path is not so flowery now – there are none of those little love songs we used to sing together when no one else heard. Many a time in the day I comfort myself with the sweet joy of folding my beloved again to my heart.'

The causes for Mary's excessive attachment to Anna must be sought in her own life. Her marriage was emotionally unsatisfying. We know that Isaac set no spark to the tinder before the wedding and it seems unlikely that he succeeded in satisfying 'that always hungry place, my heart' afterwards. The couple remained profoundly different by temperament; he steady, businesslike and mildly humorous, she poetic, enthusiastic and dedicated. In an age of large families, the fact that they had only two children is significant. The man in Mary Sewell's life was her father, not her husband, and after both men were dead, it was with her father that she dreamt of being reunited. All her other close friendships were with women, and notably with women younger than herself. Elizabeth Boyd Bayly, the daughter of her biographer Mrs Bayly, said of her, 'She delighted in the sons of men and particularly the daughters.' She was herself one of Mary Sewell's 'very dear' young friends.

> I well remember how delighted I was when, about the time of my leaving school, I first began to know her and found in her a friend who could view things from my standpoint, and who understood all about me, and standing, as it were, on the same level with me, seemed to take me by the hand, and point me upward. Her whole soul was thrown, for the time, into my youthful interests – my studies, pursuits,

and pleasures; and as we roamed over the moors, I felt what a wonderful new friend I had in my mother's old friend.

If we accept that Mary dominated her daughter as she dominated young Miss Bayly, one aspect of the mystery of her illness still remains unsolved. Why was it that Anna did not succumb to hypochondria until she left Brighton? The answer may be that there were signs of the complaint even at this period. Indeed, they can be detected even in the Buxton letter. It will be recalled that her stay in Yarmouth was spoilt by an 'obstropolus' cold and that this fact was the only incident that she considered worthy of comment in connection with her visit to the town where so many of her relatives lived. This is surprising in view of the fact that tragedy had struck Uncle Edward's family. His wife Martha and her ten-year-old daughter Elizabeth had both died and been buried in the same grave only a few months earlier. Yet we hear no comment from Anna on how the family had survived their loss. Only a rather detailed account of the symptoms and the remedies provided for the cold. This is all the more surprising in view of the fact that Anna was a far from selfish person.

The acceleration of Anna's hypochondria after her removal to Lancing was probably caused in part by the removal of the distractions of life at Brighton. It was probably caused in greater part by the removal of Philip. He had now finished his training as a civil engineer and had secured his first appointment abroad. When he boarded the channel steamer at Shoreham a lifelong companionship ended. The brother and sister had been unusually close for the first twenty-five years of their lives since Philip had never left home either to attend boarding school or university. For the next twenty-five years he was destined to live mostly in distant places. To use Mrs Bayly's words, 'Mrs. Sewell and her daughter were now more than ever all the world to each other as companions.'

Although Anna was now a semi-invalid, she was not a burdensome one. According to her mother:

> Her sufferings never made a gloom or a cloud in the house. She never brooded over her loss of power, or the loss of the changes or amusements which others enjoy. Her own mind was always a storehouse of refreshment to herself; it was a rich garden which circumstances

never allowed to be fully cultivated, but it was full of thoughts and ready appreciation of the genius and talents of others.

No parent could have been more concerned about her child's ill health than was Mary, who may have been the unconscious cause of it. Not only Mary, but Isaac also, for, as Margaret Sewell pointed out, 'she was idolised by both mother and father'. In the words of Mrs Bayly, 'Many infallible cures were tried, and proved most fallible. Much was spent upon physicians, but the poor patient was nothing the better.' Mary wrote, 'We tried everything as far as our circumstances would allow, for I always kept alive the hope that the healing-time would come.' Of all the remedies attempted, hydrotherapy seems to have given the most relief, and for the next ten years Anna's life consisted largely of a pilgrimage by rail from one spa to the next.

The cult of the water cure was at its height at this time. The Romans, of course, had believed in the therapeutic powers of mineral water, but it was a German, Vincenz Priessnitz (1799–1851), 'the peasant philosopher of Graefenberg', who revived interest in it. Priessnitz believed that all water, whether mineral or not, had curative powers whether taken internally or applied externally. In 1815 he was condemned for practising illegally. By 1835 his cure was all the rage and in 1842 an English doctor, James Gully of Malvern, was converted to his method and became its chief apologist. In his book *The Practice of the Water Cure* (1846) Dr Gully claimed to have cured aristocratic patients of diseases as diverse as syphilis, gout, impotence and T.B. He recommended many methods of applying the water, including wrapping in a wet sheet, cold bathing after sweating, bathing of particular parts, the douche or spout bath, cooling compresses and animating bandages. Dr Gully also recommended drinking water in very large quantities. At first the dose should be only two or three glasses before breakfast and about half that amount in the evening. The dose should be sipped gradually while walking up and down, and breakfast, if health will permit, should not be taken for an hour after the task is completed. By the end of his stay the patient should be consuming fifteen pints of water daily.

Hydrotherapy was chiefly recommended for middle-aged persons with chronic diseases, frequently those resulting from over indulgence at the table. To this class Anna Sewell could hardly be said to belong. There was, however, another class of people who resorted to spas and this was one of younger persons suffering from hypochondriasis and hysteria, a fact which lends support to our theory that Anna Sewell's complaint had a psychological cause. Parthenope Nightingale sought the healing waters of Carlsbad when nervously prostrated by her famous sister's determination to take up nursing. Alfred Tennyson retired to a series of English watering-places after he lost his fortune in a patent wood-carving venture.

Life at a spa was very similar to life at Brighton and the fact that Anna found watering-places congenial suggests that she was missing, rather surprisingly, the diversions of the south coast resort. Spas were the playground of the rich and idle and health was by no means the only commodity sought at them. We can turn again to Surtees for a picture of a typical English one at this time (probably Tunbridge Wells).

> When ... the London season closed, there was a rush of rank and fashion to the English watering-places. There were blooming widows in every stage of grief and woe, from the becoming cap to the fashionable corset and ball flounce ... lovely girls who didn't care a farthing if the man was 'only handsome'; and smiling mammas ... who would look very different when they came to the horrid £.s.d. And this mercantile expression leads us to the observation that we know nothing so dissimilar as a trading town and a watering-place. In the one, all is bustle ... in the other people don't seem to know what to do to get through the day ... they have generally little to do but stare and talk to each other, and mark the progress of the day by alternately drinking at the wells, eating at the hotels, and wandering between the library and the railway station. The ladies get on better, for where there are ladies there are always fine shops, and what between turning over the goods, and sweeping the streets with their trains, making calls, and arranging partners for balls, they get through their time very pleasantly.[*]

The first spa that Anna Sewell visited was Marienbad, in 1846. Philip accompanied her there, in spite of the fact that he had only just

[*] Surtees, Robert, *Mr. Sponge's Sporting Tour*, 1853.

returned from France. This suggests that the family recognised that the parting from him had been one of the causes of Anna's break-down. Also of the party were her mother and her Aunt Ellen, who was unfortunately taken ill at Brussels on the way home. Anna stayed on for several months after they left although the cure required a maximum stay of only six weeks.

Marienbad stood 2,000 feet up in the mountains of Bohemia (now Czechoslovakia) between Prague and Nürnberg. The area had been converted from an almost impenetrable wilderness of trees into a charmingly situated watering-place only thirty years earlier. There was no railway to it and it was surrounded on all sides but the south by hills which, according to a brochure, 'were clad with fragrant pine forests intersected by lovely walks'.

There is a vivid picture of the place in Murray's Handbook of *Southern Germany* for 1853.

It consists of about 50 or 60 buildings, chiefly lodging-houses, arranged in a crescent on the slope of the wood-clad hills, which surround the spot on all sides but one, … and all around may be seen stumps of trees cut down but not rooted up, just as in the back-woods of America. Within the crescent of houses stands a splendid Assembly-room and the Pump-room and a colonnade for shops, occupied by itinerant traders during the season, a church, and a theatre. The lower portion of the valley is tastefully laid out in pleasure-grounds, in the midst of which most of the mineral springs are situated, inclosed within elegant buildings in the form of temples, etc. Marienbad has the advantage of possessing two different kinds of mineral springs – two saline purgative, viz, the *Kreutzbrunnen*, which is sometimes warmed before drinking, and is then said to resemble in taste veal broth: … and the *Ferdinandsbrunnen,* about a mile distant … Three of the springs are chalybeate – the *Carolinenbrunnen,* surrounded by a circular Corinthian temple – *Ambrosiusbrunnen*, covered by a Gothic canopy – and *Marienbrunnen*. … The enormous quantities of carbonic acid gas evolved by the Marienbrunnen, and by the peat-bog adjoining, have given rise to the establishment of *Gas-Baths,* where, by a peculiar apparatus, a stream of gas can be applied to any part of the body affected by disease. When the whole person is subjected to the gas, the patient enters a sort of box, provided with a lid, through which

his head projects: the gas is admitted from below in pipes, and care is
taken to prevent his breathing it, which would be injurious or fatal.

Anna no doubt stayed at the Stadt Weimar, Baron Brussick's or
Klinger's Hotel. (Those who stayed at Klinger's were advised to
make their bargain beforehand.) Marienbad had fewer gaieties than
Carlsbad or Teplitz. 'To be sure,' Murray's handbook says, 'it has a
theatre, and balls and concerts are sometimes given in the course of
the season; but visitors who repair hither will find the chief attrac-
tions of the place, beyond the relief which its waters are likely to
afford, to lie in its quiet solitude and pretty situation.'

We can imagine Anna leading very much the kind of life that Kitty
of *Anna Karenina* led when she was sent to a German spa (probably Marienbad, for Tolstoy states that it also lacked the gaiety of
its neighbours Carlsbad or Teplitz) to recover from her unfortunate
passion for Count Vronsky. Kitty, however, unlike Anna, was only
permitted to attend the spa on condition that she didn't 'let the
German quacks get at her'. Like Kitty, Anna no doubt found her
place in the pecking order of her compatriots, and, like them, spent
warm mornings drinking from the springs beneath the pillars of
the Corinthian temple and wet ones avoiding being run down by
the invalid carriages in the arcades. No doubt there were the daily
outings in the gardens, and the development of friendships with
other invalids she met there daily. If her ankles were strong enough
there may have been walks in the 'fragrant pine forests'. There must
certainly have been carriage excursions to some of the local sights,
for no one left Marienbad without going to see the views from the
top of Podhorn, or the seventeenth-century Teplitz Abbey. Anna may
also have visited the castle of Prince Metternich near by. She little
suspected that its occupant, the great Austrian statesman, was soon
to be an exile in Brighton.

We are not told whether Anna's health improved as a result of the
visit. The waters at Marienbad were chiefly noted for their purgative
effect which was much greater than those of the neighbouring town
of Carlsbad. They were chiefly sought by the liverish, the gouty and
the obese, most of whom were restricted to rigid diets. However, as
Dr Cullimore, a writer on the subject, frankly pointed out, 'Much
of the good … arising from a course at the baths, is due to the rest,

the quiet, the altered conditions of life.' To that list we might add 'and the absence of Mamma'. Indeed, Mary Sewell herself admitted that a visit to a spa conferred more than purely medical benefits. In a letter to a friend, describing another of Anna's visits, she wrote, 'She has made dear and valuable friends, and gained a great deal of experience, and seen much variety, which, to such a prisoner as she is, is a great advantage.' No doubt it was only at spas that Anna was able to lead a life independent of Mary and make friends who did not immediately become Mary's friends.

Anna learnt to speak German while she was at Marienbad and came back with a repertoire of German songs which her niece Margaret Sewell remembered her singing. Anyone familiar with the intricacies of German irregular verbs will conclude that she had found a remedy at least for the weakness in her head. No sketches of the Bohemian mountains, however, were found among her effects and it seems that this means of self-expression had dried up for ever.

During the years of ill-health Anna did discover another distraction. She came to love poetry as passionately as her mother, but with more discrimination, as Mary was the first to admit. 'And there, darling Anna would say her beautiful lines of Wordsworth and Tennyson and Shakespeare – such a soul in them! – and I had only my old *Byron* (with an accent of supreme contempt) and *Moore* to come in with!' Tennyson was the poet whose work Anna loved above all others. Margaret Sewell had vivid memories of her aunt 'repeating poem after poem of his. We used irreverently to consider her delivery exaggerated, but English youth is chary of emotion.' It was Tennyson's shorter poems and lyrics that Anna loved and her annotated copy of *In Memoriam* can still be seen.

On a visit to a spa Anna actually met Tennyson. Her niece, Margaret Sewell, who recorded the event, thought this meeting occurred at Matlock some time after the visit to Marienbad. Neither the biographers of the poet nor the authorities at Matlock have any record that he paced the gardens overlooking the gorge of the Derwent. On the other hand there is no doubt that he stayed at Umbers Hall, an eighteenth-century mansion in the forest of Arden, in 1847, and it seems likely that here was the scene of the meeting. Tennyson found Dr Edward Johnson's cure a 'terribly long process' that required continuous 'washing and walking'. In a letter written at this time he admitted that he lacked 'woman's long enduring patience in these matters'. Could the woman whose long-enduring patience he admired have been Anna? In another letter he asked for two copies of his poems, explaining that 'two persons in this house want them'. Could one of these persons have been Anna?

According to Margaret Sewell, 'she must have seen a good deal of the poet; she used to tell of walks and talks with him, and he gave her a signed portrait of himself which we possess'. Surely this was one of the great occasions in Anna's life, perhaps the nearest she ever came to romance. Not only was Tennyson her favourite poet, he was on the way to becoming the nation's favourite poet. *In Memoriam*, it is true, had yet to be published and so had *The Idylls of the King*, but a two-volume edition of the poems, which included such masterpieces as *The Lotus Eaters* and *The Lady of Shalott*, had firmly established his reputation. He was also, according to Carlyle, at the age of thirty-eight, 'one of the finest looking men in the world. A great shock of rough, dusty, dark hair; bright, laughing hazel eyes, almost Indian-looking.' His marriage was still three years away.

Yet here the curtain falls again. If any letters were exchanged they are lost and so is the signed photograph. We can only speculate upon the relationship between the crippled spinster and the melancholy poet. Tennyson had at this time been through a period of frequent breakdowns. Since 1842, when he lost all his money in the Patent Decorative Carving Company, he had suffered from severe hypochondria. The grant of a pension by Peel in 1845 seems to have cured him but a brief relapse in 1847 brought him to Umberslade.

He was not normally at ease with women. Jane Carlyle related that he 'Entertains at one and the same moment a feeling of almost adoration for them and an ineffable contempt. Adoration I suppose, for what they *might* be – contempt for what they *are*!' It was surely because Anna was what she was that he was able to talk to her. Certainly he would have been grateful for cultured company of either sex at Umberslade, for he frequently complained of the country gentlemen at such establishments who talked of nothing but dogs and horses. He said he could have borne them 'if they would only be a little kinder to the poor', a sentiment with which Anna would surely have sympathised. No doubt he found her a useful vessel into which to pour his complaints. The doctors had told him 'not to read, not to think: but they might as well tell me not to live'. He complained to his friends at this time that he could stand neither 'the chattering and conceit of clever men, or the worry of society, or the meanness of tuft hunters, or the trouble of poverty, or the labour of a place, or the preying of the heart on itself'. Let us hope that he occasionally rewarded his confidant by 'crooning' one of his magnificent lyrics to her.

Two years after Anna's probable meeting with Tennyson, her father made a decision so shocking that it was passed over in silence by Mrs Bayly. He became a brewer. In March 1849 he had an interview with the directors of the bank and informed them that in consequence of his having engaged in the brewing business he felt it his duty to tender his resignation.[*] The full enormity of Isaac Sewell's decision can only be appreciated in the light of future events. Within the next few years his wife was to become one of the most ardent workers in the field of Temperance. In the more distant future his son was to turn down an offer of £10,000 for a site he owned in Kennington rather than see a public house built on it and his daughter was to write a book about a fine horse whose life was ruined by a drunken rider. One can only guess at the effect his decision had on his family. It must surely have increased the gulf between husband and wife and brought mother and daughter still closer together. It was probably the cause of the family's move to Haywards Heath. Perhaps the brewery was situated in this small Sussex town, now growing fast as a result of the decision to carry the London to Brighton line through it. The Sewells lived in a large house called Petlands which stood in several acres of land on the corner of Hazeldene Road and New England Road. In their day it was backed by fields and farms but now the area is densely built up. Petlands itself, built about 1830, ended its days as a private hotel and was finally demolished in 1955 to make way for a housing estate. Part of the land was taken by New England Road School.

We know very little of the four years that the Sewells spent in Haywards Heath. Mary was unusually quiet about her experiences there (perhaps understandably). We can assume, however, that

[*] I am indebted to Stanley Godman for unearthing this information and giving it to the public in the *West Sussex Gazette* of 9 January, 1958.

Anna and Mary enjoyed drives in the pony-trap through the lanes and villages of the Weald. Lindfield, with its famous common and eighteenth-century main street, was only two miles away. Ardingly, Horsted Keynes and West Hoathly were not much farther, although the steep wooded valleys that surrounded them would have obliged Mary, with her kind heart, to get out and walk to relieve the pony. Perhaps the ladies preferred the flatter drive across the common to Ditchling at the foot of the South Downs. Mary must have rejoiced to see the Sussex bluebells in May. While she still lived in Brighton Isaac occasionally took her by rail to some country place to see the spring flowers. It was on one of these excursions (very probably in the neighbourhood of Haywards Heath) that they lost their way in a wood. They had passed a woodman some time before and Isaac went to try to find him. While he was gone, Mary came upon a bank of wild whitewood sorrel, the first she had seen since leaving Felthorpe as a child. 'It was so beautiful,' she said, 'I stood before it, and could scarcely help praying that Isaac mightn't find the man, that we might be lost, and have to stay there all day long and look at it.'

In the year of the Great Exhibition Philip moved south from Skipton, where he had been working on plans for the Carlisle and Settle line, to work on improvements to the harbour at Shoreham. Shoreham was a mere twenty miles from Haywards Heath by rail, but Anna could hardly hope for a revival of the old companion ship, for Philip was now married to Sarah and the father of Mary Grace and Margaret Amie. We know very little of Sarah apart from the fact that she made him a dutiful wife. Mary's comment on her was 'Sarah was very *lovely*', and this comment she repeated often. The only photograph that remains of her is of a rather stolid young matron, so we must assume that the loveliness was moral rather than physical. Mary always valued beauty of character above beauty of face or form.

The reunion of brother and sister was in any case destined to be brief, for two years later Philip left for Spain. For the next eleven years he was employed upon the construction of the railways which linked the Atlantic ports of Santander and Bilbao to the wine-making cities of Logrono and Tudela situated on the Ebro in the mountainous province of Navarre. Spain had dropped behind the rest of Europe in the race to build railways. The first stretch of line, a mere twenty-eight kilometres, linking Barcelona to Mataro, was not opened until

1848 and resulted in the striking of a medal which showed the Bishop of Barcelona sprinkling the train with holy water. Despite enthusiasm in certain sections of the government, no money could be found for more, and the sale of railway concessions at the court of Isabella II became such a scandal that it was a major cause of her downfall. There were also grave fears that the muleteers would turn into highwaymen and rob the trains if they were ever introduced.

Spain was still a primitive country at this time. It was not included on the Grand Tour and only travellers of considerable experience exposed themselves to the discomforts and even dangers of the smaller Spanish inns. Fifty years later Baedeker was still warning the traveller against the minor enemies to repose to be found in these which 'may be repelled by Persian or Keatings insect powder, a supply of which should be brought from England'. The view from Théophile Gautier's hotel window was of 'some pillars on which the heads of three or four malefactors were exposed to view; this is always a reassuring sight, and proves that one is in a civilised country', he remarked.

Anna read Philip's letters home with interest. She shared his love of travel and it could almost be said that she saw the world through him. Philip, like Anna, had a gift for languages and no doubt became as fluent in Spanish as he was in French. In the South of France his knowledge of French had saved his party from an unpleasant experience. While boats were being prepared for a crossing of the Rhône, he overheard the boatmen planning to take him and his fellow engineers into the middle of the river and then rob and, if necessary, kill them. He conveyed the information to his chief who, as his biographer charmingly put it, caused the programme to be altered. He was to have equally exciting stories to tell about his adventures in Spain. On one occasion he was travelling at speed on the footplate of an engine when it was derailed, killing one of his companions and badly injuring the other. On another he lost his outside corner seat on the top of a stage-coach to a stranger who refused to return it to him. In the middle of the night there was a fearful scream. The stranger had been killed by a blow from the angle of a roof which caught him in the chest when the coach cornered too sharply. Such mishaps were not uncommon in a country where the roads were abominable and the coaches were pulled by teams of eight mules whom the *zagal*, 'a Fury in human form', never permitted to travel at any pace but a gallop.

It was in the year that Philip sailed for Spain that his parents moved to their third home in Sussex since leaving Brighton. Isaac, restless as ever, had taken up an appointment as manager of the Chichester branch of his old bank, presumably because the day-to-day management of the brewery either proved uncongenial or did not sufficiently occupy his time. The London and County Bank at Chichester stood at 5 East Street where its successor, the National Westminster, still stands. Isaac and his family, however, did not live on the premises. Presumably they had by now developed a taste for country living for they moved to an old-fashioned country house at Grayling Wells. Grayling Wells was an old country estate near the barracks upon which the West Sussex Lunatic Asylum was eventually to be built. The Sewells probably rented Grayling farmhouse itself, for its owner was Thomas Smith, a leading Chichester Quaker, appointed fellow representative, with Isaac, to the Quarterly Meeting at Southampton in 1855. The name of John Abel Smith of Belgrave Square, however, appears as the tenant in the register of voters of the period.

The house at Grayling Wells was probably the most beautiful that Anna had lived in. Not only was it an old manor house but it stood in an exceptionally fine garden. A woman who visited the house as a child remembered the garden many years later with the pond where bulrushes grew and the crab-apple tree loaded with bright fruit. In the spring of 1856 Philip brought his wife and four small daughters to stay on a long holiday from Spain. He had by now completed the first section of the line which linked Santander and Bilbao.

Mary Sewell was deeply interested in her grandchildren although, as we mentioned, she somewhat overawed them. Isaac also was a doting grandparent and, being playful and indulgent, a popular one. But we hear nothing of Anna's relationship with her nieces at this time and it seems probable that she was far from well. Perhaps the sight of her brother so happily married increased her sense of frustration. Certainly all her usual symptoms became acute and when Philip returned to Spain in June Anna set out for Marienberg with her mother and stayed on alone there for a course of treatment that lasted a year.

6

BLUE LODGE, WICK 1858–64

Marienberg was the name of a hydropathic establishment at Boppard, just south of Coblenz on the Rhine. According to the 1867 edition of Baedeker's guide to the Rhineland, it charged 12½ thaler a week for board, lodging, baths and medical attention. It was a former Benedictine nunnery high on a hill behind the town with a view of the mountains and had been used both as a cotton factory and a girls' school before it was converted into a medical establishment.

Boppard is a delightful little town. It is picturesquely situated above a gorge on the left bank of the river, near the rich wine-producing area of the Moselle valley. Like Marienbad it is a famous centre for excursions into the mountains but, unlike Marienbad, also contains narrow picturesque streets and buildings of historical interest within its concentric Roman and medieval walls. Anna understandably lingered in this delightful place almost a year and Mary suddenly found herself without companionship and without an occupation, for her dependence on her daughter was as great as her daughter's on her. During the years of Anna's illness she had devoted much of her time to caring for her. While the family lived at Lancing she had continued to travel to Brighton to visit the poor there, but this proved impossible after the move to Haywards Heath, and one gets the impression that from then on her poor-visiting had been considerably curtailed. She had recently suffered another loss. Her mother died about the time Anna left for Germany and her beloved father had died two years previously. Contrary to Quaker Custom, she had gone into deep mourning on both occasions although she hastens to tell us that she limited the crape trimming on the skirt to within two inches of her waist. 'Worldly people,' her dressmaker had informed her, 'have it brought up quite to the waist.'

It was during the year that Anna was at Marienberg that Mary, now sixty years old, began to write. Her first poem may well have been *The Funeral Bell*, always regarded as a dirge for her father.

> Alas for the village, alas for the day
>   The church bell is tolling a funeral knell,
> Adam Hope from the parish is taken away,
>   And a sorrowful sound has the funeral bell.
>
> Oh, what will become of the destitute poor?
>   He was eyes to the blind, he was feet to the lame!
> To the fatherless orphans he open'd his door,
>   And the widow's heart sang at the sound of his name.
>
> Oh toll for him – toll for him, funeral bell!
>   Fall sad on the heart, as you fall on the ear;
> Good neighbour, good master, good Christian – farewell!
>   Good husband, good father – in glory appear!

The reader will by now have concluded that Mary Sewell was a versifier rather than a poet but it must be pointed out in justice to her that she never pretended to be anything else. Her first volume of ballads was entitled *Homely Ballads for the Working Man's Fireside* and it was for the working man and not for the literary critic that it was intended. 'I have a knack of a rough sort of rhyming that serves my purpose,' she said, 'and all the Byron at Friends' Meeting trained me well in rhythm – that's all.' Her writing was simply an extension of her charitable work. She considered that the poor were in need of good advice and she observed that they were more inclined to take it if it rhymed. So she set about manufacturing something acceptable. No doubt she felt the touch of her father's hand on her head again as she had as a child and heard his voice saying, 'That's right, my dear. Always hope.' Unlike her sisters, he had never teased her for thinking she could 'do everything'.

In April Mary heard from Anna in Germany. She reported that her back and chest were better, her feet quite lame and her head not much better. A month later she returned home. Her feet were vastly improved and indeed for a period so successful did the treatment

prove that she was even able to walk out of doors. This was a gala
time in Anna's life and she celebrated the happy occasion with a
fortnight's holiday at Dorking with her mother. It was a holiday
Mary was to look back on with pleasure for the rest of her life. She
described it as 'a delicate plain called Ease where they went with
much content', though 'they were quickly over it, for it was but
narrow'. The weather was delicious. All day long they walked and
sat among the spring flowers, revelling in the beauty of the English
spring; and when they came home to their lodgings in the evenings,
they were so intensely interested in Carlyle's *Past and Present* that
they could hardly persuade themselves to go to bed, and drank
coffee to drive off sleep.

The reading of books together was to become a lifelong habit.
Perhaps Mary read aloud while Anna listened. Margaret Sewell recalls
that mother and daughter 'indulged in a good deal of hero worship, their heroes being social reformers or contemporary writers of
fiction and biography'. Thomas Carlyle fitted into both these cat-
egories and was always a favourite. Nevertheless *Past and Present* was
a surprising choice for holiday reading. It was an almost unreadable
diatribe published in 1843 against the materialism of the modern age.
Its attacks on the idle aristocracy 'damp with the sweat of Melton
Mowbray' might have been expected to shock Mary who was never
a Socialist. On the other hand it was full of sympathy for the working classes, and in particular for a destitute Irish widow who had to
die of typhoid and infect seventeen other persons before she could
convince her fellow men that she was their sister. Isaac Sewell did
not approve of the books his wife and daughter read.

When Anna returned to Grayling Wells her mother showed her
the ballads she had written in her absence. Anna immediately took
an active and professional interest in her mother's work. 'My Nannie
has always been my critic and counsellor,' said Mary Sewell. 'I have
never made a plan for anything without submitting it to her judgement. Every line I have written has been at her feet before it has
gone forth to the world. If I can only pass my Nannie, I don't fear
the world after that.'

Anna Sewell had the artist's instinct for form strongly developed.
It is said that her pencil drawings from nature were remarkable for
excellence of composition; if she did not edit her landscapes, she had

a genius for seizing the right point of view, and figures and objects were put in exactly the right spot; this same gift of form made her an admirable critic of manner and arrangement in word painting. She was not a lenient judge. Mrs Bayly was once present when Mary was reading some of her work to Anna.

> It was beautiful to witness the intense love, admiration and even pride that beamed in the daughter's face, but this nowise prevented her being, as I thought, a very severe critic. Nature had bestowed on her a remarkably sweet-toned and persuasive voice. I think I hear her now saying, 'Mother dear, thee must alter that line,' or 'Thee must put a fuller word there, that will give out more of thy meaning.'

On one occasion she forbade her mother to publish one of her productions, pronouncing it 'not up to the mark'. The ballad in question was on the subject of William Hunter, the young martyr of Brentwood. Mary eventually published it under the title *The Martyr's Tree* after Anna was dead, but her friends agreed that her censor had been right.

With some trepidation Mary showed her first ballads to Henry S. King, Anna and Philip's friend of Brighton days. He was still with Smith, Elder and Co. the publisher. 'I had to sit by while he turned over the leaves till at last he looked up, and said "This will do!"' Her faith in King's judgment was complete and evidently well founded. 'He was the most refined man. In everything, words and binding and paper, his taste was perfect. He always knew just the right thing to do with one's things, and what the title should be.' *Homely Ballads for the Working Man's Fireside* was printed for private circulation in 1858.

Isaac Sewell's second career as a bank manager ended in the year that his wife's career as a writer began. After only four years at Chichester he resigned. The circumstances of his resignation are not known. Sixty-three seems an early age for retirement, particularly in view of the fact that six years later he started a third career. A reference in a contemporary letter to his courage in bearing 'the reverses of life' suggests that the circumstances of his resignation may not have been entirely normal. Certainly it involved some financial embarrassment to his family. Mary confided to a correspondent, 'We shall have to be more careful, of course, than we have been and that is never very pleasant is it dear?' She added that her husband would be able to make enough to keep his family 'without his being in much more business than attending to his own', which suggests that Isaac still had an interest in the brewery.

Money was not so short as to prevent Isaac celebrating his retirement by taking his wife and daughter to visit Philip in Santander in the autumn. Philip's wife Sarah had recently been very ill after the birth of her first son, and fifth child, Edward, and her parents-in-law were no doubt anxious to see her. 1857 was a year of almost continuous foreign travel for Anna, for she had only returned from Germany in May. The fact that she was capable of it is a measure of the success of her treatment at Marienberg. She would have been quite at home in Santander, for one fashionable watering-place is pretty like another and by 1857 Santander was fashionable. Most of the wide promenades and public gardens for which it is famous had been laid out by this time and Philip no doubt drove his family along the famous Muelle de Calderon (the equivalent of the front at Brighton) and pointed out the view of the Solares mountains that can be obtained from it. He must have hustled them past the bull ring, one of Santander's favourite places of entertainment, and instead drawn their attention to the thirteenth-century Gothic cathedral in the old part of the town where were preserved the remains of the saints Emeritinus and Celedonius, twin patrons of the city. Although Philip never became a Catholic, he was more tolerant of Catholicism than his mother and, according to his biographer, 'though holding his own opinions strongly, recognised goodness wherever he found it'. He even lent money on several occasions to some nuns who were greatly attached to him. Another Spanish lady prayed for him whenever he set out on a journey, and years later, when he revisited Spain, a local paper spoke of the joy of the people at seeing him again.

It is tempting to suppose that Philip took Anna for a ride on the newly completed railway. It ran from Santander to Bilbao through fine mountain country and was accounted by Baedeker one of the most picturesque in Spain. During the second half of the four-hour journey the line followed the River Caranza through picturesque ravines and reached its highest point in the Ecita tunnel which burrowed under the crest of the Fresnedo mountains.

When the Sewells returned from Spain they moved to a house in what was then considered a remote corner of Gloucestershire, on the boundaries of the Beaufort Hunt country. The six years that Anna spent there were, after the period at Brighton, probably the happiest of her adult life. Blue Lodge was not near anywhere. It stood within a drive of Bath and Bristol between the mining villages of Liston and Wick. Mary described its situation in a letter.

> We are situated ... on a high hill which is frequented more by the wind than fogs – though many fine trees round us offer a pretty good screen: it is healthy and almost as inconvenient as it can be. It is a long way from everything, with neither postman, carrier, omnibus, nor rail; neither shop, needlewoman, nor char woman to be had, so that everything has to be done and obtained with the greatest difficulty. For instance, our letters every day take two good hours to get and post. We are two miles and a half from the school, etc. and the roads almost impassable in some parts for our chaise, and entirely for foot passengers in winter wet. And adhesive clay and ruts to break the springs, which was the case last week!

To add to Mary Sewell's discomfort Isaac insisted on extensive altera-tions in spite of the need to economise. The couple spent the autumn of 1858 in two rooms with their possessions stacked round them in packing cases, waited on by an inadequate girl from the village. Anna wisely went on a visit to relatives (probably Uncle and Aunt Wright) and Mary described the difficulties of composing poetry while organising the new maid in the only one of her letters to Anna that has been preserved.

> I must write my precious one a letter to go to the post when my young woman goes to chapel at Wick. I cannot call her servant, domestic, or help yet, because I have not proved these virtues, but she may not turn out quite so bad as I fear. Having constitutionally no method, and much self-conceit, she has great obstacles in the way at present. I will tell thee a funny little instance yesterday, which will make thee laugh. I told her to boil a little rice, thinking she would tie it up and have done with it. She came very catechetically to ascertain if I had a little diaper bag to boil it in and stood informing me that she

had always been used to a diaper bag, and did not think rice would look well without one; and so, while all the great outlines have to be made, she keeps worrying me about the *minutiae*, always supposing I 'have not such and such a thing'. It is very laughable to hear how she goes on, but very provoking, and she will make me a saint or a sinner according to the measure of grace and patience.

But the house, although 'very modest' had charm. It was built on the site of one of the three royal hunting-lodges of Kingswood Forest where Saxon kings had hunted. Mary set one of her poems (*The Little Forester*) in the forest and lamented its passing in the following words:

> The Forest trees are levelled now,
>   No wolves disturb our rest
> But still the wicked are accursed
>   And still the righteous blest.

The house itself was long and low and built of stone with mullioned windows. The rooms, apart from the entrance hall and a recently added drawing-room, were small. Mrs F., the poetess, described how this 'large and lofty' addition (now demolished)

swallowed the Chichester furniture at a mouthful, and gaped for more. But a skilful use of Indian matting, a judicious placing and draping of spare chairs and tables from other rooms, and above all the introduction of Anna's spinning wheel, had banished all bareness, and given the same air of distinction and simplicity to the room which was so striking in its inhabitants.

The views from the house were exceptionally fine. Mrs F. noted

the window of my room gave me the view of a sunny, park like, upland field, sprinkled with calm tree shadows, under which newly shorn sheep rested here and there. Breakfast in a sunny parlour, which gave us through the open door the same view as from my window, and through the open windows opposite, the brilliance and greenness of the flower garden.

The flower garden, where the Sewells took their tea whenever the weather permitted, was (and still is) bounded by a sunken tree-lined walk. It was up and down this Long Walk that Mary liked to pace while she was making up her verses. 'A crinkle-crankle walk is dreadful,' she said, 'it cuts off all one's rhymes.' The Long Walk was not the only feature of Blue Lodge that made it suitable for composition. It had another advantage. Nobody called. 'Our time,' said Mary, 'was not all cut up into bits with people ... Everyone who came to see us had to climb up a long steep hill, so that they had to be very much in earnest to do it.'

It was at Blue Lodge that almost all Mary Sewell's ballads and her two chief prose works were written. *The Children of Summerbrook* was brought before the public in 1859, but by a different publisher. Mary had deserted Smith Elder and Co. in favour of Jarrolds. Perhaps she had been piqued by Mr King's failure to do more than print her first collection privately, or perhaps Aunt Wright had recommended the Norwich firm who had been publishing her science textbooks over the last few years. Jarrolds of Norwich was a firm run by three brothers, Samuel, William and Thomas, who were members of the second generation of a publishing family which had started by printing books in a barn at Woodbridge in Suffolk, near Mary Sewell's birthplace at Sutton.

Sarah Stickney Ellis, who stayed at Blue Lodge the summer after they moved in, described with amusement the satisfaction that her old friend derived from having her 'little poems' so sought after. The two women exchanged visits frequently at this time, for Mrs Ellis was lonely in her house at Hoddesdon now that her husband had returned to Madagascar as a missionary. Unlike Mary, she had a sense of humour which showed itself in some, though not all, of her books. She was able to enjoy to the full the spectacle of her unworldly friend turning businesswoman. 'Two publishers,' she wrote, 'are wanting to have the poems, and they bid one against the other so that she enjoys to the full the pleasure of her own plentiful pocket-money.'

The following year Mary appears to have divided her favours somewhat unevenly between Smith Elder and Jarrold, for while Henry King was merely permitted to print publicly the collection of ballads which before he had printed privately, Samuel Jarrold was presented with the manuscript of Mary Sewell's bestseller, *Mother's Last Words*.

Mother's Last Words was a ballad which consisted of just over 200 four-line verses. It was issued as a thirty-two-page leaflet measuring roughly three by six inches in a uniform series called *Jarrold's Household Tracts*. The tracts cost twopence each and were recommended by the publisher as 'worthy the attention of all who promote the moral, sanitary and religious improvement of the people'. The series was started by Thomas Jarrold in 1854 and many of the early titles, such as *Power of Soap and Water, Self-help for Young Women* and *Measles* are thought to have been written by his wife who was an authoress. Samuel Jarrold was very active in distributing the tracts and always carried a supply under his hat when he rode to work before breakfast. He distributed them to operatives he met on the way and, according to a history of the House of Jarrold, they were accepted with gratitude.[*]

The subject of Mary Sewell's tract *Mother's Last Words*, as we have already mentioned, was the fate of two orphan boys who, mindful of their dying mother's instructions, preferred starving as crossing-sweepers to thriving as thieves. The older boy, John, fell briefly from grace when he stole a pair of boots for his younger brother, Chris. But so fearful was he of the 'wicked sprite as black as night' which pursued him that he preferred to return them and see the child die of cold. The story ended happily. John grew up an honest man and as for Chris, 'he found, once more, his mother dear'.

> Above the crowd of toiling folk,
> Above the cross above St. Paul's
> Above the fog, above the smoke.

The ballad had a success unprecedented in the history of ballads. It sold well over a million copies in this country and more were distributed on the other side of the Atlantic by the American Sunday School Union. The family were amazed. 'We always knew Mary had it in her,' said her spinster sisters at Buxton, who probably didn't. Uncle Wright's comment was typically prosaic. 'Why Mary, what

[*] *The House of Jarrolds 1823–1923*; A Brief History of One Hundred Years.

company have thee kept?' He was referring to the low social status of most of the subjects of Mary's ballads. Testimonials arrived from all quarters. A canon wrote, 'I read *Mother's Last Words* in December to nearly one thousand of my poor people.' The captain of a ship wrote, 'Some very rough fellows have been greatly impressed for good by our readings.' An ailing boy on a farm asked to have it read to him for the last time and then died happy. Dora Greenwell, in her essay on *Popular Religious Literature*, wrote, 'It would be hard to find a poem so completely answering to the end for which it was written. We have seen a class of adult criminals so sunk in the strange apathy habitual to them, … follow its course with eager eyes, with broken exclamations, with sobs, with pools of tears.'[*]

The following year Mary Sewell sent *Our Father's Care* to Samuel Jarrold while Henry King had to be content with a second series of *Homely Ballads*. The story of the fatherless watercress-girl proved almost as successful as that of the motherless crossing-sweepers. It sold three-quarters of a million copies and Mary was inundated with letters from well-intentioned ladies and gentlemen wishing to know how they could befriend little Nelly. At this stage Henry King understandably retired from the fray and left the Jarrold brothers as Mary Sewell's sole publishers.

The newly fledged authoress did not allow her head to be turned by this sudden success. 'My dear,' she remarked to a friend, 'I have nothing to be proud of; it all came in answer to prayer.' 'Yes,' she added immediately after, 'even the rhymes.' (One is tempted to add that some of these were not Godsends.) Nevertheless the success of her writing *did* persuade Mary that the practice of the art merited a larger proportion of her time and it was at this juncture that she handed over 'all the little *et ceteras* of house-keeping' to Anna.

The running of Mary Sewell's household was no sinecure. For reasons of economy she kept only one servant, apart from the boy who cared for the pony and, for reasons of humanity, this servant was usually untrained. Mary Sewell regarded it as her duty to rescue girls from unsuitable homes or situations to train them and see that they

---

[*] Georges, Mary, *Mrs. Sewell*, Number 20 in the *Excellent Women* series, London Religious Tract Society.

were 'respectably clothed, especially with shoes and under garments'. As soon as they began to be useful she passed them on to her friends. At this time she wrote the autobiography of a virtuous kitchen-maid, told in the form of letters home to her mother. Its full title was *Patience Hart's First Experiences in Service*, and it bursts at the seams with Mary's opinions on the correct management of servants.

Her own servants were encouraged to wear simple home-made clothes. The only garments they were permitted to buy ready-made were their bonnets and their boots, and these two items must be ample in size and sensible in design. The rest of their wardrobe, the washable print dress, the sensible apron wide enough to meet behind, the Alpaca gown for Sundays and the 'loose sort of jacket' for walking out (so much more practical than a shawl which slips) – all these were to be made at home under the supervision of the mistress of the house.

Not only was the dress of the servant at Blue Lodge closely super-vised, so also were her morals. Mary Sewell deplored the flightiness of the modern miss.

> Obedience and respect to parents is at a very low ebb, and modesty as low. It is no uncommon thing to hear a mother confess that she cannot manage her child though perhaps not ten years old, and at fourteen or fifteen they are quite out of her power ... The young girls of the present day are prematurely mature: as soon as they leave school they think of being women. To dress gayly, to show themselves when dressed, and to walk with a young lad, may without uncharitableness, describe the ambition of a large number of our young girls. [*]

Mary's own servants were warned against the advances of would-be suitors. Her advice to maidens was:

> Keep yourself spotless; see the man you love
> Has qualities your reason can approve.
> Do not be dazzled with his chain or pin,
> His handsome clothes, but mark the man within. [**]

---

[*] Sewell, Mary, *Thy Poor Brother.*

[**] Sewell, Mary, *Marriage as it May Be.*

She did not disapprove of servants marrying eventually, provided a
steady artisan presented himself, but she considered that they should
wait until, over the years, they had acquired a capital of some six or
seven pounds upon which to set up house. It was the duty of the
mistress to keep a small sum back from the servant's wages until this
amount had been collected. Until then Mary Sewell advised girls to
treat suitors as *Patience Hart* treated the grocer's assistant in the shop
down the street.

> He asked me if I was not the young lady from Mr. Freemantle.
> I said no – I was the kitchen-maid ... and he made me an offer of his
> hand and heart. I just asked him how old he was; at this, he coloured
> and looked sheepish, but he said he was between nineteen and twenty.
> 'Well,' said I, 'I am between seventeen and eighteen; in a few years
> we shall be grown up, and I have made up my mind not to think of
> marrying till I am five-and-twenty; so if you hold in the same opinion
> so long, and like to ask me then, I can turn it over in my mind.'

Mary Sewell regarded the spiritual as well as the moral welfare of
her servants her responsibility. They were expected to attend prayers
in the drawing room in the evening and were encouraged to discuss
with her any spiritual problems they might have. Like Anna and
Philip as children, they were also encouraged to sacrifice their food
to the needy and to give up their leisure to sewing garments for
those worse off than themselves. The servants in *Patience Hart* set a
shining example by clubbing together to rescue a girl from a life of
shame and sewing a complete wardrobe for her.

Mary Sewell spent a great deal of time in the kitchen herself
and took an active interest in the cooking. She was a good cook and
indeed there was an occasion when she caused considerable offence
to her own cook by insisting on her trying out a guest's recipe entitled
Warren's Hotpot. Mistresses were advised to keep a close watch also
on what became of left-overs. Mary inherited her mother's frugality.
In Ann Wright's kitchen at Felbridge 'there was never any waste nor
any pinch. The first thing she would do when she went out in the
morning was to look out such a nice breakfast for the dogs and cats!
They never had a scant meal, and yet there was never any waste.'
Mary wrote with strong disapproval of households where the cook

exercised her right to perquisites by selling so-called refuse to old women who called at the back door.

> In a well-managed family there need to be very little broken victuals; and that little, every lady ought to give away to deserving people, to get a blessing on the rest. You know, my dear, that I do not think it right, that every piece of cut bread should be called broken victuals, nor yet that new bread should be eaten in the kitchen; many a battle I have had with our servants because I would have the good pieces of bread eaten; it is a sin and a shame to throw them away. I have known a cook cut a thick top crust and bottom crust off every baker's loaf before she set it on the kitchen table.[*]

In the Sewell household nothing was wasted. Bones were boiled up to make 'a nice jug of broth' for a needy neighbour and many a 'nourishing dish for a sick person' was made from scraps.

Anna was a successful housekeeper. A guest has left an account of the domestic peace and order that prevailed at Blue Lodge.

> The 'plain living' which they loved to associate with 'high thinking' was marked by exquisite order and nicety, such as one rarely sees. Yet all seemed to spring up naturally around them with no petty anxieties or fatigues to themselves and no worrying of dependents. All was lovely calm, and yet full of cheerful activities that never jostled each other. Our first visit to Blue Lodge was early in winter, in the flowerless season and there was no greenhouse from which to supply the vases in the drawing room; but I well remember the tasteful arrangements of ivy sprays that filled these, and adorned odd nooks and bare corners.

The task of supplying this background of plain living to her mother's high thinking seems to have suited Anna admirably. Sarah Stickney Ellis wrote, 'Anna now takes the housekeeping, and it seems to suit her well; she is very brisk.' Mrs F., the poetess, who stayed at Blue Lodge the year before the family left, also gave the impression that the work suited Anna.

---

[*] Sewell, Mary, *Patience Hart*.

Meanwhile Anna would appear from time to time at the garden door of the house, shading her eyes with her hand, and trying to discover our whereabouts, anxious to meet any possible want or wish of her mother's ... At the time I speak of Anna was unable to stand for more than a few seconds at a time, though she moved freely about the house. Wherever Mrs. Sewell and I might be working at our proofs or discussing questions they suggested, if household affairs brought the daughter to her mother's side, she was obliged to kneel on the nearest support for the minute she remained. But her general appearance had little or nothing of the invalid, and the calm radiance of her expressive face was remarkable. My husband chancing once to meet her in a shop in Bath, came home saying, 'I've just seen Anna Sewell's beautiful face.' And beautiful indeed it was, with the beauty of nobility and purity.

There were no more visits to spas now in spite of the fact that Anna was only nine miles from the most famous of them all. It is true that since her father had retired from the bank there was less money to spend on such excursions but no doubt Mary Sewell could have found it from her literary earnings if it had been necessary. It seems more probable that the visits ceased because they were no longer required. Anna now had an occupation and although her symptoms, did not vanish they were no longer incapacitating. Her back was so much stronger that she could ride side-saddle to the village several times a week.

Anna's mount at this time was evidently an animal of some spirit to judge from an account of an accident that befell its groom during the first summer at Blue Lodge. The catastrophe is not mentioned by Mrs Bayly but described by 'Sarah Stickney Ellis,[*] for it happened during her stay.

The boy, a fine youth of 17, the son of nice people living near, had gone out with Anna's pony, when, as we were sitting reading in the afternoon, a loud knock came to that almost untouched door, and tidings that he had had an accident. Isaac and Mary both went out in

---

[*] *Life of Mrs. Ellis* by her nieces.

the tempest of rain; Anna and I sat alone wondering. Presently another knock, and tidings that the poor boy was quite dead. He had been trying to pass a cart; the pony slipped on the wet ground, and the boy fell with his head on the hard road, and the wheel of the cart went over it; and three days afterwards, when I walked over the spot, the stains of the blood were all about the place to such an extent as seemed almost impossible. In the stillness and solitude of that out of the world place thou mayst suppose what a sensation was created. Mary and Anna were greatly troubled and the servant wept night and day; nobody liked to be left alone. I could not help thinking of the difference between that place and this, where it would have been all forgotten in a week; there every poor person we met stopped and talked sadly and solemnly about it.

Two years after Sarah Stickney Ellis's stay, Anna's four nieces came on a visit from Spain. Margaret, the second oldest, a child of ten at the time, has left us a vivid, if not entirely flattering picture of her Aunt Anna. Anna was forty-one now and the years of spiritual conflict and physical suffering had transformed the eager writer of the Buxton letter into a rather grim spinster. It was Mary, not Anna, who enlivened the afternoon play hour by encouraging the four little girls to jump into the rocking boat in the hall and row for their lives to escape an imaginary enemy. Anna did not encourage such games. Margaret wrote of her aunt: 'She had a very high moral standard and her code was exacting ... Nothing but absolute truth would do with her.' Mrs Bayly bore this out. 'Anna had no acquaintance with fear – not even enough for mercy; it was impossible for her to understand terror that would make others, children especially, tell lame falsehoods simply from want of presence of mind.' Anna also set a high standard in consideration for others. Margaret Sewell wrote, 'Thoughtlessness, carelessness or indifference to the feelings of others – especially the poor – were always rebuked.'

Nevertheless her nieces were fond of her. 'She was just, and we knew it. We liked being with her. She told us appealing stories and found interesting jobs for us to do.' She also drew 'with great facility' for the amusement of the girls, and best of all, took them for long drives in the pony-trap with her. On these drives her talk was about 'trees and flowers and all animals, especially horses; we liked to listen to the conversations she held with the horse she was driving'.

Mrs F. gave a more flattering picture of Anna at this time.

> There was about her [she said] such a rare distinction that the first
> impression she made was not only lasting but lastingly localised, clearly
> seen through the accumulated treasures of a longer after-friendship.
> This distinction is hard to describe. It was not mere intellect, or mere
> goodness, or even mere nobility, though it had much of all these in
> its composition. Perhaps some impression of it may be conveyed by
> saying that it was the general effect produced by uncommon intel-
> lectual powers, combined with still more uncommon integrity and
> simplicity, and directed by a 'charity' that can only be fittingly described
> in the words of St. Paul's inspired lyric.

It must be remembered, however, that Mrs F. was a poet and more
than a little in love with both Anna and her mother. A diary she kept
of her four days at Blue Lodge is worth quoting for it gives a picture
of their daily life there.

> *Monday July 27th* [1863]. Pony chaise met me at Keynsham station.
> Lovely drive through quiet and sunny country. After dinner com-
> menced reading *Thy Poor Brother*, and went on for an hour, Mrs.
> Sewell reading, and I offering criticism. Tea on the lawn under wide
> tree shadows, with beds of brilliant flowers spread all about. After tea,
> more MS. till moonlight drew us again to the garden. A long talk
> there on things in heaven and earth and ranging between the two.
> Delightful company!
>
> *Tuesday, July 28th.* Walked in the garden for a quarter of an hour after
> breakfast with Mrs. Sewell. Then she established me in her private sit-
> ting room with letters to write and Bushnell's Inner Life. At twelve we
> met in the drawing room, Mrs. S., Anna, and I, and went on with *Thy
> Poor Brother*. Tea again on the lawn. After supper recited Wordsworth's
> *Ode on Intimations of Immortality.* Talked of his poems generally.
>
> *Wednesday, July 29th.* Mrs. Sewell claimed my promise to read her
> parts of my MS. Drove in the evening with Anna to Wick. Afterwards
> another spell at the MS.
>
> *Thursday, July 30th.* The last day of this most delightful visit … Four
> whiter days have seldom illuminated my life calendar.

It was during the same summer, a month or two earlier, that Mrs Bayly paid her first visit to the Sewells. She had met Mary and Anna for the first time the year before at Sarah Stickney Ellis's house. She gave a similar picture of their family life to that of Mrs F. Mary was still writing the last chapters of *Thy Poor Brother* when she paid her visit.

> As we three sat together in the drawing room she read me some of the earlier chapters. They were so suggestive, we talked and talked, complaining of nothing but the lapse of time. Anna was lying on the sofa – her mother sitting at her feet, with one hand rubbing the lame foot, and with the other holding the manuscript out of which she was reading.

It was at the end of Mrs Bayly's stay that the drive to the station occurred mentioned in a previous chapter. Under the dripping umbrellas on that drive a conversation took place about a work by an Anglican theologian which was to have far-reaching consequences. 'It was during this drive that I told Anna of something Horace Bushnell had written about animals.' Mrs Bayly was unable to find a copy of the *Essay on Animals* from which she had quoted but she summarised it roughly as follows. Man is constituted with a brain power capable of using and directing a far greater amount of physical force than he himself possesses. Animals, especially horses, were created that he might have a vast amount of strength at his disposal, dependent upon his will, by the aid of which he might accomplish much more than would otherwise be possible. Man is made for God, and just as his happiness depends upon the degree in which, in his life, he lives to do the will of God, so with animals – they instinctively know that their vocation is to do the will of man; and were we as wise and kind to animals as we might be, and ought to be, their lives in doing our will would be supremely happy.

> Soon after the publication of *Black Beauty* I had a little note from her, written from her sofa, in which she says, 'the thoughts you gave me from Horace Bushnell years ago have followed me entirely through the writing of my book and have more than anything else helped me to feel it was worth a great effort to try at least to bring

1 Joseph Stickney Sewell, Madagascar missionary and Anne's first cousin

2 John Wright of Dudwick, Mary Sewell's brother, known as Uncle Wright

Left: 3 Anne Wright of Dudwick, known as Aunt Wright

Below: 4 The London Yearly Meeting of the Society of Friends *c.* 1835. Painted by Samuel Lucas of Hitchin. William Sewell, Anna's grandfather, sits in the back row on the left

Opposite above: 5 'A silent meeting.' Watercolour by Joseph Walter West

Opposite below: 6 The children of Joseph and Elizabeth Fry (1830)

7 Mary Sewell, mother of Anna Sewell

8 Lord Lyndhurst of Behnes, 1841. Mary Sewell was said to resemble him

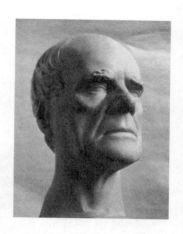

Right: 9 William Sewell, Anna's grandfather, from a death mask

Below: 10 Church Plain, Great Yarmouth. Birthplace of Anna Sewell. The mock Tudor façade was added about 1930

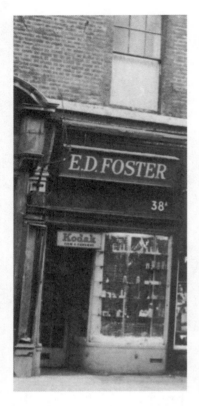

11 The shop in Camomile Street, London, E.C.3. Anna lived mostly in the basement of this house until she was two

12 Anna and Mary Sewell. Anna is seated because of her lameness

13 Anna Sewell, aged sixteen, from an oil painting formerly at Dudwick House

14 Philip Edward Sewell, Anna's brother, aged twenty-seven

15 Philip Edward Sewell in old age

Left: 16 Sarah, first wife of Philip Edward Sewell

Opposite above: 17 The White House, Old Catton, Norwich, where *Black Beauty* was written

Opposite below: 18 The City premises of Jarrold & Sons, first publishers of *Black Beauty*

19 Thomas Jarrold, publisher of *Black Beauty* until his death in 1877

20 Hannah Elizabeth Jarrold, his widow, who took over its publication after his death

21 Eliza Louisa Jarrold, widow of
Samuel Jarrold, assisted Hannah
Elizabeth with the book's
publication

22 William Tillyer, Jarrold's
London manager, who accepted
the manuscript

Left: 23 The earliest surviving example of Anna's handwriting, part of a letter written to her mother at the age of sixteen. The page has been written across to save paper

To my dear Aunts
E, M, & E Wright
from their loving &
grateful niece
the Author
Jany, 1878.

Above: 24 The last example of her handwriting, a note written in the copy of *Black Beauty* presented to her aunts Elizabeth, Maria and Ellen, now in Norwich Public Library

Opposite above: 25 Dudwick House, Buxton, Norfolk, home of Anna's Uncle and Aunt Wright, and probably the original of Birtwick Park in *Black Beauty*. Dudwick Cottage is on the left

Above: 26 Dudwick House seen from the park

27 An illustration from the first edition of *Black Beauty* portraying the horse after the fall of the drunkard, Reuben Smith, now in Norwich Public Library

28 Lucy Kemp Welch's portrayal of Black Beauty after Reuben Smith's fall in the 1915 Dent edition.

Cruelty.

29 An illustration showing the ordinary bearing-reign (above) and overcheck bearing-reign (below) from an early American edition of *Black Beauty* published by Lothrop Shepherd in 1910.

30 The rare first edition of *Black Beauty* presented by Anna to her three Wright aunts. The cover is blue, the decoration and lettering black and gold, now in Norwich Public Library.

the thoughts of men more in harmony with the purposes of God on this subject'.

The writing of *Black Beauty* was still some years ahead, however, and Anna's time was fully occupied with acting as the family coachman and housekeeper. She also had a new interest. For the first time since leaving Brighton she had begun to teach. Three evenings a week all through the first winter at Wick she rode alone into the village to give classes to the local miners and labourers. No doubt the crying needs of the villagers provided the necessary incentive for this arduous work. Mary described the state of the parish in a letter to another friend, Mrs R. soon after her arrival at Blue Lodge.

> We have settled in a thoroughly neglected parish, where there have been many changes and quarrels, and now for some time everybody has given it up, not being able to pull together. There is one sermon from the curate on Sunday and that is all he does for the souls of several hundred parishioners. There is a Sunday and day school, which no one but the poor discouraged master ever enters.

Anna's lessons were not confined to reading and writing. Her lifelong interest in natural history now began to bear fruit, for the labourers at Wick were treated to lessons in elementary biology. On her way to the night school, she would stop at the butcher's for a bullock's or sheep's eye, and dissect it before her scholar's astonished gaze, showing them what a wonderful and delicate organism must be at work to make it possible for us to see. These lessons would draw out such observations as, 'Well, it do look as if somebody were a-looking after us, and a-minding us.'

When the classes were well established Mary began to help with the running of them. The night journeys in the pony-trap must have been filled with terror for her and indeed they were not without danger. Charles Kingsley, who gave similar classes at Bramshall, confessed, 'I expect to finish in the ditch – but this rain has made it soft lying,' an easy enough fate perhaps for a man to accept who was a noted athlete. Mary, unlike Anna, also had psychological terrors to contend with. As the pony splashed along the dark muddy lane she peered anxiously for the headless form of Brand, the suicide, who was said to run beside carts in Brick Lane at Felthorpe. The night drives to Wick must certainly have provided her with material for the murderer's flight in her ballad *The Drunkards*.

> The gusty wind, in fitful moans,
>   Went wailing through the rustling trees;
> His flesh was creeping on his bones,
>   His very life blood seemed to freeze.
>
> Dull, murky clouds flew wildly past,
>   The moon just seen, then pitchy night;
> A shrouded form is gliding past –
>   A shriek appals him with affright.

With Mary's help, Anna acquired a cottage in the village. Its one room measured fourteen feet by ten and in it she established a Working Man's Evening Institute where she continued to hold her classes. Mary's boundless energy soon found subsidiary uses for the cottage. Mother's Meetings were held there and a lending library was established. The inclusion of James's *Anxious Enquirer* in the library caused the three local clergymen (the Institute served three parishes) to fear that they might have Dissenters on their hands.

It was while living at Wick that Mary's eyes were first fully opened to the horrors of rustic poverty. She had seen something of its domestic aspect in the South Down villages near Chichester and recorded it in *The Children of Summerbrook*. In that verse cycle she described cottages where

> There was a puddle at the door
>   In which the children played,
> And ashes, sticks and broken pots,
>   Before the house were laid.

Yet the conditions Mary found in Wick were far worse and she was soon as unpopular with the local landlords as with the clergy, for she considered it her duty to shame them into making a few basic improvements. In *Thy Poor Brother* she wrote, 'There are several cottages built in our immediate neighbourhood which are unprovided either with pumps or wells. The women in these families have, in all weather, to cross two or three fields to a shallow brook, from which they have to scoop the water into their pails.' Others were without a chimney and had no alternative to a room full of smoke but to keep the door open in all weathers. 'A case like this,' wrote Mary, 'has been going on for two or three years in a dwelling not far from my own. One day, going into this house and seeing all the smoke as usual coming down instead of going out at the chimney, I sent for a bricklayer and a chimney pot; and as soon as the pot was placed on the chimney the smoke ascended in its right direction.'

Mary felt as deeply for the men of Wick as the women, which was unusual for her. No doubt on her walks about that solitary countryside she had opportunities to talk to the ploughman resting at the headland and the weary miner returning from his shift. She was hard put to it to decide whose lot was the harder.

Look at the life of a collier [she wrote]. I will give you a little sketch of the common life of a friend of mine. His home is about four miles distant from his work in the pit. About three o'clock in the morning his wife creeps downstairs and makes him a cup of tea, that he may set out warm. She goes to bed again; and away he goes – rain, wind or snow, all the same – plunging in the dark of winter through miry roads and over ill-trodden tenacious field paths till, in the dark or early dawn, he arrives at his post of labour. He is then lowered down into the close atmosphere of the pit, and makes his way along the subterranean path to his place of work, and there lies down, half naked, perhaps – often wet – in a seam of coal, to pick it out, – his eyes nose and mouth exposed to the dust, and his skin covered with it. Here, hour after hour, he lies in his black sepulchre quarrying out our comfortable fires. The allotted hours of toil finished, he walks his four miles home again. He is not a young man, and I have often noticed his weary steps as he ascends the hill to his own house. Then he must wash all over, to avoid the injurious effect of coal dust on the skin. We, who are accustomed to find the bath a luxury, with our comfortable provisions for it, can hardly appreciate the disturbance and inconvenience of the one room where the great pan of warm water has to be prepared for the man to wash in, and the children and young people have to be put away – if there be a place to put

them in, which is not always the case. After a supper of potatoes and
a scrap of bacon to relish it, my friend goes early to bed, that he may
gain sufficient rest for the next day's toil.

Yet to Mary Sewell the life of the labourer seemed almost as bad.

Poets [she said] are prone to write sweet fictions about our 'rustic
hinds', as though they might live upon the breath of morning, always
rosy, and the perfumes of flowers always in blossom. These illusions
have long been dispelled from my mind as I have seen them com-
batting with all states of the atmosphere and with all states of the
earth – following the slow plough soaked through with drizzling rain,
spreading the manure, with the wind cutting through them, or baking
under the sultry heat of the sun, – often crippled with rheumatism,
the effect of wet or insufficient clothing, – but still steadily sticking
to their work through fear of dismissal.

And what reward did either of these men receive for this life of
continuous labour? The average wage was ten shillings a week and if
this ceased the man's wife must go out to wash or work in the fields.
And at the end of the road, when they were no longer strong enough
to guide a plough or wield a pick, the workhouse waited. There they
would be left to rot among strangers on a bed of filthy straw until
they obliged the overseer by dying and making way for others.

It was not surprising that such men frequently sought consolation
in hard liquor. It was an easy matter to get drunk for a penny or dead
drunk for twopence in one of the publichouses at Wick and no doubt
on Friday nights Anna's pony often shied at a body lying in the ditch
or, worse still, at a creature making its way up the village street on all
fours. Such sights were not uncommon in English villages a hundred
years ago. The financial consequences of these drinking bouts could
be as grave as the physical and moral ones. A man would often spend
his week's wages in an evening and then go home penniless and beat
his wife and children when they asked for food. In a few months he
could reduce his family to a state of destitution.

Mary Sewell became so concerned about the problems of
drunkenness that she persuaded a clergyman to accompany her to
a London gin palace so that she might see for herself the victims in

the grip of the 'grasping fiend of drink'. Mrs Bayly, herself a writer on temperance, always averred that what Mrs Sewell saw there was too dreadful for her to describe, but in fact Mary was quite ready to talk about her experiences.

> The rain poured down the whole evening. No one would remain in the street who could find a shelter; and, without disturbing oneself by thinking of the consequences, how inviting, how cheerful, did those great palaces look, both without and within. How warm, how bright they were. How savory with the scent of spirits and tobacco, – scents not abhorrent to everyone, and certainly preferable to some scents in some small rooms. Whilst my excellent companion was giving tracts and speaking to clusters of men, I looked into those dull half-alive faces, at those half stupified bodies which had crept from the cold and wet outside into a warm dry and cheerful place, the like of which they could not find in their own homes. They were not all talkative, nor intoxicated. The larger number of those I saw looked under a spell, – stupid, apathetic, drowsy; some few were noisy and argumentative … As I stood there in the warmth and light, and thought of the rain outside and of the miserable homes in alleys and attics, I said to myself, 'I should come here and do as they do if I did not know better.'

Mary and Anna Sewell became convinced that it was the lack of alternative places of refreshment that was the chief cause of drunkenness in Wick, as elsewhere.

> In the village I live in [wrote Mary] there are three public houses and three beer shops, and not a room of any kind where a sober man, if his home be not at hand, can sit down to rest himself, to eat his dinner, protect himself from the weather, spend an evening or transact his business. For all these necessities he is obliged to go to the public house, and then as a matter of course, he must drink for the good of the house. Thus our labouring men are compelled to drink, whether they would or not. In our village there are mills of different kinds, which sometimes draw men from a distance. The public house must be their home, unless they can meet with a comfortable lodging. There is also a considerable traffic through our village in the conveyance of goods to large adjacent towns. The roads are hilly, and the horses often require

to stop. In the distance of eight or ten miles there is not a place where a man can sit down, or get a drink of water for his horse, except at the public houses. There are very many of these along the road. I heard of a carter, the other day, who had stopped twelve times in the space of eight miles and spent four shillings in drink. Another carter told me that he was refused water for his horses at public houses when they found he would not drink something himself, although he offered to pay for the water. He assured me that he knew many men who would accept it as the greatest boon to themselves if places of sober refreshment could be provided along the roads and in villages; and he felt sure that after a while they would pay if well managed.

Mary and Anna were determined to supply this sober refreshment and formed a local brotherhood of working men whose aim, like that of Alcoholics Anonymous, was mutual help. In doing this they were following the advice of a well-known writer on temperance, Mrs Wightman, the author of *Haste to the Rescue*. Somewhat to Mary's embarrassment, the men immediately elected her their president. She described one of their first meetings in a letter.

Brother George, Timothy, and all the other ten of us were there. We had such a nice meeting in talking over the subject and making arrangements. I began with reading a small portion of the Scriptures and a prayer and George B – ended with a prayer, and they all sang a hymn – and then they had coffee, cocoa, and currant cake, and we were very happy together.

The brotherhood grew rapidly. By June no less than 120 local men had agreed 'to take to *water* and to *sign*',[*] and one of the three hostile clergymen had so far succumbed to the charm (or determination) of the combined force of Mary and Anna that, although he had not actually signed, he had agreed to try 'whether he could do without stimulants'. The ladies celebrated their success with a Whit Tuesday meeting for their pledged abstainers on the lawn at Blue Lodge.

---

[*] Sewell, Mary, *The Drunkards*.

We had tables on the lawn, and a capital cake and bread and butter. After we adjourned to the barn which had been prepared for the occasion, and had an excellent meeting. Mr. C. in the chair, Mr. Charleton, an excellent Quaker, and two Methodist working men, addressed us in very telling speeches – an Independent minister and a clergyman of the Church of England were in readiness to speak, had there been time.

The culmination of Anna and Mary's Temperance work was a visit from Mrs Wightman herself. 'She was staying with a relative at Bath,' wrote Mary, 'and hearing that the author of *Mother's Last Words* lived in the neighbourhood, she drove over. She was so pleasant and gave us valuable advice and information about our "little cause".'

Mary Sewell wrote several poems about 'The Monster Evil' and the sufferings of those who are

> left to sink
> In the o'erflowing sea of maddening drink.[*]

It is worth singling out *The Rose of Cheriton* if only because Anthony Trollope considered it one of the worst poems ever written.[**] The Rose was a model young woman who was brought home by a thriving farmer as his bride. To quote Trollope's summary of the plot, 'Everything goes well till the farmer takes to drink and then everything goes ill.' The Rose dies waiting for her husband to return from an orgy. Her children go to the bad, the family property is lost. The second half of the poem is devoted to remedies for the drink problem put into the mouth of an old servant in conversation with a strange gentleman. These remedies are very simple. Shut up the beer shops and gin palaces; prevent brewers from brewing and distillers from distilling (in cases where these were Quakers like the Barclays gentle persuasion would be sufficient) and spend the seventy millions thus saved on feeding the poor. Trollope's chief objections to the poem were that, like so many of 'the small pietistic books that have

---

[*] Sewell, Mary, *The Rose of Cheriton*.

[**] *Fortnightly Review,* 1867.

come my way ... (it) was written without much regard to either literary excellence or to truth of argument; as though, for such work, the manifest good intentions of the writer would stand in lieu of all other merits'. He hastened to add that 'Mrs. Sewell must be put in a very different category from that in which we would class the general writers of such little books; but here in *The Rose of Cheriton* she has fallen into the ordinary faults of such writers, and has produced a work which will hardly do much to stem the tide of drunkenness'. In fact the British public showed as little liking for the poem as did Trollope and it did not sell well. Mrs Bayly attributed its unpopularity to its price (Mary Sewell had once more changed publishers. Partridge retailed it at sixpence instead of twopence). But even she admitted that the indictment against strong drink and the liquor laws 'breaks in jarringly upon the finest poetry she ever wrote'.

Trollope was not the only one among the great nineteenth-century writers to dislike pious literature of the kind Mary Sewell specialised in. Thackeray also had a peculiar horror of 'tracts, and Low Church verse'. In *Vanity Fair* he lampooned them mercilessly and even caused one of his more disagreeable characters (Lady Southdown's daughter, Emily Sheepshanks) to compose one entitled *The Washerwoman of Finchley Common* and distribute it liberally. Matthew Arnold, however, is said to have had a high opinion of Mary Sewell's work.

In 1864 temperance work, the Evening Institute, the lending library and the Mother's Meetings all came to an end abruptly. Isaac had been appointed to be manager of the new branch in Bath of the London and South Western Bank (later amalgamated with Barclays). During the six years at Blue Lodge he had been as idle and bored as his daughter and wife had been busy and fulfilled. On more than one occasion Mary Sewell remarked on how restless he had become with only ploughmen for company, and expressed the wish that he had been brought up to some useful manual occupation that might have supplied him with a hobby. 'Were men more generally handy,' she sighed, 'how many little jobs they could do in the evening!' Although Isaac approved of the good works of his wife and daughter he did not share in them and although he was always charming and considerate to the guests who came to the house, these guests were their friends and not his. His chief interest was in the Friends' Meeting at Frenchay near Bristol. His name often appears in the minutes of this meeting.

The degree to which Isaac had become a mere appendage in his own home is illustrated by a comment Mary Sewell made on a book she read after Anna's death entitled *Patience Strong's Outings*. The author was a prolific writer of girl's stories and an inhabitant of Milton, a small town outside Boston, Massachusetts. The subject was the relationship between an unmarried woman of thirty-seven and her 'little young – old mother'. The two women's lives were 'all quilted together' and they spent their days happily sewing, reading and reminiscing side by side. 'Patience and her mother made me think much of my Nannie when we were together, when we fought the fight of life with one heart and one soul united in a vigorous fellowship of thought and action,' wrote Mary Sewell. She omitted, however, to mention one big difference between Patience Strong's household and her own. Patience Strong's mother had been a widow for ten years. One suspects that Mary Sewell almost thought of herself as one. Her life with Anna was complete without Isaac.

The people of Wick were sorry to see the kind ladies at the big house go. Mary Sewell loved to dwell upon the kindness they always received from their country neighbours. One woman she remembered with particular affection. Although she was poor and ailing and lived in a house that Mary could only describe as 'a crazy dwelling', she could never give enough to the Sewell ladies. 'Her first fruit,' wrote Mary, 'is sure to come to us; basins and baskets full are smuggled in by contrivance; and I have to manage a kind of payment with as much delicacy as if she were a duchess.' When Mary was ill, 'but few days passed, during several weeks, without some present being sent me from one or other of our poor neighbours. The best fruit and vegetables which their gardens produced, little cakes of home-made bread, new laid eggs, watercresses, flowers.'

Perhaps the best proof of the affection in which the ladies were held can be found in a letter from one of the scholars at Anna's Evening Institute.

My very Dear and Honoured Lady,

   I hope you will take these few lines without offence, from the hand of one who feels it his Bounden Duty to render to you my many thanks for all your kindness to me, and to my family, and to all of us.

I understand to well that you are about to leave us, and I feel deep regret on account of it; tis always Good to have a friend and Bad to be without one; yet still my Jesus is precious to my soul, and I know he will never go away.

I hope you are better. I have heard you have been ill, and I hope dear Miss Sewell and Mr Sewell is Well.

Dear Lady I felt I could not let you go off, without sending you these few lines. But I feel much Contrition while writing to you – my heart is full while I write. I feel like the Disciples when Jesus was going to leave them, but I hope the Lord will still Bless us all and Bless you most wherever you go. When I think how Beneficial you have been to the inhabitants of wick how they will all mis you and Miss Sewell when you are gone away.

I hope dear Miss Sewell got home safe – when I met her in the road to wick, I was so overjoyed I felt like one lifted out of the Body. I couldn't help my tears after we parted.

Dear Lady, I should like to tell you a good deal but I cannot in the Space of a Letter. I am not well the cold winds upset me and my wife had the Rhumatics. I get about as usual but my little trade is verry Bad. Please to pardon my faults. We send our united love to you dear Lady, and Mr Sewell and dear Miss Sewell.

7

MOORLANDS, BATH 1864-67

The first few months at Bath were not happy ones. The Sewells took lodgings in a house high up on Combe Down, near the quarries from which the famous Bath stone is taken, and as Mary put it, felt it 'very hard ... to be cramped up in little rooms with no garden of our own, and all strangers about us, and no welcome from the faces we met'. Anna again lost a good deal of her walking power, a fact which her mother attributed to the fatigue of leaving all right at Blue Lodge although it may have been an unconscious protest against the loss of her interests and occupations. Even Mary, cut off from these interests, went through a period of depression and went as far as to describe herself as a 'poor, empty, barren, hard-hearted, pitiful wretch'.

Fortunately the period in lodgings was short and by the winter of 1864 the Sewells were installed at a house called Moorlands, which stood on a green hill opposite Bath just off the Wells road with its back windows overlooking the city. Mrs Bayly's daughter described the place as 'a green paradise'. To her the double-fronted stone mansion 'nestled in a curve of the hillside', gave the impression of a place shut out from human ills, and only open to sweet flowers and sunshine. It was approached through its own meadows from above. Another field at the back of the house ran down to the embankment of Brunel's Somerset and Dorset railway line. The Sewells bought a couple of milking cows called Daisy and Fanny to inhabit these fields and also pigs to fill the empty sties. With the addition of a grey Welsh pony who had the run of the stable block on the left of the house and a brown dog called Lion, the establishment almost merited the name of farm.

The garden, like so many of the Sewells' gardens, was large. There was a gently sloping lawn in front of the house where fruit trees grew and when Anna first saw it the tallest of these was bending under a load of small red apples. An attractive feature of the garden was a fresh-water spring and circular lily pond with a large ornamental rock in the centre. The Sewells soon set about improving the property which had been neglected. One of Mary's first undertakings was to build a terrace behind the house where Anna could walk. She planted it with old-fashioned flowers, salvias and lupins, carefully arranged to look as if they were growing naturally.

The house itself was handsomely proportioned, with a large intricately tiled entrance hail from which rose a staircase with wrought-iron banisters bent outwards to accommodate crinolines. On the right of the entrance hall was a large drawing room divided in two by an archway and with windows at both ends. From the window at the back a magnificent view of Bath on the hill opposite could be obtained, with the houses of Landsdowne Crescent appearing to stand on the roofs of those of Royal Crescent.

Moorlands still stands and has not changed greatly. A former owner added a tower at the left-hand end, the present one (the Bath Corporation) has pulled down the stable block and the barn. The grounds, however, have been sadly curtailed. Yellow blocks of flats rise between the house and the railway embankment, half of Mrs Sewell's croquet lawn has been taken for the playground of a new primary school and the meadow where Daisy and Fanny grazed is now a park for the children who live in the suburban semi-detached houses of Englishcombe Lane, above. The house too is probably due for demolition. At present it houses nineteen old gentlemen but a far larger number are due to be accommodated on the same site. If the old house is sacrificed in the interests of progress let us hope someone will preserve a tea-chest that stands in the store-room under the tower. It contains Mrs Sewell's croquet mallets, small-headed and slim-handled compared to their modern counterparts.

Once she was established at Moorlands, Anna's walking power quickly returned. Mary reported in a letter, 'Anna is much better; we are getting on well, working like – Trojans, shall I say? Or English women? I think the last, because the cause is better and *bloodless*.' Anna continued to keep house while Mary wrote. In 1865 the ballad entitled *The Lost Child*, which melted hard hearts in the women's prison at Brixton, was published. Nevertheless, the bulk of her creative work was now done. The ladies were once more within humanity's reach and the daily routine of morning calls began again. Etiquette demanded that all the local families visit them, particularly as Mary was now something of a celebrity, and the time left over for writing was sadly curtailed. 'Those who do not write poetry at all,' commented Mary Sewell sadly, 'think it is just as easy as mending a glove – but they make a great mistake.'

Nevertheless one gets the impression that Anna found life pleasant enough at Bath. The hectic charitable work seems to have ceased with the demand for it. She bravely drove out to Wick several times during the first winter at Bath in an attempt to keep the Evening Institute going, but Mary put an end to the impossible venture by becoming ill for several weeks. After that Anna was content to teach at a local Sunday school.

She had always, paradoxically, thrived in the worldly atmosphere of watering-places and Bath will surely always be the queen of these. Mary reported that her daughter enjoyed the close proximity to 'church, chapel, schools, shops etc. which she had not before'. She also enjoyed driving in the Cotswold countryside and found the banks and hedgerows rich in colour at every time of year. It seems that even Mary allowed herself to dabble in some of the more frivolous pleasures of life at this time. Mrs Bayly's daughters were taken to meet her for the first time in 1866. 'We found her learning to play at croquet in her seventieth year, because a friend staying with her represented that she ought to have some knowledge of a game which then occupied so large a share of her fellow-creatures attention. With girlish briskness of movement, she threw down her mallet and came to meet us. I rather think the study we interrupted was not much further pursued.'

It was at this time that Mrs Bayly's daughter, Elizabeth Boyd Bayly, became a close friend of Mary Sewell. One of Mary's more remarkable characteristics was her ability to make new friends in her old age. The closest of those she made in Bath was Mrs Williamson. Mary kept up a lengthy and very intimate correspondence with Mrs Williamson for the rest of her life. She was a woman 'of large executiveness and organising power', a quality which Mary Sewell admired.

It was one of her dearest wishes to spend eternity with Mrs Williamson although she pointed out modestly, 'I shall not be put into such a high class as you.' Mrs Williamson had come to live in Bath for the health of her husband, a clergyman, and almost as soon as she arrived she set about founding a home for orphan girls and followed it up quickly with another for boys. Both the homes were conducted on the family system. Up to that time it had been the custom to bring up orphan children in barracks – with disastrous results, especially for girls. Mrs Williamson aimed at making the lives of her orphans as natural as possible. They went out to the district schools as other children did, and always had credit for good behaviour there. Her own house being very near to the Girls' Home, she was able to take an especially motherly interest in them.

In their last summer at Moorlands the Sewells gave a tea for the orphan girls on the lawn. Elizabeth Boyd Bayly has left us an account of the occasion.

Jessie and I arrived to find Mr. Sewell very busy and concerned about the provender, and while Miss Sewell went to attend to his wishes, the other visitors appeared – Mrs. Williamson on her little pony, the children skipping about her, and a carriage for Mr. Williamson and two orphans. It was a pretty sight when Mrs. Sewell stood before the house to receive them, in her black silk dress without a furbelow, and quilled net cap, and with her duchess look – Mr. Sewell bending down his tall white head to the little ones and making them so heartily welcome. In a few minutes they were scattered about the grounds to do just what they liked.

One little child mounted the wall beside the pig-sty and sat absorbed in gazing at the pigs, to the great amusement of Mr. Sewell and his gardener. 'She'll be the farmer,' the gardener said. They were to have seen the cows milked, and have tea on the lawn, but it came on to rain, and all the out-door diversions had to be given up. It did not signify, with such a tide of good spirits flowing: there was all the fun of running to and fro from kitchen to barn with the tea things. At tea the great excitement was to coax Lion, the brown dog, to eat from their hands. Proud was the little girl whose cake he gobbled up… Miss Sewell is not as *unstiff* as Mrs. Sewell, but very kind … It seemed like Eden, everybody so good and so happy.

8

THE WHITE HOUSE,
NORWICH 1867–77

If Philip's wife Sarah had not died in her early forties, *Black Beauty* might never have been written. It was Sarah's death that set in motion a train of events that culminated in the creation of the book. Philip and his family had been living in England for three years when the tragedy occurred. He had returned from Spain in 1864 when the Bilbao–Tudela line was finished, in spite of further offers of work abroad. He returned home partly to please Uncle Wright who was anxious to have him living near by, partly because he felt that families should be united but chiefly for the sake of his wife and his children's education.

In the course of constructing the railway he had performed some remarkable feats of engineering and no doubt felt he had earned the right to rest on his laurels. The terrain through which the line passed between Bilbao and Miranda had presented sufficient problems. The River Nervion had to be crossed eleven times and, among the 5,000-foot peaks of the Cantabrians, a rise of 140 feet was achieved in no more than twenty miles. Yet these problems were slight in comparison with those presented by the gorges of the River Ebro whose course the line pursued from Miranda to Tudela. At one point the river actually had to be diverted. A new channel was dug during the heat of the summer when the bed was dry and Philip sent home vivid descriptions of the immense masses of rock that had to be displaced by the blasting, of the honey of wild bees that was discovered in the crevices of the rocks and finally of the breathless wait for the rains. The operation was successful: he woke one morning to find a new river running through his dry channel. At another point the river had to be spanned by a 300-foot iron bridge which is still one of the marvels of the line, just beyond Miranda. A navvy was killed during the construction and it was typical of Philip to attempt to procure the man a Christian burial, for he was thoughtful of his work people. The local priest would not allow a Protestant to lie in holy ground but the sexton confided to *el señor ingles* that he had dug the grave at a spot outside the cemetery where the shadow of the cross would fall upon it.

After such exertions, life in a quiet English town like Norwich must have seemed attractive and at forty-two, Philip started the career for which his father had originally trained him. He took a job in a bank owned by Quaker neighbours he had known all his life, the Gurneys (the bank was later amalgamated with Barclays), and moved into a house in Norwich. The sudden death of Sarah at this point left his children sadly in need of a mother. The youngest girl was only seven or eight years old and the oldest barely sixteen. The disaster was accentuated by the fact that, a year before Sarah died, he had become the guardian of seven orphans. He was a man of very strong domestic affections and the loss of Sarah seemed to him irreparable. Indeed her death very nearly caused his, and he had to go to Panticosa in Spain to recover his health.

Mary decided that the family must move to a house near Philip. Isaac had no cause to disagree with her. Rather the contrary. He had resigned his post at the bank two years earlier as a result of defalcations by a cashier. He was not in any way connected with the defalcations but he was considered culpably negligent in allowing them to be possible. (Mrs Bayly makes no mention of the episode.)

When the Sewells arrived at Norwich, other familiar faces besides Sarah's were missing. At Buxton the families both at Dudwick House and Dudwick Farm were depleted. Anna's grandparents were dead and the aunts had moved into Dudwick Cottage, a charming flint-built house with gothic windows which still stands, surrounded by high beech hedges, in the park, close to Dudwick House. They had been joined by their sister Elizabeth and now formed a formidable trio. Canon Marsham, who used to live at Rippon Hall, remembers being afraid of them in their black bonnets when he was taken for walks past their house as a child. Even his mother was more than a little in awe of them.

Aunt Wright was no longer at the big house. She had died unexpectedly six years earlier while nursing her husband through what was expected to be his dying illness. After a period of widowhood, during which Aunt Maria kept house for him, John Wright had married again.

The White House that Isaac bought at Old Catton was in fact of red brick. It was a handsome L-shaped building flanking the main road from Norwich to Aylsham. It was considerably smaller than any of the houses the Sewells had inhabited in the last twenty years. Mrs Bayly was able to leave us a detailed description of the room in the house where *Black Beauty* was written, for she was a frequent guest there.

The drawing-room was over the dining-room, each taking the whole width of that part of the house, with an outlook behind over the garden and the fields beyond it to the village church and trees – in front across the highroad to a grove of beech trees in Mr. Buxton's park, where the deer would come to lie in the cool shade. The roof of the verandah made a balcony outside the large back window of the drawing-room; there Mrs. Sewell trained flowers and creepers in boxes to make a garden for Anna when she was unable to leave that floor. A tempting lump of mutton suet hung, enclosed in a piece of net, for the special benefit of the tom-tits who were constantly to be seen hovering about, and pecking at the dainty morsel, in no danger of being trapped, or frightened from their meal. The room itself had an old-world look, a low subdued harmony of colour, and a scent of pot-pourri, in keeping with the quaint speech, the silver hair, and antique, old-world courtliness of the lord and lady of the home. An exquisite perception of the effect of colour was seen in every part of the house – or rather felt; all was too simple and harmonious to have any striking effect. The paper on the walls was of the quietest tone – no showy patterns, no one piece of grand furniture to spoil the look of the rest, but plants at the windows, and flowers in vases arranged lightly, never in solid clumps; at meals, no profusion of dishes, but simple delicacies daintily served.

It has always seemed to me that there is a peculiar charm in visiting at the houses of Friends ... Friends who are not in a position to give great entertainments ... will yet allow themselves to have much enjoyment in entertaining, in their own simple way, those whom they love and esteem, or to whom they feel a short sojourn in their house may be helpful. This was quite the custom at The White House at Old Catton and all who went there cherished the memory of its graceful, heartfelt hospitalities. The door of the little bedroom, carefully prepared, stood open, as if to welcome you. The room would have looked almost too white and clean, but for the flowers and books placed exactly in the right position, to relieve the effect. The atmosphere of thoughtful love pervaded the place, for you could scarcely be conscious of a want without finding, on looking round, that it had been anticipated. Whatever business Mrs. Sewell had on hand was held second to the pleasure of a guest.

The garden afforded abundant scope for the new inmates' love of improving.

A rather low wall had divided its garden from the next door neighbour's. On this a high lattice-work was put up, and creepers planted to train over it, which formed by degrees a beautiful leafy screen. A broad, sloping bed under the wall was given up to wild things transplanted from lanes and hedgerows. There, in time, grew flowers of all seasons – primroses, wood-sorrel, speedwell, wild geranium, lilies of the valley, and climbing things full of blossom in spring and berries in autumn. A little lawn rose steeply in front of the paved verandah outside the French window of the dining-room; on its brow, a straight, level walk, running the length of the garden, supplied the requirements of composition. Two large beech trees flung their shadows down the slope, and beside every root and stump, little wild flowers came to bloom. A thick hedge cut off the farther part of the garden, previously given over to vegetables. Mrs. Sewell had these exchanged for a second little lawn and flower beds.

The flowers in the beds of this enclosed upper lawn had special personalities for Mary and she invented stories about them and drew improving conclusions. The white anemone–japonicas were 'happy schoolgirls with such open faces', the pansies all had different expressions ('So look at that pert little thing, did you ever see any thing so saucy?') and some wild ferns that she had planted in rich soil beside a garden pool, were typical *nouveaux riches*. They had thrown out a crop of green curls above their natural fronds. 'It's a perfect caricature of fashion,' she remarked to Mrs Bayly at breakfast after a morning walk in the garden. 'They are just like mankind … when they get well fed … instead of developing in a nice orderly way, they go … mad for new fashions, all the frills and furbelows that you could think of.'

The garden was filled with pleasant sounds as well as sights. There were beech trees next door as well as in the park across the road. Indeed, the garden was walled in by trees. The cooing of the pigeons in the branches of these made a pleasant background to the ritual of tea on the lawn. Anna started to keep bees again as she had at Palatine Cottage, and there was a bark-covered bee-hive at the end of the walk. An acquaintance of the Sewells once had the misfortune to call it an apiary and Mary turned upon him and said, '*It's a bee-hut*,' for she hated pretentious language. The bees, like those at Palatine Cottage, came to a sad end one autumn of heavy rains. Mrs Sewell recounted the tragedy in a letter to a friend. 'Having observed no going in and out since the great rain, I felt anxious, thinking it must be too early for them to go to sleep, and when G. was here I got him to lift off the top of their house, – and they were all dead corpses. As I turned sorrowfully away, a gracious pigeon said, "That *be* a pity!"'

There was also a strip of garden at the front of the house, bordering on the road, which Mary called Anna's Garden. It was kept filled with bright flowers intended to give pleasure to the artisans of Norwich who often brought their families for a country airing along that stretch of road. Sometimes a man returning from work at the end of the day would pause to look at the flowers and if Mary was near the gate she would pick him a bunch to take home with him.

The White House still stands at 125 Spixworth Road, about three miles north of Norwich near the Maids Head Inn. The room where Anna wrote her book has changed little, although the balcony at the back has gone. Even the outlook from the windows is essentially the same. The Buxton's park across the road is still there. The view across the garden at the back, however, is somewhat marred by a bungalow built in one corner. The stable, which formed part of the ground floor, is still there, although it is now used as a garage, and a plaque commemorates the famous occupant of the house.

Norwich, which someone once described as 'Either a city in an orchard or an orchard in a city', was a worthy successor to Brighton and Bath. Anna enjoyed driving her chaise along the winding medieval streets, every one of which seemed to end with a view of either a church tower or the cathedral, but her pony considered cobbled streets a poor recompense for the long train journey from Bath and if he found there were two ways to a place by one of which the cobbles could be avoided, he flatly refused to cross them. Neither coaxing nor scolding nor the most reasoned of arguments about his moral obligations to his kind owner would move him. His mistress must go round the other way. It is to be hoped that the road to the newly remodelled 'Ye Olde Booke Shoppe' owned by Mary's publisher, Jarrold, was not cobbled. The shop connected London Street to Exchange Street and contained twelve stock-rooms full of books. It must have been a favourite resort of Anna and her mother.

The flat countryside round Norwich no doubt suited the pony better but his owner less well. Anna missed the variety of the Cotswold countryside. The Norfolk lanes were shut in between high banks and stiff hedges at that time. Returning to the county of their birth had another drawback for Anna and her mother. The morning callers had been a trial at Bath but they were a worse one at Norwich, not only because they were more numerous but because they were not people who, as Mary put it, had 'sought us for ourselves'. These were friends of Uncle Wright, of the Miss Wrights and of Philip and, as they sat passing commonplaces in the pretty upstairs drawing room, the precious hours for writing trickled away. Mary put up a valiant fight to preserve her art. A note in her hand runs, 'Must write during long calls.' Presumably she hoped to jot down a few verses while Anna kept the conversation ball rolling. If so, her hopes were dashed, for she published very little during the last fifteen years of her life. Instead she resumed her role of mistress of a well-run household with many guests.

Anna, however, was not deprived of all occupation, for she took her role as companion to her widowed brother, and aunt to his many motherless children, seriously, and the road her fat grey pony had to travel most often was the one to Clare House, on the way in to Norwich. Philip must have amassed a considerable fortune in Spain, for the house was a large one and had probably only been built a few years before he bought it, of specially made grey local bricks. Of all the houses inhabited by the Sewell family, it is the only one that lacks charm, and the fact that it was in the process of being demolished when I visited it did not distress me unduly. It stood in a network of high-tension cables and notices saying 'Danger. Keep Out' were everywhere. The floorboards were already up and most of the windows were broken. Some of the eight hundred pupils at Blyth School (Norwich Grammar School for girls) in whose grounds Clare House now stands evidently did not feel as I. There were slogans painted over the walls like 'We love you Grey House. The Heart of the school is here.' The headmistress who showed me round (at some risk to both of us) said the sixth-formers had insisted on giving a dance in the old house the night before the wreckers moved in. They took out the school desks and refurnished the series of vast reception rooms with chairs and sofas. Wood fires burned for the last time in the Victorian grates and the house for an instant looked something like it must have looked when Philip and his children lived there a hundred years ago.

For the five little Sewell girls and their brothers the garden of Clare House was its best feature. A member of the next generation of children to play in that garden, the daughter of Mr Griffiths, the local vicar, remembers Philip as a very old man and the two daughters who remained at home, Grace and Ada, with their welcoming cry to her mother of 'Dee-ar Mrs. Griffiths.' She tells me that the garden covered several acres. On one side of the house, at some distance from it, was a huge brick and tile barn with stalls and a loft at one end. This barn still stands and is being turned into a 'Project Room' for the school. It is much older than Clare House itself and was probably part of a former farm that stood on the same site. (Sections of walls have been discovered during the present excavations for a gymnasium.) Philip's horses were kept in this barn and cared for by his groom, Simons. Beyond it was a large, walled kitchen garden. At the back of the house was 'a most beautiful dell full of great trees with rooks perpetually calling' and at the front were the formal gardens with lawns and flower beds, separated by a ha-ha from a 'pleasant field which filled the angle between Constitution Hill as it was then called and St. Clement's Hill'. Philip made this field available every Thursday afternoon in summer for school treats and after his death his children presented it to the City of Norwich as a park in his memory. On the railings at the lower corner of the park, where

Constitution Hill meets St Clement's Hill, is a metal plaque bearing the following inscription. 'Sewell Park. This open space once used and loved by Philip Edward Sewell is dedicated to his memory and to the use and love of his fellow citizens.' Next to it is a triangular stone drinking-trough for horses. It bears the inscription: '1917. This fountain was placed here by Ada Sewell in memory of her Aunt Anna Sewell, Authoress of Black Beauty and of her sister Edith Sewell – two lovers of animals.'

Playing in the open space was not, however, the activity that Aunt Anna considered it her duty to encourage in her nieces although no doubt she informed them about the fauna and flora they encountered there. She was chiefly concerned about their moral growth and felt deeply the responsibility of guiding them during the formative years of their childhood. It is true that the children were under the care of a remarkably competent nurse and Philip himself gave them a daily Bible lesson before their eight o'clock breakfast, but Anna did not feel that this was enough. Like her mother, she equated morality with plain sewing, and saw that they got plenty of it. Many not very happy hours were spent by Grace, Margaret, Edith and Ada attempting to sew seams that would satisfy her. 'She was a very good needlewoman and taught us to sew,' wrote Margaret ruefully. 'And we had to do it well!' The youngest girl, Anna, was probably treated more leniently, for she was as much a favourite with her aunt as she was with her sisters, but even for her there was no spoiling.

For the last seven years of her life Anna once more kept a diary. It was very different from the discursive, introspective one she had kept in her twenties. This one chiefly consisted of brief factual entries and filled no more than fourteen pages of what Mrs Bayly described as 'an old, haggard-looking account book'. 1870, the first year covered by the diary, seems to have been full of charitable activity and, although one suspects that this was chiefly carried on by Mary and merely recorded by Anna, she obviously took an interest in it, particularly in individual cases of need. The first three entries in the diary for 1870 give something of its flavour.

January, 1870. – At Old Catton. Father is in his seventy-seventh year and active. Mother in her seventy-third year, very well and wonderfully active and competent. I in my fiftieth year, as well as usual.

April 8. – Mother is now engaged in getting signatures to Miss
Preusser's Memorial to the Poor Law Board about pauper children.

October 28. – Metz capitulated, 173,000 troops laid down their
arms with Marshal Bazaine.

The reference to the Franco-Prussian war is worth noting. Both
Anna and Mary took an interest in current affairs and were zeal-
ous readers of newspapers. Public disasters particularly engaged their
attention. Mary was so affected by the Indian Mutiny that in *Patience
Hart* not only the heroine but also the governess were destined to
lose brothers in it.

The summer that the French army capitulated was a particularly
fine one and, in a letter written in August, Mary admitted: 'We
have done little, but be happy.' There were visits to friends and to
the seaside but, best of all, there were long days in the garden of The
White House. 'We have allowed ourselves to enjoy the sunshine all
day long, and no harm of any kind has come near us.' It was during
this summer that Mary caused the summer-parlour, as she called it,
to be built on the small upper lawn. It stood against the wall and was,
in effect, a large greenhouse. It was specially planned for Anna, in
spite of its distance from the house, and Mary hoped that she would
spend many hours there. She never imagined that this was to be the
last summer the two of them would spend out of doors together.
Towards the end of that same year 'the shadow of death began to
steal over The White House' and, to pursue Mrs Bayly's metaphor,
it was 'never wholly lifted until the last of the household had passed
where shadows flee away'. First, in November, Isaac began to suffer
from attacks of faintness and giddiness which the doctor thought
might be the precursor of 'something serious'. On 1 March 1871,
Anna made the following brief entry in her diary. 'I have not been
well. Dr. R. thinks it is a troublesome case.' She did not go beyond
the garden gate again until her death.

Anna's final illness is as mysterious as her earlier one, and one
suspects it was as much misunderstood by her contemporaries. Mary
considered that she contracted a mortal disease at the age of fifty-one
and died of it seven years later. Doctors assure me, however, that no
disease with symptoms such as those Anna complained of would be

of such long duration. Tuberculosis could take seven years to kill, but tuberculosis in its early stages is not painful and Anna, during the first year, was often in considerable pain. It seems almost certain that the disease she eventually died of was not the one she contracted in 1871. Indeed, one questions whether at this stage she was suffering from a disease at all in the accepted sense of the word. Certainly her doctor thought she was ill, for he gave her only one and a half years to live, but doctors knew very little in those days. Certainly at times during the first year she suffered a great deal. At the end of that year she wrote in her diary, 'I am quite poorly with pain.' Yet during the summer and autumn Mary, who was Anna's chief nurse, had found time for an amazing number of outside activities and Anna, equally surprisingly, found the strength to record them. Extracts from the diary she kept during the first year of her illness do not suggest complete prostration.

> August 9. – Mrs. Riches' class of thirty girls came to tea.
>
> Sept. 1. – We gave a tea and frolic to thirty-four children, Miss H.'s Band of Hope. G. and E.[*] helped.
>
> Sept. 13. – Mother's Sun Lane Infants (50) had tea and play. A. and A. helped famously.[**]
>
> Nov. 6. – Mother's Sun Lane School was inspected by Mr. S. The week previous she went every day, and since then goes one day each week, taking her dinner at Mrs. A's. She is trying a new plan of teaching to read without spelling, by making words with loose letters. She is also making clothes for the R's. Little Caroline R. comes three days a week. Mother gives her two lessons a day.
>
> Nov. 11. – Mother also began a class for the girls of Miss H's Band of Hope on Saturday mornings every other week.

By the following summer Mary reported the disease was no worse and in October 1873 Anna was able to write in her diary, 'I am very well and keep good nights,' and Mary, for the first time, went away for a week. During this summer she wrote her last book, *Davie Blake the*

---

[*] Probably her nieces Grace and Edith.

[**] Probably her nieces Ada and Margaret Amie.

Sailor, designed for the edification of seamen, and said by a sea captain to show a remarkable knowledge of maritime affairs. By now Anna had settled into the routine that she followed for the remaining four and a half years of her life. Mary described it in a letter to Mrs Williamson at Bath. 'She is usually in bed till midday, and then dresses, resting between whiles. She lies on the sofa for the rest of the day, sometimes sitting down to meals with us only for a very short time. She requires almost complete quiet; conversation and reading are usually too fatiguing for her.' In the same letter Mary added, significantly, 'Sometimes she has such a lovely colour and looks so animated.' Dr R. had now ceased to attend her. 'He gave no hope and was only discouraging.'

Seen through the knowing eyes of the twentieth century Anna's condition seems more the result of an unwillingness to face the world than of actual disease. Yet her retirement was by no means complete. Unlike Florence Nightingale, whose case so much resembles hers, she spent only the mornings in her bedroom. During the afternoons she lay on the sofa in the upstairs drawing-room. Nor, perhaps was the condition itself as debilitating as has sometimes been suggested, for as we have observed she was able to sit at table and the dining room at The White House was downstairs.

It remains to discover what were the causes of Anna's second with-drawal from the world. After a brief review of her situation in 1871 one comes to the conclusion that they were very similar to the causes that led her to retire in 1845. In 1870 Philip had once more married, and in taking Charlotte Jane Sole as his second wife, he not only deprived his sister of his companionship but also of her chief inter-est in life at that time; the supervision of his children. Furthermore, there was no alternative interests to take the place of 'our children' as she always called them. There were no manuscripts to correct now that Mary had ceased to write, there were no household affairs to supervise now that her mother had resumed the role of housekeeper, and the intellectual poverty of the shoemakers of Norwich, although no doubt considerable, was evidently not as urgent or appealing, as that of the miners of Wick.

The hours that Anna spent in apparent idleness on her sofa were, however, not unemployed. A brief entry in the diary for 1871, fol-lowing immediately upon the ones already quoted, ran as follows. 'Nov. 6. I am writing the life of a horse and getting dolls and boxes

ready for Christmas.' The retirement from the world this time was
to bear fruit. At the end of it *Black Beauty* was given to the world.
The book was not 'written', in the normal sense of the word, for
Anna was as incapable of writing as she was of reading. Her ability
to think and imagine scenes, however, was unimpaired, and she spent
much of the first year of her illness forming scenes in her head and
dictating these from time to time to her mother.

It is perhaps significant that *Black Beauty* became Anna's constant
companion at the time that the last real horse went out of her life. Since
she had become ill there had been no one to drive her pony. For the
summer she lent him to a small girl who learnt to ride on him. Then
she asked Philip to drive him to Buxton and donate both him and his
chaise to the headmaster of the Red House School and his wife. It was
typical of her unsentimental attitude. She would not have kept a pony
in injurious idleness (and idleness is injurious to ponies) just to gratify
her desire to have him near her. As she lay on the upstairs sofa and heard
the hoof-beats of the fat grey cobble-hater pass under her window she
must have thought of all that horses had done for her. Without the
willing service of the series of cobs and ponies she had owned there
would have been many occasions when she would have been unable
to go beyond the garden gate. It was as a gesture of gratitude to these
animals that she undertook the labour of piecing together the book.

The living horse that now became Anna's chief interest was Bessie,
Philip's black mare. She was a fine creature, both fiery and wise, and
every Monday she drew Philip's carriage safely to the Red House
School at Buxton, often in the dark, for he could not leave Norwich
until the bank closed. (Philip had become owner of the school since
Uncle Wright's recent death.) Bessie was still alive when Mrs Bayly
wrote her book, although she must have been at least twenty-five
years old.

> She is a splendid creature, [she wrote] holding rank with the fastest
> trotters in the county, with any amount of go, courage and spirit in
> her; yet when, in the fading light of the short winter afternoon, she is
> brought to the door, and the master takes her reins in his hands, then,
> as if she divined the responsibility of her task, she seems to be made
> up of caution and care. How in the pitch darkness and narrow lanes,
> where guiding must be impossible, she manages never to let a wheel

get entangled, is only known to Him who asks, 'Hast *thou* given the horse his might?'

On one occasion Bessie carried Philip across country through deep snowdrifts to the school. Mary described the adventure in a letter to Mrs Bayly.

> Philip has been to Buxton twice – he was much wanted at the Reformatory, and mounted his horse (the one you said seemed to have the spirit of the family). He knew the road was blocked with snow, so that no wheels could pass, but he determined to get there in some way. He called on me as he passed, to assure me he would go no further than he could. You know well how I charged him, and how I kept praying while he was away. At a little before seven o'clock he called on his return, retailing his adventures in high spirits. In some places a way had been cut through the snow-drifts just wide enough for him to pass, his knees frequently touching the sides, and the snow higher than the horse's back; when the way failed altogether, he went into the fields on either side, and with his cheerful perseverance, in which his horse entirely participated, he overcame all difficulties. The last time he went was in a sledge – he accomplished ten and a half miles in fifty-two minutes, Bessie delighted and excited by the bells and the lightness of the burden she drew.

On his way to the Reformatory Philip would always stop at the White House and pay a call on Anna and his parents. On his way home he would call 'goodnight' to them as he rattled by. Mrs Bayly described the silent expectation in which this shout was awaited in the upstairs drawing room at The White House.

> It was always difficult on Monday evening to get the mother's undivided attention to anything. Soon after nine o'clock we gave up all attempt at making ourselves interesting, and caught the infection of listening. Shortly before ten o'clock the welcome sound of distant wheels would be heard, and Bessie's well-known step. As the carriage flew by, a loud 'Goodnight' penetrated the walls of our room to which we heartily responded; and when the dear mother had said 'Thank God he is back safe again,' we returned to our normal condition.

The Red House School was not the only property that Philip inherited from Uncle Wright. He also inherited Dudwick House and the neighbouring manors of Buxton and Brampton and an estate in Kennington. It is interesting to note that Philip personified in his own lifetime the general tendency, observed by Trevelyan in his *Social History*, of the sons of the Quaker shopkeepers of the early nineteenth century to develop into the landed gentry of the late nineteenth century. Philip, however, although a landed gentleman, never lost his strong social conscience. According to his biographer: 'Anything connected with the well-being and elevation of those around him, physically, mentally or morally, excited his warm interest. His abiding idea was to leave the world better than he found it, and to put down oppression wherever he could.'[43] He never lost the habits of self-denial that Mary Sewell had inculcated in him as a child and his way of life was simple and abstemious. 'Laziness was his great abhorrence. He would give no quarter to a lazy person, and was so strong himself that he scarcely understood that some needed more rest than he would take himself. Tolerant in general to a marked degree, he was yet intolerant of anything that savoured of unreality or posing.' He was 'an active worker on behalf of the Discharged Prisoners' Aid Society. For nearly fifty years he held the secretaryship of the Norwich City Mission and as an Evangelical Churchman he gave public countenance and support to various other movements of philanthropic character.' He was a Justice of the Peace and one of the original Aldermen appointed on the formation of the Norfolk County Council. An appealing aspect of his philanthropy was his fondness for children. He was a Sunday school teacher at New Catton, where he lived and

> had a great talent for speaking in a bright and interesting manner to children … This talent was partly due to his simplicity of character, and to his cheerful and optimistic way of looking at life. He always seemed young himself, and it was a pretty sight to see him walking down St. Clement's Hill talking to tiny children, who were taking hold of his hand or clinging to his coat.

Philip succeeded his uncle not only as the owner of the land on which Red House Farm School stood but also as its manager. The school became a great source of interest to the family at The White House.

---

* *A Sketch of the Life of Philip Edward Sewell*, Jarrolds

It was already the main concern of the three Miss Wright's at Buxton. Indeed, it is said that Aunt Elizabeth was still busying herself with the contents of the boys' linen closets when blind and bedridden at the age of ninety-four. Aunt Wright also had continued to visit it until the end of her life. She founded a library for the boys and drove over several times a week to impart instruction in religion and 'of a useful nature'. On her deathbed she thought she heard the boys singing hallelujahs.

The history of this Reformatory, otherwise known as the Red House Farm School at Buxton is an interesting one. Previously young boys were sent to Buxton Old Union, where tradesmen from Norwich and neighbourhood went to procure apprentices for their various trades. On one occasion a chimney-sweeper, wishing to have a boy from there, picked out several successively as likely to suit him, but, in each case their parents objected; at last a little boy was pointed out to him who had no friends or relations to care for him, so the master sweep was told he would have no trouble about him; no one would enquire what had become of him; the sweep was then about to remove the boy, but John Wright happened to be present at the time, and, turning round, said, 'What, because this boy is friendless is he to be forced into a trade where boys who have friends are not allowed to be placed? No, he shall not.' This was the incident which first made him think of founding the establishment, and, as he used jocularly to remark, 'Buxton Reformatory sprang from soot.'

The original reformatory was a square red-brick building, with governor's house in front and in the centre a large courtyard; there was also a plot set aside for a playground; the boys were instructed in seamen's duties, for which purpose there were two masts rigged in the playground, and they were also taught shoe-making, tailoring, farming and agricultural duties; for the latter purpose there were forty acres under cultivation by spade.

The institution is still very active and still maintains the strong Christian stamp put upon it by its founders. The original buildings still stand although they are somewhat obscured by the modern ones that have grown up round them, and Mr Hurley, the present head, showed me the commemorative plaque to Philip Sewell that still hangs in the chapel.

Records of each boy's career at the school going right back to Frederick Woods, the first pupil, are still preserved there. The proportion of successes was eventually high considering that six months in Norwich Prison was an obligatory qualification for entry into the school and most of the boys were orphans whose early childhood had been spent in the back streets of the city. But the records of the earliest pupils were not entirely satisfactory. Their ages ranged from fifteen to twenty-two and one was dismissed at the latter age as 'a confirmed tramp', while another, in 1855, solved his own problems by running away to join the army. He was last heard of at Constantinople and no doubt perished from starvation with thousands of his comrades on the heights of Sebastopol. Things reached a crisis when the boys mutinied one Sunday and locked the superintendent in one of the cells. A master mounted one of the farm horses and galloped to Dudwick House where Uncle Wright happened to be in converse with Thomas Babington, a lay scripture reader for a Norwich Society. Babington was a man of enormous stature and it was probably this combined with his eloquence that enabled him to persuade the boys to submit to his authority. John Wright appointed him headmaster on the spot and he held the post for forty-two years and was succeeded by his two sons. Mary Sewell used to describe him as 'a Martello Tower in the sunshine, a veritable Christian with a heart as tender as a mother's'.

Philip Sewell supported the school largely out of his own purse and, without drawing attention to his generosity, made many improvements. He provided the school with a swimming-pool when such luxuries were rare for more fortunate children. Anna's niece and nephew, Margaret and Edward, became managers of the school after Philip's death. Margaret had a head for figures and did all the accounts. The school was recognised by the Home Office as an Approved School in 1933.

Anna had other interests besides the Red House School. With her mother she continued to read books and discover new heroes, and of these the greatest was Charles Kingsley. All the early editions of *Black Beauty* bear the following quotation from Mrs Kingsley's life of her late husband.[*] 'He was a perfect horseman, and never lost his

---

[*] *Charles Kingsley: His Letters And Memories Of His Life*, edited by his wife, C. Kegan Paul and Co., London, 1876.

temper with his horse, talking and reasoning with it if it shied or bolted, as if it had been a rational being, knowing that, from the fine organisation of the animal, a horse, like a child, will get confused by panic fear which is only increased by punishment.'

The Kingsley biography was published in 1876, only a year after its subject's death, and seen through the press by the Sewell's old friend, Henry S. King. Mary and Anna read it as soon as it came out and Anna no doubt would have echoed Mary's verdict expressed in a letter to Mrs Williamson: 'Kingsley was a wonderful man … you could not help admiring him. He worked too hard, and wore out a splendid constitution comparatively early.' Certainly there was much to attract the pious maiden lady in the fiery Broad Church vicar of Eversley Canon Kingsley was a handsome man and a very distin- guished one. In his day he had been the Regius Professor of History at Cambridge and Chaplain to the Queen. All his life, however, his most abiding concern had been to better the lot of the poor working people. He had campaigned ceaselessly for clean water and adequate drainage in the 'stifling workshops, reeking alleys … roofless and crowded cottages … these nests of typhus, consumption and cholera'. His philanthropy was practical and Anna must have been touched by Mrs Kingsley's account of him, during the diphtheria epidemic, going from cottage to cottage in his parish with bottles of the green medicine which he considered a preventative.

Yet there were sides to Kingsley's character that could not have been so easily accepted. He was not the conventional subject of the pious biography. He was moody and full of contradictions He had a delightful sense of humour but he also had 'violent and unreason- able prejudices (he once condemned the twelve centuries of church history before the Reformation as a period of meaningless hysteria). One moment he was on fire with enthusiasm for a cause, the next he only wanted to die. He would go a week without sleep during a cholera epidemic in his parish and spend three months recover- ing among the molluscs of the Devon shore. Worst of all, he was a Socialist. Under the name of Parson Lot he had contributed to the Christian Socialist; and he had been denounced by the incumbent of a London church after preaching freedom, equality and brotherhood from his pulpit. It is true that his gentlemanly upbringing made some of his associates in the cause distasteful to him. The appearance of a colleague in blue plush gloves 'quite upset and silenced him ... he did not recover from the depression produced by these gloves for days'. Nevertheless he had associated with men in blue plush gloves. There were other blots in his copy-book. He did not approve of teetotalism, he considered money spent on the abolition of slavery wasted, he upheld the German side of the war of 1870, he called Irish peasants white chimpanzees and he hunted whenever anyone would lend him a horse.

> Dinner was just coming on the table yesterday ... when the bow-wows appeared on the top of the Mount, trying my patch of gorse, so I jumped up, left the cook shrieking, and off. He wasn't there, but I knew where he was, for I keep a pretty good register of foxes (ain't they my parishioners?) and as the poor fellows had had a blank day, they were very thankful to find themselves in five minutes going like mad.

Hard words for Anna to swallow yet swallow them she did. It says a good deal for her broadmindedness that she regarded Kingsley as a hero in spite of them. The effort would have been beyond a good many of her mother's friends, Mrs Williamson included. To her, Mary had written of the Kingsley biography, 'I somehow fancy you would not enjoy the book as I do – you would find more wrong.'

During this period Anna continued to take a lively and detailed interest in the affairs of other members of the household. The Sewells now had two servants, Emily the cook and Jane the housemaid, and Mrs R. recalls Anna advising Jane, who was about to be married, about a quilt for her future home.

> The arrangement of colours in that quilt was a matter to which the closest attention of both Mrs. Sewell and her daughter was given. It was made quite a study. The quilt was brought in and spread upon the floor; the effect of one colour tried, and then another, till after much consultation, a harmonious arrangement was at last arrived at, and the maiden despatched to work out the design of her mistresses.

Anna also took an interest in her mother's district visiting. Mrs Bayly recalls these visits in her biography.

Any little improvement in Anna's health gave Mrs. Sewell the opportunity she much valued of seeing more of her poor neighbours. When I was staying at Catton she would occasionally leave me in charge, saying she was going into the village. Before leaving the house, she would return, in her walking dress, to have one more look at her darling, and would be greeted with 'Mother dear, how nice thee look!' or 'Mother dear, don't thee hurry back, I am quite comfortable. Couldn't thee call on Lucy Smith? It is not her washing day, and she would be so pleased to see thee.'

Anna also undertook a new form of charity on her own account. Her mother called it 'Sixpenny Charity' and became so enthusiastic an advocate of it that the last winter of her life she wrote a short book called *Sixpenny Charity* – a plea for regularity in giving help to cases of chronic poverty, were it only to the amount of sixpence a week, so that the receiver might count on it, and have a little sense of thrift in managing accordingly.

Mary Sewell gave a graphic picture of a family in which an extra sixpence a week could make the difference between abject squalor and some degree of comfort.

We will take a case [she wrote]. A widow with three young children. She will receive 2s. in money and 1s. worth of bread; her rent is 1s. 9d. When this is paid, she will have 3d. left and the bread. If she has a fire, the very smallest cannot be kept alight with less than 1 cwt. of coals for the week, and every coal will have to be watched lest it burn up too fast. It is wondrous pitiful to see these coals put on. They will cost 1s. 3d., leaving her 1s. in debt. Besides this, she must have candles and soap to keep up the tidy appearance we so much applaud in the poor.

It is into a home like this, of which there are thousands, that the 'Sixpenny Charity' enters like a handmaid of mercy.

Suppose the mother to have been able to keep starvation from the door, she will find bread upon the table. To this the sixpence will add tea, sugar and dripping in the very small quantities the poor allow themselves. No one who has always plenty to eat and plenty to drink, and the choice of what they will take, can imagine what tea is to a poor woman. It somehow has the faculty of keeping her in society, as it were; the tea-pot makes the table smile, whilst the dry bread with hot water poured upon it and a sprinkle of pepper and salt, cries out 'Pauper'. It is the gauge of extreme poverty.

Anna had no great wealth to dispose of. Her will is a brief document by comparison with Philip's.[*] Yet she took as much thought over the allocation of her few hundreds of pounds in railway shares as he did of his tens of thousands, and the receivers of sixpenny charities were not forgotten.

It was the practice of both Anna and her mother to spend the 'twilight hour' playing literary games which involved quoting from the poets or inventing fresh verses. In their household, as in all well-conducted households at that time, the candles were not lit until it was absolutely necessary and an occupation was sought that did not require much light. Margaret Sewell recalls capping verses and games involving the stringing of rhymes. 'They liked the young people to join in these exercises,' she wrote, 'but we made a sorry show by comparison.'

There was another pastime of which Anna was very fond. She would get someone to give her a few words, which, notwithstanding their diversity of meaning, she managed to work into a little story in verse. Mrs. Bayly quotes the following specimen from among many.

Prawn, Yawn, Tall, Wall, Missed, Kissed.

O Henry dear, don't yawn so loud,
   The tea will soon be here;
But Jane has had an accident
   Which might have cost her dear.

In coming up with that tall urn,
   She caught a sight of Jem,
She missed the step, and kissed the wall,
   Instead of kissing him.

---

[*] For Anna's will, see Appendix III.

> I do not think the girl is hurt.
> But still she's vexed and fluttered;
> So cook will bring the prawns and toast,
> And tea-cake, when 'tis buttered.

Many people came to stay at The White House during the long years that Anna spent on the sofa in the drawing room. There were new 'dear young friends'. 'We have several young people round us,' wrote Mary, 'who are earnestly desirous to lead a vital, practical Christian life, and we are deeply interested in them. They are often here to question the old pilgrim, and all this keeps my dear Anna full of external interest, which is so wholesome and happy for her.' There were also friends of longer standing like Mrs Bayly, Mrs Williamson and Mrs F. But Sarah Stickney Ellis was to come no more. She and her husband had died suddenly of 'severe colds' caught on a railway train in 1871. There was, however, a visit from Anna's first cousin, Joseph Stickney Sewell, who had finally achieved his ambition to be a missionary and had just completed a nine-year stint in Madagascar after a lifetime of schoolmastering at Ackworth. In Madagascar he made up for lost time. During his stay there he wrote the first grammar of Malagasy and it is said that his translations into that language of the hymns 'Abide with Me' and 'Whither, Pilgrim, art thou going?' are still sung by the natives. He also made a valiant attempt to map the island, as his companion on this venture, a gentleman of the name of Pickersgill, recorded in the Malagasy Annual for 1877.

> There were two of us. One was a hale grey-headed Friend, carrying a small tripod and a trap to catch mountain tops with, strapped to the side of his palanquin. As for the other, he was not without concern for the mountain tops, but he also had a rather keen interest in small game. The good Quaker gradually grew accustomed to the presence of loaded firearms in the tent, and once or twice, I believe, when our larder was reduced to a gravyless drumstick, inwardly wished him a chance of rejoicing in bloodshed.

No doubt the subject of this anecdote had many stories of his own to recount to the ladies at The White House, although one suspects they were moral and uplifting rather than humorous. He had a high opinion of the courage of the native converts and used to give many examples of their steadfastness under persecution. Fortunately Anna did not live to hear of the story of those who failed his daughter Lucy Johnson and her child and left them to be massacred by a band from the forest. The story of the atrocity was told in a book entitled *Faithful Unto Death*. Joseph wrote the preface to the book, freely forgiving the murderers.

Anna, however, was to have the sorrow of parting with a child closer to her than little Blossom Johnson. On a cold autumn evening in October 1873 her youngest niece, who had never been strong, died. The event inspired the only poem of a serious nature that has survived in Anna's hand.

Seven young trees grew close together,
All fresh and green in the summer weather.
A little one, beautiful, tender, and tall,
Grew in the middle, the joy of them all;
And lovingly twining their branches together,
They circled it round in the fine summer weather.
On the Sabbath eve of an autumn day
The beautiful plant was taken away,
And left a lonely and leafless space,
And nothing was found to fill the place –
Nothing of rich, nothing of rare,
Could fill the spot that was left so bare;
Nothing below, nothing above,
Could fill this empty spot but love.
Then closer the young trees together,
In the chilly days of that autumn weather;
And every branch put forth a shoot,
And new life quickened at the root.
They grew in the winter, in spring they grew,
Silently nourished by heavenly dew;
And when they came back to summer weather,
One beautiful group they stood together;
And their greenest leaves hung o'er the place
Where the youngest had stood in its tender grace.
Nothing below, nothing above,
Nothing can heal the hurt but love.

The summer after the death of her niece, Anna underwent a spiritual experience so profound that it almost amounted to a second
conversion of the kind she had had at the age of twenty-five. To out-
ward appearances she was already exceedingly pious, and indeed the
whole Sewell household had become increasingly oriented towards
the things of the next world during her illness. The day at The
White House always started by Mary going into Anna's bedroom,
accompanied by any guest who might be staying in the house, and
reading with her the verse from *Daily Light* that she had meditated
upon alone in the garden before breakfast. The day ended with family
prayers, of which Mrs Bayly has left us an account.

> At the time of my visits to Old Catton, Mr. Sewell was unable to
> conduct family prayers – or, to speak more correctly, family reading.
> At half-past nine the servants came in; Mrs. Sewell read a chapter,
> occasionally making a few remarks as she went on, and then a hymn
> or piece of poetry. Now and then she read a short extract from a
> magazine or paper. If any subject of local or national interest was just
> then occupying attention, she would refer to it in a way that put us
> into sympathy with the times. Now and then, but rarely, the sweet
> voice from the sofa was heard, always beginning with 'Mother dear,
> don't thee think' so-and-so. When the servants rose, the master rose
> also, and remained standing until they had closed the door, saying in
> his courteous way, 'Goodnight, Emily. Goodnight, Jane.' … When the
> servants had gone, and the weary master had retired for the night, we
> sat round Anna's couch and spoke together of the coming Kingdom
> and its exceeding glory.

Yet inwardly Anna was not completely reconciled to her fate. The
long and apparently incurable illness had brought back the religious
doubts that had plagued her from time to time all her life and,
according to Mrs Bayly, it was not until she read a devotional work
by the Philadelphian Quakeress, Hannah Pearsall Smith (mother of
Logan Pearsall Smith, the author), that her submission to God's will
became complete.

Mrs Bayly named the crucial book *A Word to the Wavering Ones*
but I have been unable to trace such a work. It is more likely that
she intended *The Christian's Secret of a Happy Life* published about

this time. Mrs Pearsall Smith's attitude to spiritual conflicts was an astringent one. In the chapter entitled 'Doubts' she wrote:

> Spiritual conflicts! Far better would they be named did we call them spiritual rebellions! … Just as well might I join in with the laments of a drunkard, and unite with him in prayer for grace to endure the discipline of his fatal appetite, as to give way for one instant to the weak complaints of these enslaved souls, and try to console them under their slavery … You ought to be free, you can be free, you MUST be free!

Anna evidently responded to this hearty treatment. Now at last she felt wholly emptied of self, a hollow reed through which only God spoke. She wrote to a friend that, though she had loved her Saviour for so many years, that summer was the first time that she had really known what it was to abide in Christ. To Mrs Bayly she confided:

> I had always taken my petition and request to Him, but then I knocked from without, somewhat in the spirit of a beggar. Now He has shown me that I have a place in the household, I belong to the family of God, and my very frailty has given me a place among the weak ones in whom His strength is perfected. I know now the meaning of that word, 'No longer a servant, but a Son.'

Now even the long nights of sleeplessness were turned to good account. Mrs Bayly, going into Anna's room one morning to enquire how she had slept, received the following reply: 'Oh, I have had such a happy night; it was nice to be awake and ready to listen to His teaching about the Kingdom. He not only gives me "songs in the night" but instructs me in the night season.'

Both to Anna and her mother the next world seemed very close, 'another room', as Mary put it, into which they would shortly pass. The following year Mary spent four days at the Brighton Convention for the Increasing of Holiness and came back laden with visions of heaven.

> I cannot tell you [she wrote to Mrs Bayly] how thankful I am for the four days I had at Brighton – you truly divine that Nannie and I have been feeding together on the feast ever since. I feel as if I had been into a land of fountains and brooks of water and seen all the

figs and pomegranates and honey and drunk a little of the wine –
oh, so sustaining! and as I and my dear Nannie talk about the good
land, we keep venturing a step further in, seeing there is no stint, but
a free invitation from the glorious Lord of the Country to take full
possession, and live in plenty and in perfect peace.

Anna was equally filled with gratitude. 'How good it was of those
people to make such an effort to share with many others their own good
things! How they poured themselves out to do us good, and kept back
nothing, delighting to spread forth all they had seen and handled!'

It was at this time that Anna's friends noticed a change in her. The
old severity against herself, the strain of great-grandfather Holmes,
had gone. If she had appeared calm and radiant before, she was doubly
so now. 'We are very happy,' wrote Mary. 'Even these cold, wet days
cannot make more than skin deep impression upon us. My darling has
more assurance than ever, so full of cheerfulness and sweetness – the
drawing-room is always bright, and oh if you would only come!'

The spiritual revival seems even to have affected Anna's physical
condition, for the next year, quite suddenly, she began to write.
Not continuously, admittedly, or with a pen. But from time to time,
during the year 1876, the greater part of *Black Beauty* was transferred
from its storage place in Anna's mind to pencilled slips of paper
which were passed to Mary for fair copying. For the first time since
the original entry in 1871 there is a mention of *Black Beauty* in her
diary. It runs with typical terseness, 'December 6, 1876. I am getting
on with my little book, *Black Beauty*.'

Perhaps Anna was inspired to make a final effort by the example of
her aunt, Maria Wright. Maria was the fourth late-flowering authoress in the family. Her writing career had begun in the fifties when,
perhaps inspired by the example of her sister-in-law up at the big
house, she had published two books of stories from the Bible; one
from the Old Testament and one from the New. (*The Bow of Faith and
The Anchor of Hope.*) During the 'sixties her pen was still (no doubt
because she was keeping house for her widowed brother) but in the
'seventies she ventured into fiction with *The Forge on the Heath* and
The Happy Village. Her novels were romantic and had rustic settings.
They are still by no means unreadable and *The Forge on the Heath*
deserves to be remembered if only for the description of the hero's

worldly mother as 'a beautiful icicle wrapped in fur'. When Anna was putting the finishing touches to *Black Beauty*, Maria published a novel that was also about a black horse. His name was Midnight and he was a rare piece of horseflesh endowed with almost human intelligence and capable of keeping up an easy gallop for a distance of thirty-three miles a day without whip or reins. The novel in which he appeared was entitled *Jennet Cragg, the Quakeress*, and the plot hinged upon his lady owner's 200-mile ride from her farm to rescue her orphaned grandchildren from London after the plague of 1660. There are many touches in the book that suggest that Maria Wright was not ignorant of the ways of horses. Strangely enough, Mary Sewell seldom mentioned the fact that her sister was also an author. She did, however, remark that Jennet Cragg was 'a pretty story'.

The person most closely connected with the composition of *Black Beauty* after Mary, was Philip. He always came to tea at The White House on Sunday afternoons. These visits, more prolonged than his brief calls on Mondays, were reckoned the bright spot of the week for Philip brought with him news of the outside world. Anna once remarked, after reading aloud a letter of condolence from a friend, 'I don't think I can appropriate all this pity. No one need be pitied who has Mother and Philip.' Anna's conversations with him on those Sunday afternoons often centred on Bessie in particular and horses in general. With him she discussed points about driving, breaking, stable-management and harness. But Philip was not her only source of practical information. The drawing room it will be remembered had a window overlooking the street as well as one over the garden, and Anna evidently had the strength to lean out of this and conduct conversations with people below. Among her sparse papers Mrs Bayly found a record of one of these conversations. It appeared to have become separated from something else to which it belonged; whether it was part of a letter or intended as a kind of journal, she had no means of knowing.

> I have for six years been confined to the house and to my sofa, and have from time to time, as I was able, been writing what I think will turn out a little book, its special aim being to induce kindness, sympathy and an understanding treatment of horses. In thinking of Cab-horses, I have been led to think of Cabmen, and I am anxious, if I can, to present their true conditions, and their great difficulties, in a correct and telling manner.

Some weeks ago I had a conversation at my open window with an intelligent Cabman who was waiting at our door, which has deeply impressed me. He led the conversation to the Sunday question, after telling me that he never plied on the Sabbath. I found there was a sore, even a bitter feeling against the religious people, who, by their use of cabs on Sunday, practically deny the Sabbath to the drivers. 'Even ministers do it, Ma'm,' he said, 'and I say it's a shame upon religion.' Then he told me of one of the London drivers who had driven a lady to church – as she stepped from the cab, she handed the driver a tract on the observance of the Sabbath. This naturally thoroughly disgusted the man. 'Now, Ma'am,' said my friend, 'I call that hypocrisy – don't you?' I suppose most of us agree with him, and yet it might not have been done hypocritically – so few Christians apparently realise the responsibility of taking a cab on Sunday.

When the book was finished, Mary took the manuscript to Jarrold's London office in Paternoster Row. She saw Mr Tillyer, the London manager, with whom she had had dealings in the past and asked him to give her an opinion on 'this little thing of my daughter's', and left the manuscript with him. A few days later a letter arrived from Mr Tillyer offering an outright payment of twenty pounds for the copyright of the book.[*] Mary advised Anna to accept. She pointed out that the unknown author of a first book could not expect more. Admittedly in modern currency the sum would have been worth ten times as much, but even so it seems a pity that Mary did not drive a better bargain. If she had insisted on a percentage, however small, on future sales, the sum realised would have been of a very different order. As it was, twenty pounds was all the money that either Anna or her family ever received from a book that was to make millions.[**]

---

[*] William Tillyer was still working for Jarrolds when they published their history in 1924.

[**] In 1921 a change in the law of copyright enabled Margaret Sewell and her brothers and sisters, Anna's nephews and nieces, to obtain from Jarrolds a half share in the rights of the first film of *Black Beauty*. This amounted to £38 10s 9d for each of them. By the time the two later films were made the book was out of copyright.

The final proofs were seen through the press by the widows of Samuel and Thomas, for Thomas, the last survivor of the three Jarrold brothers, had died suddenly. On 21 August 1877, Anna made a third and final entry in her diary about *Black Beauty*. It ran, 'My proofs of *Black Beauty* are come – very nice type.' The book was published on 24 November 1877.

PART III

BLACK
BEAUTY

1

EARLY SUCCESS

The original title of Anna's book was *Black Beauty: his grooms and companions. The autobiography of a horse*. It was ascribed to no human author, but was described as being 'translated from the original equine' by Anna Sewell. All the early editions bear the following dedication.

To

my dear and honoured

MOTHER

whose life no less than her pen

was devoted to the

welfare of others

this little book

is affectionately

DEDICATED

The first edition was a modest enough affair. It was about the size of a pre-war Everyman and contained only one illustration, a crude woodcut of Reuben Smith's accident. It was bound in red, blue or green cloth. A rustic trellis in black flanked each side of the cover and up each climbed a golden oat plant. The title *Black Beauty* was written in specially cut capitals graded to diminish in the centre of each letter. Below this was a gilt horse's head looking to the right. This edition, which retailed for '2/- in cloth boards, 2/6 in extra board, gilt edges', has now become very rare indeed. Even the British Museum does not possess it, no doubt because life in the nursery is not conducive to survival in books. Norwich Library, however, possesses two copies, one of them having been formerly in the possession of the three Miss Wrights. It bears the following inscription in Anna's hand:

> To my dear Aunts
> E. M. and E. Wright from their loving and
> grateful niece
> the Author Jan. 1878

On the cover of a much commoner early edition the horse's head looks to the left instead of the right. Many people who possess this one (described as 'Variant C' by John Carter, the binding expert[*]) are under the impression that it was published simultaneously with the first edition, but this is by no means certain. Both editions carried advertisements for the complete works of Mary Sewell at the end.

The immediate public reaction to the publication of *Black Beauty* was silence. Jarrold's gloomy prognostications about the book's chances of success seemed justified. Their town traveller, having made his rounds of the London booksellers, could report a subscription of only one hundred copies for the entire trade. Anna bought several copies and gave them away to her friends and relations for Christmas. The one she gave to her cousin Lucy containing a letter in her hand, still exists. Several appreciative letters were printed in Mrs Bayly's book, including one from Philip regretting that a horse who had suffered so much in this life could not be granted a share in the next. Another cousin wrote:

> I am so delighted, so proud of my cousin, that I can never thank you enough for my Christmas present. Read it! – I should think I did. Do you remember, when you and Philip were children, how you used to have Christmas Day for your 'very own' – choose your own amusements, your own pudding? Just such a Christmas Day did I promise myself, with your capital book for my special delectation. I could not quite carry out my wishes, for J.A. had to be invited to dinner – but directly he was gone, I petted *Black Beauty* and enjoyed myself.

---

[*] Carter, John, *More Binding Variants*, Constable, 1938.

I do like the book exceedingly, it is so good; and, forgive me, so unladylike that but for 'Anna Sewell' on the title-page, and a certain gentle kindliness all through the story, no one, I think, would believe it to be written by a lady. Where you have obtained your stable minded-ness I can't imagine, but that you fully understand your business is a fact. I like your grooms, only I am afraid you had the pick of some most exceptional ones. Manly, James, and even little Joe Green are just the jockeys for me. Would they could be counted by thousands!

The story of poor *Black Beauty* and Ginger is most touching, and the different characters of the horses admirably carried out. The only fault I find in the translation is making Ginger exclaim 'Thank Heaven!' that being, as I suppose, a place not dreamt of in Equine philosophy; but were I to tell you of all I admire, I should not get this letter posted tonight. The best bit of writing according to my ideas, is the drive through the City – that is really wonderful. Are you sure you have never stood on the steps of an omnibus to collect passengers and watch the traffic?

There were many letters in a similar vein:

Norwich December 24, 1877

You will be shocked to hear that a work intended to benefit mankind has been the cause of my neglecting all my duties – I *could not* leave *Black Beauty* till I left him safe in Joe's care. I cannot think how you could ever write such an Equestrian story. One would think you had been a horse-dealer, or a groom, or a jockey all your life.

...You have so filled my mind with the thought of what these poor animals suffer from the bearing-rein, that I feel quite breath-less as I look at some of them, and only my sex, and fear of the police, prevent my cutting the leathers and setting them free.

...To induce fashionable ladies to forego the style of the bear-ing-rein is simply to wait for an altered fashion; nothing short of that arbitrary foe will have any very evident effect, I fear; but the book is a thoroughly good step in the right direction. May it circulate widely and may many a neglected *Black Beauty* find a resting-place in the kind consideration of some happy home.

Torquay, January 18, 1878

As an imaginary entrance into the minds of horses, it is extremely clever, – as a study it is thoroughly well planned and told; and last, not least, it must do good among all, high and low, who have the care of these noble creatures … It has made me cry more than twice or thrice. Poor Ginger! Then the fall on Ludgate Hill! My dear Anna, you have been doing angels' work in writing this book, bringing messages of peace and goodwill from the Lord of all to these His poor dumb creatures, of whom man too often proves himself so unworthy a guardian.

A letter that Anna appreciated more than all these, however, was not received from a relative. It was written by a Mrs Toynbee on behalf of Edward Fordham Flower. Mr Flower was the author of several pamphlets on the humane treatment of horses and was considered an expert on harness. The letter ran as follows:

January 29, 1878

Captain Toynbee and I went yesterday afternoon to see our friends the Flowers, in Hyde Park Gardens, and found Mr. Flower in a complete state of enthusiasm over *Black Beauty.* 'It is written by a veterinary surgeon,' he exclaimed; 'by a coachman, by a groom; there is not a mistake in the whole of it; not one thing I wish altered, except that the cabman should have taken that half-crown. I shall show Mr. Bright the passage about horses in war. I must make the lady's acquaintance; she must come to London sometimes – she is my Araminta!' (Do you remember Miss Edgeworth's Araminta, or the Unknown Friend?)[*] He particularly wished me to say that he would like to write himself, but writing is troublesome to him, from the weakness of his hand. Are we right in supposing that the book is written (translated, by-the-by) by your daughter? Is it being actively circulated? That was a point Mr. Flower was very anxious about … Will you forgive so many questions, but Mr. Flower could talk of nothing else. Now and then, when the conversation strayed to the war, or anything else, he would exclaim, 'How could a lady know so much about horses?'

---

[*] Mr Flower referred to *Angelina*, or *L'Amie Inconnue*, a book which he evidently had not read, for the unknown friend is a novelist admired by the heroine who turns out to be a drunken old slut.

Mary Sewell wrote the following letter to Mr Flower on Anna's behalf.

I should have thanked you for your most welcome letter the day it came, but an infirm household and an invalid friend staying with us, obliged my pen to be quiet.

Your letter was indeed a great encouragement both to me and Anna. It was the first of the kind that had come to hand, and was accordingly treasured. Many letters followed, but when I took yours to Anna, I said I was come to put her crown on. I assure you it was a triumphant moment. She had ventured to send a copy of her book to Mr. Flower, but had thought, if he noticed it at all, it would be chiefly to point out inaccuracies. But when his entire approbation came, it brought indeed a full measure of gladness and confidence. If he would add to his kindness by writing a few lines expressive of his commendation, he would be giving it a standing beyond what anyone else could do.

We are expecting every day the proofs of the School Edition; we have both a great desire that it should become a reading-book in Boys' Schools. This also was the sanguine hope of the publisher, but his sudden death, just before its publication, has deprived it of his energetic aid.

Perhaps Mr Flower obliged by writing the few lines of commendation requested and perhaps Mary Sewell brought these to the notice of Jarrold. Certainly at this point the publishers began to exert themselves on the book's behalf. By advertising, by lobbying editors, by galvanising the trade through their local travellers, Jarrolds got the book moving at last. The reviews, carefully preserved by Mary, began to roll in. They were laudatory enough to satisfy the vainest author. The publisher's selection is given below.

We are prepared to say of this story, that the readers are few who, having commenced the book, will fail to read its every page – or who, having reached the last page, will not regret that they cannot again read it with the first freshness of interest.

Isle of Wight Advertiser

The more often we have turned over the leaves of *Black Beauty,* the greater has been our delight.

Its circulation amongst boys will do a world of good.

Hand and Heart

Wherever children are, whether boys or girls, there this should be.

School Guardian

Black Beauty will be a favourite with the boys.

Schoolmaster

We do not know what could teach kindness to horses better than this story.

Christian World

We have rarely read a book with so much genuine pleasure as this. The narrative is managed with no little skill, and is full of variety and interest.

Eastern Daily Press

We are glad to see that it has already reached a fourth edition, and we hope it will be extensively circulated among owners and users of horses.

Mark Lane Express

A capital book for the young – boys and girls.

Freeman

If the Society for the Prevention of Cruelty to Animals had published the Autobiography of Black Beauty we should have said it had published its best work.

Hand and Heart

We most cordially recommend the book.

Literary World

The story is simply told and cleverly put together, and while it may be read with pleasure and profit by educated people, it is an excellent book to put in the hands of stable boys, or any who may have to do with horses.

Essex Standard

2

THE STORY

It seems appropriate at this point to enquire into the contents of a book that was so phenomenally successful.

Black Beauty, the narrator, was a well-bred gelding with a good deal 'of the racing blood' in him. His grandfather had won at Newmarket and his brother, Rob Roy, died before his eyes in the hunting field. Although he was primarily used in a carriage he was not of the 'regular tall carriage horse breed' favoured by the gentry who show off in London parks and probably did not stand above 15½ hands high.

He was an exceptionally fine-looking animal with a black coat that shone like a rook's wing, one white foot and a white star on his fore head. His mane and tail, when well brushed, were almost as smooth as a lady's hair and, as his first mistress observed, he had 'a sweet, good-natured face and … a fine, intelligent eye'. His character was as perfect as his appearance. In the words of a coachman, 'he is as fleet as a deer, and has a fine spirit too; but the lightest touch of the rein will guide him'.

This perfection of character was due to the good start he had in life. The exact date of his birth is not given but it must have been around 1855 because at the age of eleven he shared a stable with a sixteen-year-old survivor of the Charge of the Light Brigade. His dam was a sensible grey mare called Duchess and he was raised by the kindly Farmer Grey, who also broke him in.

When he was four years old he was sold to Squire Gordon of Birtwick Park. As he spent the three happiest years of his adult life there (and one-third of the book) it is worth describing the place in some detail. Birtwick Park skirted the village of Birtwick and stood within easy reach of the City, being on the London side of the imaginary Beacon Hills. 'It was entered by a large iron gate at which stood the first lodge, and then you trotted along a smooth road between clumps of large old trees; then another lodge and another gate, which brought you to the house and gardens. Beyond this lay the home paddock, the old orchard and the stables.'

Within this haven man and beast lived in perfect accord. Squire Gordon was, in the words of an old hostler, 'a fine judge of horses' and 'the best rider in the country' but since the death of his only son George in the hunting field he had ridden little. Instead he busied himself with the running of his estate. He also had interests in the City. Although wealthy, he cared more for the well-being of his work-people and horses than for making an impression on his neighbours. He and his family walked to church on Sundays, on weekdays he drove himself in a two-wheeled gig when not accompanied by Mrs Gordon, and even when he did order the carriage he would not allow the use of the bearing-rein and tolerated a pair of unmatched horses. (Black Beauty's partner in double harness was a chestnut.)

Mrs Gordon was a sister of Sir Clifford Williams of Clifford Hall. An illness which started soon after Black Beauty's arrival soon reduced her to little more than a sweet voice and a gentle touch of the hand, but she was as devoted as her husband to the welfare of her dependents. It was she who, having rejected the names Ebony and Blackbird (and, to her coachman's relief, not having even suggested Marengo, Pegasus or Abdullah) settled upon Black Beauty. Her two remaining children, Miss Jessie and Miss Flora, were seldom seen and never heard, but they occasionally escaped from their governess into the orchard with their little dog Frisky and played games with their pony, Merrylegs, holding buttercups under his chin to see if he liked butter. They were allowed to play with the children of the rector, Mr Blomefield, who lived next door, although his older boys were a little rough.

The stable staff at Birtwick Park were as kindly as their master. The name of the coachman was John Manly; he had a wife and one little child, and they lived in the coachman's cottage, very near the stables. John was devoted to his master and extremely knowledgeable about horses. Neither hand nor voice was ever raised in anger in the light, sweet-smelling stalls under his care, and as for the groom, James Howard, 'you never saw such a kind boy as James is'. When he left, his place was taken by Joe Green, the gardener's son, who was cheerful and willing but, being only fourteen years old, had much to learn.

And so we come to the all-important horse characters. When Black Beauty was first led into his loose box at Birtwick Park he noticed a little fat grey pony in the stall next door. He had a thick mane and tail, a very pretty head, and a pert little nose, and was about twelve years old. He introduced himself as Merrylegs and assured the newcomer that he was a great favourite with the family and sometimes took the mistress about in the low chair.

Black Beauty received a less friendly welcome from a chestnut mare in the stall on the other side of him. She was Ginger, the most complex and tragic horse character in the book, and a few years Black Beauty's senior. The brutal method by which she had been broken in might have subdued a milder animal but she was high-mettled and it had made her vicious. Maddened by the pain of the gag bit and the bearing-rein her first owner had used on her, she had kicked herself free of his carriage and was sold at Tattersalls not warranted free of vice. By the time she came to Birtwick Park she had, in her own words, 'made up my mind that men were my natural enemies and that I must defend myself'. She snapped at anyone who came into her box and once even bit James in the arm. Kind treatment gradually improved Ginger's temper and she lost 'the watchful defiant look she used to turn on any strange person who came near her'. But she had made a truce, not a treaty with mankind. And though the flame of rebellion burnt low while she was at Birtwick Park it was ready to flare up at any moment.

Squire Gordon owned two other horses that stood in another stable. 'One was Justice, a roan cob, used for riding or for the luggage cart; the other was an old brown hunter, named Sir Oliver; he was past work now but was a great favourite with the master who gave him the run of the park; he sometimes did a little light carting on the estate.'

Life was peaceful at Birtwick Park. Black Beauty was either used in double harness with Ginger to pull the carriage or alone in the dog-cart or gig. Sometimes all the horses went out on a family ride with the master on Ginger, the mistress on Black Beauty and the young ladies on Merrylegs and Sir Oliver. On Sundays in summer there were idle hours in the orchard when the horses stood under the shade of a great chestnut tree and talked.

Life was peaceful but it was not uneventful. On one occasion Black Beauty was nearly burnt to death in a stable fire at a coaching inn. On another he saved his master's life when a river in flood had washed away the centre of a bridge. On a third he almost gave his life for his mistress by galloping sixteen miles by moonlight for a doctor. But, alas, that life could not long be preserved and as its sands drained away so the happy days at Birtwick Park came to an end. Mrs Gordon was ordered to a warmer climate and the last service Black Beauty performed for her was to draw her carriage to the railway station. The departure of the train was symbolic, for it carried with it not only the Gordons but also happiness. The outer and the inner gates of Birtwick Park had been stormed and an alien world was about to break in.

The new home at Earlshall Park appeared at first as good as the old. The house was very grand and three or four times as large as at Birtwick Hall. The stables were under the supervision of a knowledge-able coachman, Mr York. But life there for a horse was made wretched by one invention, the bearing-rein. Ginger and Black Beauty had been bought to pull the proud Countess of W—'s carriage and, in the words of Mr York, 'it must be tight up when my lady rides'.

Mr York had been warned that the two horses were unaccustomed to the hated device and at first he buckled it on loosely and Black Beauty found that although it was a nuisance not to be able to get his head down now and then he was not forced to hold it higher than he usually did. This state of affairs however did not satisfy the proud countess and each day she insisted that the bearing-reins should be tightened a hole. Now both horses began to feel the strain. When pulling the carriage uphill they were no longer able to put their heads forward and pull with a will and the strain came on their back and legs. Finally the breaking point came. The countess was calling on a duchess and insisted that the horses heads be pulled up even higher. That final hole in the bearing-reins settled Ginger's fate. Unable to stand any more she began plunging, rearing and kicking in a most desperate manner and finally threw herself on the ground and had to be cut from the traces.

Black Beauty's undoing came not through the bearing-rein but through that other scourge of Victorian horses, a drunken rider. Reuben Smith was the under-coachman at Earlshall. He had been left in charge while the family were in London for the season. The fateful accident occurred on an occasion when he had orders to take a brougham to be repaired in the local town. He was an excellent driver and very clever in his management of horses, but every now and then he would have a serious bout of drinking. He indulged in such a bout after delivering the brougham and set off for home on Black Beauty at a gallop knowing that the horse had a loose shoe. Black Beauty came down on his knees on the stony road and Reuben was thrown and killed. Although the inquest cleared the horse's character, his knees were so badly blemished that he was no longer considered fit to stand in a gentleman's stable. He was turned out to grass for a few months and there was joined by Ginger. For her, also, the good days were over. After she had ceased to be used in the carriage, the earl's son, Lord George, had taken her over as a hunter. Lord George was young and would take no warning; he was a hard rider and would hunt whenever he could get the chance, quite careless of his horse. Soon after Black Beauty left the stable there was a steeple-chase, and he determined to ride Ginger in it. She came in with the first three horses, but her wind was touched, and her back was strained. 'And so,' she said characteristically, 'here we are, ruined in the prime of our youth and strength, you by a drunkard, and I by a fool.'

Chapter Twenty-Seven of the book is headed, ominously enough, 'Ruined and Going Down Hill', for Black Beauty now became a job horse in Bath, hired out by the hour to people who wished to drive themselves. In this place he was to get experience of all the different kinds of bad and ignorant driving to which horses are subjected. He was also to learn the discomfort of being driven in double harness with an uneven-paced horse. Peggy, the mare he was partnered with, had short legs, and to keep up with him she had to break into a canter every few steps. When she was sold to a lady driver, Rory, 'a good honest fellow' took her place until he was disabled in an accident and sent off to cart coal. 'What that is, up and down those steep hills, only horses know.'

A happier fate awaited Black Beauty, for a kind man in Pulteney Street, after hiring him a few times, recommended him to a business man who had been advised by his doctor to take horse exercise. With Mr Barry it seemed as if Black Beauty had found a good home, but here he was to discover the discomforts not of bad drivers but of bad grooms. For Mr Barry was deceived by two grooms in succession. The first was Filcher, a retired ostler from one of the big Bath hotels. He was a hard-working man but he kept rabbits, and it was the rabbits that got three-quarters of Black Beauty's oat ration. Soon the lack of concentrates in his diet began to tell on the horse's condition. A farmer friend of Mr Barry's (who lived, incidentally on the Bath—Wells road) noticed that the horse was damp after a short ride. The police were alerted and discovered Filcher's son leaving the stable at six o'clock one morning with a basket full of oats. The father was sentenced to two months' imprisonment.

Filcher was followed by Smirk, a personable fraud who would do anything to please his master except work for him. Not only did he fail to groom Black Beauty, he also neglected his stall. 'He never took all the straw away and the smell from what lay underneath was very bad.' As a result, the horse contracted thrush and stumbled twice when carrying his master down Landsdown into the city. By this time Mr Barry was understandably so disgusted that he determined to give up keeping a horse and Black Beauty was sent to a horse fair.

The horse fair commences Part III of the book, a long section devoted to the three years Black Beauty spent working for Jerry Barker, a London cabman. With Jerry, Black Beauty learnt that a horse can be better off in a good poor home than in a bad rich one. Jerry was rather small, but well made, and quick in all his motions. He was kind and good, and as strong for the right as John Manly; and so good-tempered and merry that very few people could pick a quarrel with him. He owned a four-wheeler cab (popularly known as a growler) and two horses which he drove and attended to himself. The horses were stabled across the way from his house and were treated almost as members of his happy family. Polly, his wife, was a plump, trim, tidy little woman with smooth dark hair, dark eyes, and a merry little mouth. His son Harry was nearly twelve years old; a tall, frank, good-tempered lad; and little Dorothy (Dolly they called her) was her mother all over again, at eight years old.

Black Beauty and his stable companion, Captain, were well cared for by Jerry. Captain was the survivor of the Charge of the Light Brigade. He was a tall, grey, rather large-boned animal who must have been splendid in his youth; he still had a proud way of holding his head and arching his neck. He worked alternate shifts with Black

Beauty in the cab. Black Beauty's first shift was an afternoon one and on it he made his acquaintance with the cab rank which was outside the railings of a large city church opposite a row of shops. He also made his acquaintance with London traffic.

At first he found the noise and hurry, the crowds of horse carts and carriages harassing; but he soon found that Jerry was as good a driver as he had ever known. He never used the whip unless it was gently drawing the end of it over his horse's back when he was to go on. He was a man of principle and refused to sacrifice his horse for an extra shilling. He would not carry passengers who were late for an appointment and expected a horse to be flogged along to make up for their idleness. He always went a fair pace, however, and was not averse to 'putting on steam', as he said, if he only knew why.

Not all the horses in London were as fortunate as Black Beauty in their owners, and he saw many sad sights among them. There was the butcher's horse in St John's Wood that was driven at such desperate speed to deliver last-minute orders that it ended the morning's work with 'heaving sides and trembling legs'. And there was the little pony no bigger than Merrylegs, 'doing his best to pull a heavy cart, while a strong rough boy was cutting him under the belly with his whip and chucking cruelly at his little mouth'. Worst of all was the horse he saw at a cab-stand outside a fashionable park. The horse was an old worn-out chestnut, with an ill-kept coat, and bones that showed plainly through it. It was Ginger! But how changed! The beautiful arched neck was now straight and fallen in; the clean straight legs and delicate fetlocks were swelled; the face, that was once so full of spirit and life was now full of suffering and the once glossy sides heaved with a frequent cough.

Ginger told how she had never recovered from her old strain and had passed through many hands until she was sold to the man named Skinner who kept a number of cabs and horses and let them out. When Skinner discovered Ginger's weakness he ordered that she be put into one of the low cabs and used up. Since then her life had been one long round of whipping and working with never a day's rest. But rest after all was on the way for her. A few days later a cart with a dead horse in it passed the cab-stand. The head that hung out of the cart-tail was that of a chestnut horse with a white streak down the forehead.

For Black Beauty also evil times were coming. The happy life with Jerry came to an end as the result of illness, just as had the life at Birtwick, for Jerry contracted bronchitis after a long wait for a fare on New Year's Eve. Eventually he recovered but it was decided he would never be strong enough to drive a cab again and he was offered a post as coachman in the country to his wife's former employer. This was sad news for Black Beauty who was no longer a young horse.

In the fourth and final part of the book his career reached its lowest point. Jerry sold him to a corn dealer where he thought he would have good food and fair work but he did not count on the foreman who was always hurrying everybody and would frequently order the carter, Jakes, who drove Black Beauty, to takes on something extra when he already had a full load. To add to the misery of overloading he had to submit once more to the hated bearing-rein which had become the fashion among carters. The hard work in this constricted position soon pulled him down and he was sold to the work he most dreaded. He became one of Skinner's team of hirelings.

Now Black Beauty experienced for himself Ginger's misery and his life nearly ended as hers had. His driver was a hard man who laid on his cutting whip without mercy. Eventually the horse collapsed pulling a cab overloaded with luggage up Ludgate Hill. As he lay perfectly still he was convinced that he was going to die but in fact life was not over.

The farrier who nursed him back to health persuaded Skinner to send him not to the dogs, but to a horse fair. His wind was not broken and all he needed was six month's rest. At the second fair Black Beauty was as fortunate as he had been at the first. A gentle man farmer, Thoroughgood, recognised the breeding in him in spite of his fourteen years and was persuaded by his grandson, Willie, to buy him. After a year of perfect rest on the farm he regained some of his lost youth and was sold to a 'quiet genteel place' with the three Miss Blomeflelds who needed a horse to draw their low chair. When the Miss Blomefield's groom was cleaning Black Beauty he recognised the white star on his forehead. The groom was none other than Joe Green! And so the story ended on a cheerful, if slightly nostalgic note. Black Beauty concluded with the following words: 'My troubles are all over, and I am at home; and often before I am quite awake, I fancy I am still in the orchard at Birtwick, standing with my old friends under the apple trees.'

3

PEOPLE AND PLACES

Inevitably one seeks, in Anna Sewell's life, the originals of the characters, places and events in her book, and for Black Beauty himself one does not have to seek far. Margaret Sewell never doubted that he was simply Philip's Bessie after a change of sex. Even the names of the two horses are similar, for Bessie's full name was probably Black Bess, like Dick Turpin's famous mare.

The Sewell family used to tell many tales of Bessie's wisdom and foresight and one feels the incident of the flooded bridge in *Black Beauty* must almost certainly have been based on an event in her life. It occurred when Black Beauty was being driven home one stormy evening by Squire Gordon in the dog-cart.

By the time we got to the bridge it was very nearly dark; we could just see that the water was over the middle of it; but as that happened sometimes when the floods were out, master did not stop. We were going along at a good pace, but the moment my feet touched the first part of the bridge I felt sure there was something wrong. I dare not go forward, and I made a dead stop. 'Go on, Beauty,' said my master, and he gave me a touch with the whip, but I dare not stir forward.

'There's something wrong, sir,' said John, and he sprang out of the dog-cart and came to my head and looked all about. He tried to lead me forward. 'Come on, Beauty, what's the matter?' Of course I could not tell him, but I knew very well that the bridge was not safe.

Just then the man at the toll gate on the other side ran out of the house, tossing a torch about like one mad.

'Hoy, hoy, hoy! halloo! stop!' he cried.

'What's the matter?' shouted my master.

'The bridge is broken in the middle, and part of it is carried away; if you come on you'll be into the river.'

In one respect, however, Bessie did not resemble her fictional self. She was a restless horse and would never have suffered the long hours on the cab-stand that Black Beauty did. She had a strong sense of propriety and would not allow social calls to last beyond the prescribed fifteen minutes. When she brought Anna's nieces to see her they would put their heads out of the window and plead with her to wait an extra five minutes, but Philip found it hard to hold her and the carriage was usually moving away down the road before the last one had climbed in, laughing and protesting. In the book Bessie's restlessness was transferred to Ginger.

The original of Merrylegs is also not hard to find. I am assured by Miss Lee Warner that her mother learnt to ride on this pony, lent to her by Anna when she became too ill to drive, and that he was the fat grey pony that took such an objection to the Norwich cobbles. Certainly it would have been very like Merrylegs to know better than his driver what was good for her. It will be recalled that he always knew what was best for his rider and used to end riding lessons by gently tipping his rider off backwards. 'Boys,' he explained, 'must be broken in as we are broken in as colts.' In a conversation with Black Beauty he described how he dealt with the Blomefield boys.

They rode me by turns, and I galloped them about, up and down the fields and all about the orchard, for a good hour. They had each cut a great hazel stick for a riding whip, and laid it on a little too hard, but I took it in good part, till at last I thought we had had long enough, so I stopped two or three times by way of a hint. Boys, you see, think a horse or pony is like a steam engine or thrashing machine, and can go as long and as fast as they please; they never think that a pony can get tired, or have any feelings; so as the one who was whipping me could not understand I just rose up on my hind legs and let him slip off behind – that was all. He mounted me again, and I did the same. Then the other boy got up, and as soon as he began to use his stick I laid him on the grass, and so on, till they were able to understand – that was all. They are not bad boys; they don't wish to be cruel. I like them very well; but you see I had to give them a lesson.

The original of Ginger is not known and it seems unlikely that Anna would have owned such a vicious animal. A mare she was much more likely to have driven was Peggy, the short-paced cob at the livery stable in Bath. Although not well-bred, 'she was a strong, well-made animal, of a bright dun colour, beautifully dappled, and with a dark brown mane and tail'. She stood in the next stall to Black Beauty and was able to explain her strange paces to him.

> It really is not my fault; it is just because my legs are so short. I stand nearly as high as you but your legs are a good three inches longer above your knee than mine, and of course you can take a much longer step and go much faster. Men will go so fast and if one can't keep up to other horses it is nothing but whip, whip, whip all the time. And so I have had to keep up as best I could, and have got into this ugly shuffling pace.

Peggy's story ended happily for she was sold to two ladies living in Bath who drove themselves and wanted a good safe horse. These two ladies can surely have been none other than Anna and Mary Sewell.

Anna herself crops up several times in the course of the book. She makes her first appearance, one feels sure, as Jerry Barker's eight-year-old daughter, Dolly. Indeed Dolly and her brother Harry bear a strong resemblance to Anna and Philip as they were at Palatine Cottage, when they helped their parents with the running of the little farm. 'Harry was as clever at stable work as a much older boy, and always wanted to do what he could. Then Polly and Dolly used to come in the morning to help with the cab, to brush and beat the cushions, and rub the glass, while Jerry was giving us a cleaning in the yard and Harry was rubbing the harness.'

As an adult, Anna first appears in a somewhat idealised guise as Lady Anne, the daughter of the Earl of W— who was so romantically run away with by the skittish mare Lizzie and was rescued by young Colonel Blantyre on Black Beauty. 'She was a perfect horse woman, and as gay and gentle as she was beautiful.' It was true that she had 'followed the hounds a great many times', but she also had a heart that could be touched by suffering. One of the labourers who came to her aid after her horse fell said, 'I'd risk my neck for the Lady Anne; she was uncommon good to my wife in the winter.'

Anna was also almost certainly Miss Ellen, the youngest of the three Miss Blomefields, a good and fearless driver with dark eyes and a merry face. But she makes her longest appearance in the chapter entitled 'Jakes and the Lady'. Jakes, it will be recalled, was the cruel carter who overloaded Black Beauty and drove him in a bearing-rein.

> One day I was loaded more than usual, and part of the road was steep uphill. I used all my strength, but I could not go on, and was obliged continually to stop. This did not please my driver, and he laid his whip on badly. 'Get on, you lazy fellow,' he said, 'or I'll make you.'
>
> Again I started the heavy load, and struggled on a few yards; again the whip came down, and again I struggled forward. The pain of that great cart whip was sharp, but my mind was hurt quite as much as my poor sides. To be punished and abused when I was doing my very best was so hard it took the heart out of me. A third time he was flogging me cruelly, when a lady stepped quickly up to him and said in a sweet earnest voice:
>
> 'Oh! pray do not whip your horse any more; I am sure he is doing all he can, and the road is very steep. I am sure he is doing his best.'
>
> 'If doing his best won't get this load up he must do something more than his best; that's all I know, Ma'am,' said Jakes.
>
> 'Pray, stop; I think I can help you if you will let me.'
>
> The man laughed.
>
> 'You see,' she said, 'you do not give him a fair chance; he cannot use all his power with his head held back as it is with that bearing-rein; if you would take it off I am sure he would do better – do try it,' she said persuasively. 'I should be very glad if you would.'
>
> 'Well, well,' said Jakes, with a short laugh. 'Anything to please a lady of course.'

It must be admitted that this portrait, like that of the Lady Anne, shows Anna as she would have liked to be, rather than as she was. In reality, as Margaret Sewell pointed out, the sight of cruelty drove her to such a frenzy that she was incapable of restraint. Like her mother, however, she would have preferred to have the self-mastery to address wrong-doers gently.

Several other characters in the book were recognisable members of the Wright family. There seems little doubt that Farmer Grey, who bred Black Beauty was none other than Grandfather Wright.

> Our master was a good, kind man. He gave us good food, good lodging and kind words; he spoke as kindly to us as he did to his little children. We were all fond of him, and my mother loved him very much. When she saw him at the gate she would neigh with joy, and trot up to him. He would pat and stroke her and say, 'Well, old Pet, and how is your little Darkie?'

Like Grandfather Wright, Farmer Grey was kind to the helpless but stern to their oppressors.

> There was a plowboy, Dick, who sometimes came into our field to pluck blackberries from the hedge. When he had eaten all he wanted he would have what he called fun with the colts, throwing stones and sticks at them to make them gallop. We did not much mind him, for we could gallop off; but sometimes a stone would hit and hurt us.
>
> One day he was at this game, and did not know that the master was watching in the next field; but he was there, watching what was going on; over the hedge he jumped in a snap, and catching Dick by the arm he gave him such a box on the ear as made him roar with pain and surprise.

The field near the railway line, however, into which Farmer Grey turned Black Beauty to accustom him to trains, was not on a Norfolk farm but more probably the one behind the Sewells' house at Bath.

> I shall never forget the first train that ran by. I was feeding quietly near the pales which separated the meadow from the railway, when I heard a strange sound at a distance, and before I knew whence it came – with a rush and a clatter, and a puffing out of smoke – a long black train of something flew by, and was gone almost before I could draw my breath. I turned and galloped to the further side of the meadow as fast as I could go, and there I stood snorting with astonishment and fear. In the course of the day many other trains went by, some more slowly; these drew up at the station close by, and sometimes made an

awful shriek and groan before they stopped. I thought it very dreadful, but the cows went on eating very quietly, and hardly raised their heads as the great, black, frightful thing came puffing and grinding past.

For the first few days I could not feed in peace; but as I found that this terrible creature never came into the field, or did me any harm, I began to disregard it, and very soon I cared as little about the passing of a train as the cows and sheep did.

Birtwick Park, Black Beauty's second home, must have been modelled on Dudwick House, at Buxton, the residence of Uncle and Aunt Wright. The house and grounds were certainly similar. Like Birtwick Park, Dudwick was approached by a long tree-lined avenue that wound its way through an extensive park. There was a wide sweep of drive in front of the house, and beyond it stables, a home paddock and an orchard where Anna, like Miss Jessie and Miss Flora, no doubt learnt to ride. Squire Gordon and his wife were probably portraits of Uncle and Aunt Wright, for, like them they were devoted to the welfare of those less fortunate than themselves.

Our master and mistress were respected and beloved by all who knew them; they were good and kind to everybody and everything; not only men and women, but horses and donkeys, dogs and cats, cattle and birds; there was no oppressed or ill-used creature that had not a friend in them, and their servants took the same tone. If any of the village children were known to treat any creature cruelly they soon heard about it from the Hall.

The Squire and Farmer Grey had worked together, as they said, for more than twenty years to get the bearing-rein on the cart horses done away with, and in our parts you seldom saw them; and sometimes if mistress met a heavily laden horse with his head strained up she would stop the carriage, and get out and reason with the driver in her sweet serious voice.

Like Aunt Wright, Mrs Gordon often drove herself about in a low chaise pulled by a pony and, like her, she was often confined to the house by illness for long periods.

Only two places in the book are mentioned by name; Bath and London. Bath was the city where Black Beauty served his term as a job horse working in a livery stable and Anna obviously used the knowledge of the city she had gained while living at Moorlands in portraying it. She actually mentioned two of the streets by name (Pulteney Street and Lansdown) and Black Beauty's journey from Earlshall to Bath by train was obviously based on her own grey pony's train journey in the other direction. Yet, strangely enough, the picture she gave of London in her book was far more vivid, although she knew the city less well. The only comment she made on the horses of Bath was on the misery of the coal horses struggling up and down the hills of that city. The pictures she gave of the crowded streets of London, seen through the eyes of Black Beauty pulling his cab, are among the most vivid in the book. It was the City itself she always described: Cheapside, Ludgate Hill, the Monument and London Bridge, and one is tempted to suppose she was drawing on the memories of the horse traffic she had seen there as a child when she came in every Sunday for the Gracechurch Street Meeting. Yet the horse traffic she described was the traffic of the sixties and not the twenties. In the days when she came up to town for First Day Meetings there was no such thing as an omnibus and the crush of vehicles on London Bridge, all trying to reach the station, did not exist, because the station had not yet been built. She must therefore have relied on her impressions gathered on subsequent brief visits to the City.

One of the most famous passages in the book describes a dash through the City traffic at midday to help an invalid catch a train at London Bridge Station. There was little time left but Jerry considered the case a worthy one.

It is always difficult to drive fast in the city in the middle of the day when the streets are full of traffic, but we did what could be done; and when a good driver and a good horse, who understand each other, are of one mind, it is wonderful what they can do. I had a very good mouth – that is I could be guided by the slightest touch of the rein; and that is a great thing in London, among carriages, omnibuses, carts, vans, trucks, cabs, and the great wagons creeping along at a walking pace; some going one way, some another, some going slowly, others wanting to pass them; omnibuses stopping short every few minutes to pick up a passenger, obliging the horse that is coming behind to pull up too, or to pass, and get before them. Perhaps you try to pass, but just then something else comes dashing in through the narrow opening, and you have to keep in behind the omnibus again; presently you think you see a chance, and manage to get to the front, going so near the wheels on each side that half an inch nearer and they would scrape. Well, you get along for a bit, but soon find yourself in a long train of carts and carriages all obliged to go at a walk; perhaps you come to a regular block up, and have to stand still for minutes together till something clears out into a side street, or the policeman interferes; you have to be ready for any chance – to dash forward if there be an opening, and be quick as a rat-dog to see if there be room and if there be time, lest you get your own wheels locked or smashed, or the shaft of some other vehicle run into your chest or shoulder. All this is what you have to be ready for. If you want to get through London fast in the middle of the day it wants a deal of practice.

The night drives from Blue Lodge to Wick certainly furnished material for the dramatic night journey that occurred while Black Beauty was living at Birtwick Park. Ridden by John Manly, Black Beauty had to gallop eight miles to the local town to fetch a doctor for his mistress. 'The air was frosty, the moon was bright; it was very pleasant. We came through a village, then through a dark wood, then uphill, then downhill, till we came to the town, through the streets and into the market place. It was all quite still except the clatter of my feet on the stones – everybody was asleep. The church clock struck three as we drew up at Dr. White's door.'

The most violent scene in the book is, strangely enough, the most authentic. The tragic accident that robbed Reuben Smith of his life and Black Beauty of his good home surely had its roots in the equally tragic accident that befell the groom at Blue Lodge.

Beyond the turnpike was a long piece of road, upon which fresh stones had just been laid – large sharp stones, over which no horse could be driven quickly without risk of danger. Over this road, with one shoe gone, I was forced to gallop at my utmost speed, and my rider meanwhile cutting into me with his whip, and with wild curses urging me to go still faster

This could not go on; no horse could keep his footing under such circumstances; the pain was too great. I stumbled, and fell with violence on both my knees. Smith was flung off by my fall, and, owing to the speed I was going at, he must have fallen with great force. I soon recovered my feet and limped to the side of the road, where it was free from stones. The moon had just risen above the hedge, and by its light I could see Smith lying a few yards beyond me. He did not rise; he made one slight effort to do so and then there was a heavy groan.

Help came at midnight in the form of two grooms in a dog-cart pulled by Ginger.

They came slowly over the stones, and stopped at the dark figure that lay upon the ground.

One of the men jumped out, and stooped over it. 'It is Reuben,' he said, 'and he does not stir!'

The other man followed, and bent over him. 'He's dead,' he said, 'feel how cold his hands are.'

They raised him up, but there was no life, and his hair was soaked with blood.

4

THE SOCIAL ORDER

Black Beauty tells us a great deal about Anna Sewell's attitude to life. From it we can discover what were the real thoughts of this silent woman, who at times, seemed little more than the shadow of her mother. As one reads about Anna Sewell one finds oneself constantly asking the question, did she share Mary's philosophy of life or was she secretly a rebel? A careful reading of *Black Beauty* proves that she was not a rebel. Indeed, the book is a final proof of Mary's domination over Anna, for in it the daughter's view of life is seen to be a faithful reflection of the mother's.

Anna's attitude to the social structure was feudal. She believed in the good old days when everyone knew his place; the rich man's being in his castle and the poor man's at his gate. Although she was sympathetic to the sufferings of working men, she would have no truck with Socialism and indeed she had little use for any political party, as she stated clearly enough in a conversation between Jerry Barker and his son in a chapter headed 'The Election'.

> 'Why, father, I thought blue was for Liberty.'
> 'My boy, Liberty does not come from colours, they only show party and all the liberty you can get out of them is liberty to get drunk at other people's expense, liberty to ride to the poll in a dirty old cab, liberty to abuse anyone that does not wear your colour and to shout yourself hoarse at what you only half understand – that's your liberty.'

Squire Gordon's family at Birtwick Park represented her ideal society in miniature. At the head of it was the master, Squire Gordon himself. Below him were the servants, John Manly, James Howard and little Joe Green. And below them were the horses. Just as it was the duty of the horses to serve the men, so it was the duty of the men to serve their masters.

This similarity between the position of servants and horses becomes more obvious still when we compare *Patience Hart*, Mary Sewell's autobiography of a kitchen-maid, with Anna Sewell's autobiography of a horse. It is true that Patience herself never descended the ladder of service in the way that Black Beauty did. On the other hand, the life history of her fellow servant, Honour Green, closely resembled that of the horse. Like Black Beauty, Honour was raised in a simple but happy country home, lost a good place through no fault of her own and descended to the lowest kind of work as a general servant in a boarding house. Here her final collapse occurred, and even this resembled that of Black Beauty for, while he fell pulling a load up Ludgate Hill, she fell while carrying a tray up a flight of stairs. After a period in hospital she, like Black Beauty, was rescued by a kindly old person and ended in a good home.

There are other characters in *Patience Hart* who have equivalents in *Black Beauty*. Abigail, the flighty house-maid who picks up bad habits in youth and lives to rue them, is a forerunner of Ginger, while Mrs Trubody, the cook who is so given to quoting from the Good Book, is obviously a close relative of John Manly. The advice given to young horses in *Black Beauty* echoes that given to young servants in *Patience Hart*. 'Lift up your feet when you trot and never kick or bite,' says Black Beauty's mother to him when they part. 'Be sure to do well whatever you do; and remember servants must not have tempers,' says Mrs Trubody to Patience.

But if Anna and her mother considered that servants should obey their masters as horses do, they also considered that masters had responsibilities. It was their duty to care for those beneath them, even at inconvenience to themselves. Squire Gordon walked to church on Sunday so that his servants could also attend a place of worship, and he took on John Manly as 'a raw boy from the plough tail', to save him from the workhouse.

Grooms equally had responsibilities for their horses. Indeed, Anna regarded the prevention of suffering as the duty of every human being and had no patience with those who pass by on the other side. She caused one of Jerry's passengers, named, appropriately enough, Wright, to express her doctrine on this point. (He had just reprimanded a drunken driver for brutally whipping his horses.)

'Do you know why this world is as bad as it is?'

'No,' said the other.

'Then I'll tell you. It is because people think only about their own business, and won't trouble themselves to stand up for the oppressed nor bring the wrongdoer to light. I never see a wicked thing like this without doing what I can. My doctrine is this, that if we see cruelty or wrong that we have the power to stop, and do nothing, we make ourselves sharers in the guilt.'

Ignorance, also, Anna would never allow as an excuse for causing suffering. It was through Joe Green's ignorance that Black Beauty almost lost his life after galloping for the doctor to save Mrs Gordon's life. Joe, seeing the horse was steaming 'like a pot on fire' gave him a bucket of water and left him without his rug. As a result, the horse contracted pneumonia and only just escaped with his life. Joe's father did not escape without the following castigation from John Manly:

'Only ignorance! Only ignorance! How can you talk about only ignorance? Don't you know that it is the worst thing in the world, next to wickedness? – and which does the most mischief heaven only knows. If people can say, "Oh, I did not know, I did not mean any harm," they think it is all right. Bill Starkey did not mean to frighten his brother into fits when he dressed up like a ghost and ran after him in the moonlight; but he did; and that bright, handsome little fellow, that might have been the pride of his mother's heart, is just no better than an idiot, and never will be, if he lives to be eighty years old.'

Not only did Anna Sewell believe in a strict social hierarchy in human society. She believed in a parallel one in horse society. Black Beauty himself was an aristocrat, as his mother, named, appropriately enough, Duchess, was quick to inform him. 'I wish you to pay attention to what I am going to say to you. The colts who live here are very good colts, but they are cart horse colts, and of course they have not learned manners. You have been well-bred and well-born; your father has a great name in these parts, and your grandfather won the cup two years running at the Newmarket races.'

Many of Black Beauty's associates were also out of the top drawer. Captain, Jerry Barker's grey horse, was the equine equivalent of a retired army officer, 'a high-bred, fine-mannered, noble old horse every inch of him'. Peggy at the livery stables, on the other hand, was but a common creature. 'There was no high breeding about her, but she was very pretty and remarkably sweet tempered and willing.'

Black Beauty himself descended the social scale as his misfortunes increased. He was worth £150 when Squire Gordon parted with him. Jerry Barker secured him for £24 10s. 0d. and he finally changed hands for a flyer. Not only did his value diminish but his name also became increasingly vulgar. To Lady Anne he was Black Auster, but to Jerry he was plain Jack, and cruel Jakes the carter called him Blackie, which was hardly a name at all. Yet, even when to all intents and purposes he was a broken-down screw, he was still a gentleman at heart, as Farmer Thoroughgood quickly saw. 'He might have been anything when he was young; look at his nostrils and ears, the shape of his neck and shoulders; there's a deal of breeding about that horse.'

Anna was opposed to the Industrial Revolution and the new era of technology. This was natural in one so attached to the established social order and the ideal of paternalism. Like her mother she deplored the severing of the old ties of master to man which followed upon the herding of the working classes into the manufacturing towns. Towns in *Black Beauty* were always symbols of evil. All his good masters lived in the country with one exception, Jerry Barker, and even he had finally to be transported to the heaven of a country home, for he was too good for the city. We are given one glimpse of him in his natural setting when he takes Dinah Brown to visit her sick mother in the country. 'Jerry seemed to be quite as happy as I was. He sat down by a bank under a shady tree, and listened to the birds, then he sang to himself, and read out of the little brown book he is so fond of.'

Ironically the two men in the Sewell family were actively engaged in bringing about the very revolution that the women so deplored and whose harmful effects they attempted to remedy. Isaac, as a banker, no doubt financed many of the schemes that changed the face of England, and Philip was a builder of railways. Railways indeed play a part in the story of Black Beauty, but it is a sinister one. To Black Beauty as a foal, the train that ran along the bottom of his field was a thing of ill omen and sure enough it was the 'black frightful thing' that carried away his kind master and mistress.

Besides towns and railways, there was a third product of the Industrial Revolution to which Anna, like the ladies of Cranford, took great exception, and that was the class of persons she described as Cockneys. Black Beauty came in contact with many of these people when he was working as a job horse in Bath. They were usually people from towns who had never had a horse of their own.

> Instead of starting at an easy pace, as a gentleman would do, they generally set off at full speed from the very stable yard; and when they want to stop, they first whip us, and then pull up so suddenly that we are nearly thrown on our haunches, and our mouths jagged with the bit – they call that pulling up with a dash; and when they turn a corner they do it as sharply as if there were no right side of wrong side of the road.
>
> I well remember one spring evening I and Rory had been out for the day … As we neared the corner I heard a horse and two wheels coming rapidly down the hill toward us. The hedge was high, and I could see nothing, but the next moment we were upon each other. Happily for me, I was on the side next the hedge. Rory was on the left side of the pole and had not even a shaft to protect him. The man who was driving was making straight for the corner, and when he came in sight of us he had not time to pull over to his own side. The whole shock came upon Rory. The gig shaft ran right into the chest, making him stagger back with a cry I shall never forget … The driver was one of those random, ignorant fellows, who don't even know which is their own side of the road, or, if they know, don't care.

Anna's dislike of Cockneys spread to people of all classes whose chief concern was show, be they earls or stable-boys. She did not disguise her disapproval of the Countess of W— who insisted on the bearing-rein, and the chapter of Mr Barry's groom, Alfred Smirk, was appropriately entitled 'A Humbug'.

> If ever there was a humbug in the shape of a groom Alfred Smirk was the man. He was very civil to me, and never used me ill; in fact, he did a great deal of stroking and patting when his master was there to see it. He always brushed my mane and tail with water and my hoofs with oil before he brought me to the door, to make me look smart;

but as to cleaning my feet or looking to my shoes, or grooming me
thoroughly, he thought no more of that than if I had been a cow.

For Anna, as for her mother, the ideal society was still the one portrayed
by their favourite schoolroom author Maria Edgeworth in the story
Simple Susan. For them, as for Miss Edgeworth, the good characters were
Squire Somers up at the big house and Farmer Price, his humble and
grateful tenant. The villain was the get-rich-quick lawyer, Case.

Of the social vices of her day alcoholism was the one that Anna,
like Mary, most deplored. Strong liquor was the cause of Black
Beauty's undoing. 'It was all that cursed drink; why will they sell
that cursed drink?' sobbed Reuben's widow when her husband's
dead body was brought to her. Jerry Barker, incredibly enough, had
once been a drinker, but had given it up.

> I had hard work at it for several weeks; you see I never did get
> drunk, but I found that I was not my own master, and that when
> the craving came on it was hard work to say no. I saw that one of us
> must knock under, the drink devil or Jerry Barker, and I said that it
> should not be Jerry Barker, God helping me; but it was a struggle, and
> I wanted all the help I could get, for till I tried to break the habit I
> did not know how strong it was, but then Polly took such pains that
> I should have good food, and when the craving came on I used to
> get a cup of coffee, or some peppermint, or read a bit in my book,
> and that was a help to me.

Jerry refused to vote for a candidate who otherwise represented his
view in the election because he was a brewer for, he said, 'a man who
gets rich by that trade may be all very well in some ways, but he is
blind as to what workingmen want'. Jerry had good cause to wish
the 'drink devil' in 'the bottomless pit', for it was a drunken driver
who fatally injured Captain.

> He and Jerry had taken a party to the great railway station over
> London Bridge, and were coming back, somewhere between the
> bridge and the monument, when Jerry saw a brewer's empty dray
> coming along, drawn by two powerful horses. The drayman was lash-
> ing his horses with his heavy whip; the dray was light, and they started

The Woman Who Wrote Black Beauty

off at a furious rate; the man had no control over them, and the street was full of traffic.

One young girl was knocked down and run over, and the next moment they dashed against our cab. Both the wheels were torn off and the cab was thrown over. Captain was dragged down, the shafts splintered, and one of them ran into his side … The drayman was proved to be very drunk, and was fined, and the brewer had to pay damages to our master; but there was no one to pay damages to poor Captain.

Another social evil that Anna in particular felt very strongly about was the seven-day week. It is true that Mary also considered Sunday work wrong for both men and horses. Indeed, in a ballad called *Marriage as it May be* she drew a picture of the perfect Sunday afternoon:

> The horse rolled over, snorting at his ease,
> Or with his working friends stood nose to nose,
> In quiet converse, or in mute repose.

Nevertheless, she never made the point as emphatically as Anna. Jerry Barker would never ply on a Sunday and lost his best customer by refusing to drive her to church. Mrs Briggs paid down 'fair and honourable, like a lady … no beating down or making three hours into two hours and a half as some folks do'. But, as Jerry explained to her husband, 'I had a seven-days' license once, and the work was too hard for me, and too hard for my horses. Year in and year out, not a day's rest, and never a Sunday with my wife and children; and never able to go out to a place of worship, which I had always been used to do before I took to the driving box.'

Although a Sunday's work was rare for Jerry, it was common enough for some of the other drivers on the stand. Such a one was Seedy Sam. He did not own his own cab and horse, but hired them from the notorious Skinner who charged eighteen shillings a day for them. ''Tis more than hard work,' said Sam, when accused by the governor of overworking his horses.

''Tis more than hard work; 9/- to get out of each horse before you begin to get your own living. You know that's true, and if the horses don't work we must starve. I am on the stand fourteen or sixteen, hours a day, and I haven't had a Sunday these ten or twelve weeks. I say 'tis a mockery to tell a man he must not overwork his horse for when a beast is downright tired there's nothing but the whip that will keep his legs a-going.

'You that have your own horses and cabs, or drive for good masters have a chance of getting on and a chance of doing right; I haven't. We can't charge more than sixpence a mile after the first, within the four mile radius. This very morning I had to go a clear six miles and only took three shillings. I could not get a return fare, and had to come all the way back; there's twelve miles for the horse and three shillings for me. After that I had a three mile fare and there were bags and boxes enough to have brought in a good many twopences if they had been put outside; but you know how people do; all that could be piled up inside on the front seat was put in and three heavy boxes went on the top. That was sixpence, and the fare one and sixpence; then I got a return for a shilling; now that makes eighteen miles for the horse and six shillings for me; there's three shillings still for that horse to earn and nine shillings for the afternoon horse before I touch a penny.'

A few mornings after this talk a new man came on the stand with Sam's cab.

'Halloo!' said one, 'what's up with Seedy Sam?'

'He's ill in bed,' said the man. 'He was taken last night in the yard and could scarcely crawl home. His wife sent a boy this morning to say his father was in a high fever and could not get out so I'm here instead.'

The next morning the same man came again.

'How is Sam?' inquired the governor.

'He's gone,' said the man.

'What, gone? You don't mean to say he's dead?'

'Just snuffed out,' said the other; 'he died at four o'clock this morning; all yesterday he was raving – raving about Skinner, and having no Sundays. "I never had a Sunday's rest," those were his last words.'

The tragic news was received in awed silence on the stand. Jerry felt so strongly on the matter that he actually suggested a strike. '"If you Sunday drivers would all strike for a day of rest," he said, "the thing would be done."' Such a shocking suggestion would never have come from the pen of Mary Sewell. She never considered that strikes were justified. On this point at least the daughter's views diverged from the mother's.

5

A HORSEMAN'S MANUAL

Like *Gulliver's Travels* and *Robinson Crusoe*, *Black Beauty* was not originally intended for children. It was aimed at precisely the section of
the public that Mary Sewell wrote for, the simple working folk,
for it was these who were in daily contact with horses. This fact is
driven home by a note found at the back of all the early editions of
the book. It runs:

> If any readers of this Autobiography wish to know more of the
> right treatment of horses, on the road and in the stable, the Translator
> would recommend them to procure an admirable little book, price
> fourpence, entitled The Horse Book.
>
> Its directions are short, clear and full of commonsense. It has been
> revised by no less an authority than Mr. Fleming, R.E., F.R.G.S., President
> of the Central Veterinary Medical Society and Member of the Council of
> the Royal College of Veterinary Surgeons. It has also been approved by
> the other eminent Veterinarians. It is published by the R.S.P.C.A.

The account of Black Beauty's breaking-in by Farmer Grey is
particularly full and accurate.

> Everyone may not know what breaking-in is, therefore I will describe
> it. It means to teach a horse to wear a saddle and bridle, and to carry on
> his back a man, woman or child; to go just the way they wish, and to
> go quietly. Besides this he has to learn to wear a collar, a crupper, and a
> breeching, and to stand still while they are put on; then to have a cart
> or chaise fixed behind, so that he can not walk or trot without drag-
> ging it after him; and he must go fast or slow just as his driver wishes.

He must never start at what he sees nor speak to other horses, nor bite, nor kick, nor have any will of his own; but always do his master's will, even though he may be very tired or hungry; but the worse of all is, when his harness is once on, he may neither jump for joy nor lie down for weariness. So you see this breaking-in is a great thing.

I had of course long been used to a halter and headstall, and to be led about the fields and lanes quietly, but now I was to have a bit and bridle; my master gave me some oats as usual, and after a good deal of coaxing he got the bit into my mouth, and the bridle fixed, but it was a nasty thing! Those who have never had a bit in their mouth cannot think how bad it feels; a great piece of cold hard steel as thick as a man's finger to be pushed into one's mouth, between one's teeth, and over one's tongue, with the ends coming out of the corner of your mouth and held fast there by straps over your head, under your throat, round your nose and under your chin; so that no way in the world can you get rid of the nasty hard thing; it is very bad! yes, very bad! at least I thought so; but I knew my mother always wore one when she went out, and all horses did when they were grown up; and so, what with the nice oats, and what with my master's pats, kind words, and gentle ways, I got to wear my bit and bridle.

The next unpleasant business was putting on the iron shoes; that too was very hard at first. My master went with me to the smith's forge, to see that I was not hurt or got any fright. The blacksmith took my feet in his hand, one after the other, and cut away some of the hoof. It did not pain me so I stood still on three legs till he had done them all. Then he took a piece of iron the shape of my foot, and clapped it on, and drove some nails through the shoe quite into my hoof, so that the shoe was firmly on. My feet felt very stiff and heavy, but in time I got used to it.

And now having got so far, my master went on to break me to harness; there were more new things to wear. First, a stiff heavy collar just on my neck, and a bridle with great side pieces against my eyes called blinkers and blinkers indeed they were, for I could not see on either side, but only straight in front of me: next, there was a small saddle with a nasty stiff strap that went right under my tail, that was the crupper. I hated the crupper; to have my long tail doubled up and poked through that strap was almost as bad as the bit. I never felt more like kicking, but of course I could not kick such a good master, and so in time I got used to everything, and could do my work as well as my mother.

The most technical section of the book is Part II which covers Black Beauty's period at Bath. In the chapters devoted to his experiences as a job horse Anna Sewell went into some detail about the different styles of driving and deplored equally those who drive with too tight a rein under the impression that it is their duty to hold the horse up, and those who drive with too loose a rein. Her castigation of 'loose rein drivers' suggests that Mrs Bayly's picture of Anna herself driving with the reins resting on her horse's back was not entirely accurate. She considered that a horse 'likes to feel the rein a little in going downhill … and to know that his driver is not gone to sleep'. Nor did she approve of lazy habits in a horse. 'Squire Gordon always kept us to our best paces and our best manners. He said that spoiling a horse and letting him get into bad habits was just as cruel as spoiling a child and both had to suffer for it afterward.'

A hazard to which a loose-rein driver's horse was exposed was that of travelling several miles with an undetected stone wedged in his hoof. Victorian roads did not have the smooth surfaces we are familiar with today. When newly made up they were often covered with loose chippings of the sort that caused Black Beauty's fatal fall with Reuben Smith. There were regulations about the maximum size of these chippings but, as Anna's admirer Mr Flower pointed out in his book, *Macadam versus Vestries*, these regulations were often ignored. Macadam himself recommended that a chip should be small enough to fit into the mouth of the navvy who was building the road. The vestries, however, allowed larger ones to slip through and even Macadam was occasionally deceived.

> While superintending the making of a road, Mr. Macadam one day perceived some stones of extraordinary size. His wrath was kindled against the stone breaker – a canny Scotsman – whom he forwith accused of having failed to test the stones. The man denied the accusation, and solved the mystery by opening his mouth which was of, enormous capacity and entirely bereft of teeth!

Flower included a life-size illustration of the chip that the gargantuan-mouthed navvy accommodated. Not only was it large but it was rounded at one end and pointed at the other. It was just such a stone that became wedged between Black Beauty's shoe and frog when he was being driven by a loose-rein driver.

In the chapters devoted to Black Beauty's life as the hack of Mr Barry, we are given an equally accurate account of faulty stable-management and some remarkably detailed diet sheets are given for horses under different circumstances. A cure for thrush is also given which involves packing the affected hoof with medicated wadding. In a previous chapter are included cures for pneumonia and broken knees.

Some might suppose that this detailed knowledge of horses was normal in an age of horses, for an age of horses the mid-Victorian era undoubtedly was. It is true that by 1845 the stage-coaches had gone but the trains that took their place had to be met by horse-drawn vehicles and the travelling public had never been so large. A woman who lived in this horse-drawn age, however, was no more expected to know about what went on in the stable than a modern woman is expected to know about what goes on under the bonnet of her car. Sweat and manure were not considered suitable subjects for ladies to discuss[*] and even if a lady interested herself in horses she was certainly not expected to associate with grooms. Stablemen were considered the lowest of the low. It will be recalled that it was a stable-boy who corrupted Lazy Lawrence, the villain of one of the Edgeworth stories. Even the liberal Mrs Ellis, who so strongly recommended ponies as companions for children, sternly discouraged intimacy with their keepers. 'It is a generally acknowledged fact,' she wrote, 'that the class of men whose business consists … in the management of horses are among the last whose society a prudent mother would choose.' There is hardly a stableman in the Surtees novel who is not a drunken rascal and Sir Moses Mainchance's groom was not called Wetun without reason. In creating the virtuous trio at Birtwick, John Manly, James Howard and Joe Green, Anna was breaking with tradition. The 'nice' girls today who can take positions as grooms without loss of reputation may well have Anna Sewell to thank for the new image she gave to the stable yard.

---

[*] Over one aspect of Black Beauty's life Anna did however throw a veil. She makes no mention of his gelding. The operation was presumably performed while he was still at his first home with Farmer Grey. This fact was ignored by the author of a sequel to Anna's book, *Son of Black Beauty*.

6

THE END

We have travelled a long way from the invalid at The White House who wrote *Black Beauty*. In fact she only lived a few months after its publication. Mary always said that the excitement of its success killed her, but Mary, as we have observed, was often a source of inaccurate information. Anna clearly implied in her diary that she became severely ill even before the arrival of the proofs in August. An entry in her diary runs, 'July, 1877. I began milk diet two weeks ago and hope for benefit.'

Again we are left in ignorance as to the exact nature of Anna's complaint, but the necessity for a milk diet suggests that she developed a gastric disorder of some sort soon after she finished writing the book. The milk diet led to a marked diminution of suffering, but she was unable to take the prescribed quantity and she began to lose weight rapidly. Just as *Black Beauty* was beginning to be acclaimed, in the New Year of 1878, she contracted a disease of the lungs and a rapid decline set in.

She now became completely bedridden. Mary nursed her by day and at night a professional nurse sat with her. Mary was now eighty-one and one feels that she might have spared herself this exertion. Not only was she caring for one patient who was physically ill. Another patient in the house was now severely ill mentally. For the past year Isaac had begun to suffer from those 'mental impressions of a very distressing nature' mentioned above. He needed constant reassurance and diversion. After his death, the following year, Mary often thought she heard his plaintive cry, 'Art thee there, Mary?' No doubt if the Sewells had lived today both patients would have been removed to hospital, but in the mid-Victorian era this was not the custom.

Hospitals were for the poor and those who had no one to care for
them. A good housewife took a pride in a well-conducted sickroom
and Mary's would undoubtedly have been of the best. She was an
admirer of Florence Nightingale and had no doubt read her *Notes on
Nursing*, a manual for those caring for sick in their own homes.

All her attentions, however, could do no more than ease the passing
of the patient. Anna's last weeks and death are best left to Mary to
describe in a series of letters to friends.

To Mrs Williamson

The darling has not been so well for the last few weeks, quite unable
to work or do anything but be an angel of patience and sweetness
in the house.

(Mary was always amazed at Anna's ability to bear pain without
showing it. On one occasion she asked her, 'Do you never break
down and fret about it, darling?' Anna's reply was, 'Sometimes when
I am alone I do say, "Poor Nannie!"')

To a friend

Step by step, day by day, the dear life seems to be slipping away,
gently just now, comparatively little pain, quiet and praiseful, taking
medicine, food; – but the life goes. She can scarcely be moved without
faintness. The water-bed is a great comfort. She has not been moved
to the couch for three days – it is all too much – but the Comforter
is here. We do not talk of the future – the parting, it might unnerve
us both, and we each know what the other thinks and feels. She has
done the day's work in the day, and no arrears press on her tranquil
spirit, which is resting in the arms of Eternal love. She never loses an
opportunity of sending her love to her friends; all are affectionately
remembered – thee most especially.

To Mrs Williamson

I have been wishing to send thee a line but nursing brings many
interruptions. I wanted to tell thee myself of the goodness of the Lord
– not in restoring bodily strength – but little more of this remains to
be taken away – but in restoring the soul. We are both of us kept in
such wondrous peace and trust. He is taking us down on the sunny

side of the valley, where the dew lies still, and every sharp stone as we touch it is taken away – we touch it, and feel it is there and then recognise the Hand that removes it. There is now no acute pain internally, but the poor bones, barely covered with skin, have passed through at the lower part of the back … The difficulty of raising the mucous phlegm is the most trying, but her sweet patience accepts all from the Hand of Love. The majestic grandeur of her countenance is never disturbed excepting in sleep, then we see what she suffers, and how she restrains herself from showing it. Her thought is about me – we know each other's thoughts and feeling so perfectly, that words would be an intrusion, and might overcome us both. How long it may last I know not, but think it cannot be long – she now never rises from her water-bed. I have moved her into the drawing-room, the nurse always sleeps there, and I go to my own bed.

April 1878

You are longing, I know, to hear of my Jewel, but what shall I say? A little weaker, and a little weaker – two or three words at a time is all she can say, and all she can bear to hear. I dare not say a word that would touch her tender feelings. 'My dearest Jewel,' I say, and her response is 'My dearest Mother' – we neither of us venture further. She has been sorely tried with her poor back – no ease … Her sweet patience is past description, and her thankfulness for any little change that promises ease, if only momentary, is truly touching. The dear Lord is putting on the last ornamental touches, and beautifying her exceedingly. But oh! it is too touching – with all the sweet springing of the flowers, the joyous songs of the birds, and the sunshine, and she, fading away, never to look at them again with me.

I stole out for a short walk before breakfast this morning, to be alone with the Comforter. The grass was glittering all over with dew-drops, myriads upon myriads everywhere, with all the fair colours that the glorious sun could produce; and then I saw my darling drawn up to pass into the pure light of the Sun of Righteousness, and the Comforter Himself comforted me, and I returned strengthened for the day; and so the days come and go.

To Mrs. F.

April 23, 1878

Your tenderly sympathising letter, my beloved friend, has been a real comfort to me. I read parts of it to my darling, and whilst they are fresh in my remembrance, I want to tell you the words she said, at broken intervals. 'How we have loved her, mother, and how we have admired her! I have so often wished to write to her since I had her last letter. I have been waiting till I was stronger, and that has never come. Say to her from me' (alluding to a portion of your letter to her), 'do not mourn your "dead friend".* If God takes it away, it is because He has some other work now more wanted, and therefore more worthy of being done; the other is only laid aside for the present time. I have many "dead friends" in which I delighted – they were taken away from me one by one. They might have carried my heart away. I think they would, but I think they were taken away to be restored. I shall find them when the new life begins, and rise and enjoy them without danger. Meantime God has given me a few "humble friends" to employ my small talents, and keep my thoughts from myself – little works for children and poor people, that have made me glad and busy, and thankful now. Give my most dear love to F. and F.'

Three or four days later, Mrs Bayly received a card in the well-known writing, and read:

> For ever with the Lord
> All tears wiped away.

At the end of a week came the following letter, dated 1 May 1878.

I will try to write you a few lines. It is a week today since my bright Jewel was taken from me and put safe into the heavenly casket, out of my sight.

… In the morning of the day, I went into her room about four o'clock in the morning, having heard her incessantly cough-ing for a long time. 'Oh,' she said, in her bright sunny way, 'thee

---

* Mrs F.'s word for poetic inspiration.

art not so good as thee said thee would be. Go to bed, darling; I really have had some nice sleep.' I returned again at six, with something very soft to place under her shoulders; every part of her back was so tender that no position afforded comfort. She said she would have it the next time the nurse moved her. In about an hour the nurse called me hastily, saying Anna was faint. I found her breathing with difficulty, but as soon as she could speak, she said, with one of her inexpressible smiles, 'I am not going yet, I am so strong.' She then asked the nurse if that was dying. For four and a half hours this painful breathing continued, becoming more and more difficult, and she was perfectly conscious till the last few minutes … Her lips were often seen moving, and her clear, beautiful eyes raised upwards; then her face would become overspread with an almost luminous smile as she evidently received the answer. She did not move the whole time, but her sweet eyes were ever seeking me with inexpressible tenderness, as if she would comfort me. About a quarter of an hour before she passed away, she said, 'Pray', and my Philip commended her into her Redeemer's hands, giving thanks for her full salvation, for all He had revealed to her, and for her perfect peace. She said, 'Amen; it is all quite, quite true.' Then in a clear voice she said, 'I am quite ready.' Her eyes sought me again. I laid my cheek on hers; a few more long-drawn breaths and she left me behind.

Mrs Bayly was not present on the day of the funeral, but Mrs Buxton, the wife of the local squire, was. She was standing near the window of the upstairs drawing room at The White House where the guests were gathering to follow the cortège to Lammas. Mary Sewell, who was beside her, glanced out of the window as the horse-drawn hearse drew up outside. 'Oh, this will never do!' she exclaimed to herself and hastened downstairs. When Mrs Buxton looked out of the window again she observed Mary in earnest conversation with the undertaker's man. A moment later a top-hatted figure was seen moving to the head of each horse in turn. He was removing the bearing-reins from all the horses in the train.

7

LATER SUCCESS

When Anna died several thousand copies of her book had already been sold but sales gathered momentum after her death. The first illustrated edition, brought out by Jarrold in 1894, instead of listing the works of Mary Sewell at the end, carried advertisements for a whole range of editions of *Black Beauty* from a luxury one at five shillings down through a 'cloth elegant' at two shillings, a 'school cloth' at one and sixpence and a 'popular paper' at one shilling. By the time this edition appeared the sales had risen to 192,000 and a French translation was available.

The sales of the book in the United States, where it was pirated, were even more remarkable. A million copies were circulated within two years of its publication, a feat never before achieved in the history of publishing. The man responsible for this massive achievement was George T. Angell, the founder not only of the Massachusetts Society for the Prevention of Cruelty to Animals but also of the American Humane Education Society, the Band of Mercy and the S.P.C.A. magazine *Our Dumb Animals*.

George T. Angell, it is hardly necessary to point out, was a remarkable man. He was born about the same time as Anna Sewell herself, the son of a Baptist minister of Southbridge, Massachusetts, who died when he was four years old and left his mother virtually penniless. By the time he was forty-five he had made enough money at the bar (strangely enough in partnership with Samuel E. Sewall,* a descendant of the Warwickshire branch of the family**) to retire and devote himself

---

*The name is often spelt thus in the United States.

** See Appendix I.

to philanthropic work. The causes he espoused were very varied. Not only did he campaign against cruelty to animals but also against the adulteration of foodstuffs, the use of poisonous substances in the manufacture of wallpaper and the burial of human bodies before decay set in. (From his childhood he had had a terror of being buried alive and strongly approved of the Bavarian habit of attaching a bell to the big toe of a corpse for three days before interment.)

Angell had been anxious for some years to find a book that would do for horses what *Uncle Tom's Cabin* had done for slaves. 'Many times,' he wrote in his introduction to *Black Beauty*, 'have I called the attention of American writers to this matter and asked them to undertake it. At last the book has come to me: not from America but England.' A Miss Georgiana Kendall of New York sent Angell a copy of *Black Beauty* without comment, on 1 February 1890. Within twelve days of receiving the book he had solicited $265 from one friend to have the book electrotyped, and a larger sum from another to enable him to print an edition of 10,000. He then appealed for more funds in an article in *Our Dumb Friends*. He wrote:

> I want to print immediately a *hundred thousand copies*.
>
> I want the power to give *away thousands of these to drivers of horses*.
>
> I want to send a copy postpaid to the editors of each of about *thirteen thousand* American newspapers and magazines.

The appeal succeeded and dollars from wealthy Bostonians rolled in. The book was published on 1 April and by 1 July 70,000 copies had been given away[*] or sold at twelve cents a copy (postage eight cents extra) and a half-price copy at six cents was available. By the end of 1890, 216,000 copies of the book had been sold. Twenty years later the book was still selling at a rate of a quarter of a million copies a year.

---

[*] The habit of giving away copies of *Black Beauty* to drivers and stablemen was never as widespread in England as it was in the United States. Emma Saunders, however, whose philanthropic work lay among railwaymen at Temple Meads Station, gave a copy to the driver of every horse-drawn railway van and no doubt there were others like her.

Mr Angell was a salesman of genius. Nearly half the copies of *Black Beauty* that were distributed in the first two years were paid for by big business. Many magazines were induced to award them as premiums to their readers and the makers of Frank Miller Harness Dressing ('suitable for Harness, Buggy Tops, Saddles, Fly Nets, Travelling Bags, Military Equipments etc.') brought out fifteen tons of their own version of *Black Beauty*. Chapter headings in the Frank Miller edition were decorated with a row of four horses each wearing a rug that carried a word of the phrase 'Frank Miller's Harness Dressing'. Where there was a gap at the end of a chapter, an advertisement was inserted.

Mr Angell's own first edition did not look much less strange. It was about the size of the first English edition, but far less elegant, being bound in plain grey boards and printed on cheap paper now brown with age. The cover bore the title, *Black Beauty: his grooms and companions. By A. Sewell. The Uncle Tom's Cabin of the horse.* There were only two illustrations and neither had any connection with the text. But what the book lacked in illustration it made up for in advertisements; for kindness, this time, not saddle-soap. Many pages at the beginning and end of the book were devoted to propaganda. There was a reprint of the appeal from *Our Dumb Animals*, recommended procedure for meetings of the Band of Mercy, a legal definition of 'What is overloading a horse?' and a list of advertisements for tracts on subjects ranging from cattle transportation to Band of Mercy songs and hymns. Perhaps the strangest inclusion of all, in a book that is now considered suitable for children, was a set of instructions (illustrated) for the humane destruction of a horse, a dog and a cat.

In later editions Angell added a highly entertaining account by a Captain Codman of his vision of a heaven for the carriage horses of New York. 'I saw these friends … changing their shape and floating in the air … They were dragging their carriages over the clouds – but the carriages were empty. Yes, there must be a place for good horses and a place for bad men.' Still later two more illustrations were added. One was entitled 'Cruelty' and the other 'Happy Horse'.[*] They portrayed horses with and without the bearing-rein. There were no major changes in the text of the American edition. Important points

---

[*] Colthrop, Lee and Shephard Co., 1910.

were italicised, a favourite device of Angell's, and certain words were
'translated' so that bearing-rein became check-rein, blinker, blinder
and so on. In 1906 a dramatised version of the book appeared as
a result of a competition set by the tireless Angell. It was actually
staged in a Boston theatre 'by a powerful company' (whether equine
or human we do not know) with 'most careful attention to scenic
details' and concluded with 'an inspiring allegorical scene'.

GOOD BOOKS AND GOOD PLAYS

THE ORIGINAL ANNA SEWELL PRODUCTION

OF THE

GREAT HUMANE PLAY

Black Beauty

Dramatized by Justin Adams

The Dramatist of

QUINCY ADAMS SAWYER

from Anna Sewell's world-famous story, of which
**MILLIONS OF COPIES HAVE BEEN
SOLD AND READ**

A Four Act Play, introducing **Black Beauty** and her companions,
Merrylegs and **Ginger.**   Teaching a great moral lesson and inculcating
the love of dumb animals.

Presented by a Powerful Company

Staged with the Most Careful Attention to
Magnificent Scenic Details

Concluding with an

Inspiring Allegorical Scene

Under the Direction of

Chas. F. Atkinson and James Thatcher

Angell claimed that the book was flatteringly reviewed in 'not less than a thousand American papers' and admitted to only one hostile comment. This comment, which appeared in a leading Boston newspaper, was directed not against the author but against himself and accused him, quite correctly, of pirating the book, selling it at a quarter of its proper price and paying nothing to the author. Angell was quick to defend himself in a letter to the same newspaper. He made seven points in his defence, of which a selection are given below. (The italics are, of course, his own.)

1)   The author died *unmarried* shortly after the publication of the book.

2)   Her mother, a *widow,* died soon after.

3)   The English publisher paid Miss Sewell *just £20* for the book. By the payment of *£20* it became his property and *none but the English publisher gets a sixpence from the profits.*

7)   As there is no American copyright on this book, we must undersell every other publisher – if we wish to use it as a vehicle for carrying our propaganda into every home. Under Divine Providence, the sending of this book *Black Beauty,* into every American home may be … an important step in the progress not only of the American, but the World's humanity and civilization.

Although his thinking was somewhat muddled, his conclusions were probably correct. It is true that only Anna's publisher would have benefited from the phenomenal American sales, and it is equally true that Anna herself was more concerned to improve the lot of horses than to hand on large sums of money to her nieces and nephews. In fact, it seems possible that the success of the book in the United States had an effect on the English sales. Certainly it jolted the R.S.P.C.A. into adding their recommendation to the book. The words 'Recommended by the R.S.P.C.A.' appeared for the first time in the 1894 English edition. The Society lost many of its records during the Blitz and the circumstances which led to this inclusion are unknown, but it seems very probable that George T. Angell had something to do with it. He was a tireless traveller and twenty-five years earlier had persuaded the august body to start a sister publication to *Our Dumb Animals* entitled *Animal World.*

His account of the meeting at which he suggested the foundation of *Animal World* is worth recording.

> The meeting occupied three hours; the Lord Bishop of Gloucester and Bristol in the chair and a fine-looking body of elderly gentlemen around the table ... They seemed to me a dignified, cool and somewhat non-committal body ... One thing at the close struck me as very strange, and that was the question, *Who should move the vote of thanks?* It seemed to be regarded as a much more important matter than we consider it in America, but presently Field-Marshal Sir John Burgoyne, an aged gentleman, very near the head of the British army, slowly rose, and with the utmost dignity moved the vote of thanks. [*]

---

[*] Angell, George T., Autobiography.

8

THE BEARING-REIN

It has always been said that *Black Beauty* led to the abolition of the bearing-rein and this is essentially true. A contemporary admirer wrote, 'The testimony of those who mingle most among London drivers ... has been that no society ... has induced such humane treatment, as the influence and teaching gained by *Black Beauty*.'[*] However, like all emphatic historical statements, it requires quali-fying. Anna Sewell was neither the first nor the last campaigner in the field, although her appeal reached the largest and most impressionable section of the public.

As early as 1845 a book entitled *Horse-Emancipation; or, the Abolition of the Bearing-Rein*, was published by a horse-lover who signed him-self 'Philippos'. Philippos deplored the use of bearing-reins on the horse that pulled the stage coach and described them as the most 'injuriously-tormenting part of his gear' and the worst of 'the almost innumerable cruelties ... practised on his matchless frame'. No more voices were raised in defence of the silent sufferers until the six-ties when a refinement of the instrument, known as the gag, was introduced and described in detail by Mr Flower.

> Latterly a far more complicated and powerful instrument has come into fashion.
>
> This is the Bedouin, or Gag bearing-rein, which is attached to the top of the bridle. It is then passed through a swivel attached to the separate bearing-rein bit, which has nothing to do with the driving.

---

[*] Georges, Mary, op. cit.

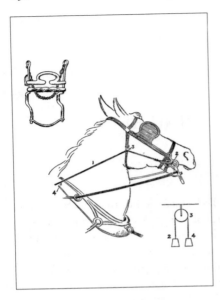

THE DISCOMFORT OF THE SIMPLE BEARING-REIN. The bearing-rein (1) is attached to the driving bit (at 2), passes through a ring (at 3) and is attached to the harness (at 4). This sketch and the one below is based on *Bits and Bearing-Reins* by Edmund Flower.

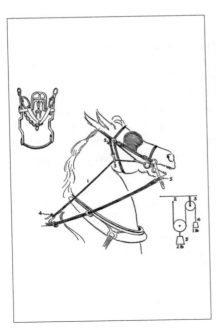

THE TORTURE OF THE GAG BEARING-REIN. The gag or Bedouin bearing-rein (1) is attached to the top of the bridle (at 2), then passed through a swivel attached to the separate bearing-rein bit, which has nothing to do with the driving bit. Thence it passes through the drop-ring (at 3) and is attached to the harness. The effect of this is to double the power by which it can be tightened since, according to a simple mechanical law, 1 lb. applied at 4 is equivalent to 2 lb. at 5. The coachman was unable to loosen this terrible bit for, separate as it was from the driving apparatus, it would fall out of the horse's mouth if not held in tightly.

Thence it passes through the drop-ring, and is attached to the pad and crupper as in the former case.

The effect of this is to double the power by which it can be tightened, for by mechanics we learn that 1 lb. applied at A is equivalent to 2 lbs. at B, a fact which every one can prove for himself.

Thus it is evident what force is brought to bear on the horse's mouth, a sufficiently sensitive organ, even when unencumbered by another heavy bit, with cruel cutting power.

Severe as is the simple bearing-rein, its evil is doubled by the gag system, for its elevating power is, as we have shown, doubled, nor can the coachman relax this terrible and dangerous gag-bit, for separate as it is from the driving apparatus, it would fall out of the horse's mouth, and to put it in again would take time and persuasion, or rather force.

Mr Flower was not the only horse-lover to raise an outcry against the gag bearing-rein. In the late sixties many veterinarians spoke out against it, some of them in the correspondence columns of *The Times*. It was in a letter to that paper in 1867 that Professor Pritchard of the Royal Veterinary College accused the bearing-rein of causing 'distortion of the windpipe to such a degree as to impede the respiration ever afterward'. Dr. Kitching of York wrote that 'Confinement of the head in a constrained position ... hinders the circulation of the blood in the head ... and causes head-aches', while Dr John Adam McBride, Professor of Veterinary Medicine at the Royal Agricultural College, gave these headaches more sinister names – 'Megrims,[*] apoplexy, coma, inflammation and softening of the brain'.

In the first years after the publication of *Black Beauty* the battle continued to be waged and the forces became more united. In 1883 five hundred British horse doctors signed a petition against tight bearing-reins. Three years later, Alfred Saunders, author of a manual called *Our Horses*, was able to report 'Bearing-reins are less used every year. Miss Sewell's *Black Beauty* and the energetic appeals and well told facts

---

[*] Megrims was a disease of the brain. Sir Moses Mainchance sold a horse suffering from the disease to the hero of Surtees' *Ask Mamma*. When an attack came on the animal spun in circles like a dog about to lie down.

of Mr. and Mrs. Flower on this subject have done wonders.' Yet even this humane writer was not averse to the use of a loose bearing-rein on certain occasions. 'When a lady has to drive a horse of doubtful docility, it is convenient to have a bearing-rein short enough to prevent a horse putting his head lower than he naturally carries it at his work.' It was not until 1914 that the R.S.P.C.A. finally persuaded undertakers, through their association, to abolish bearing-reins for funeral horses.

In America Mr Angell had a harder and more long-drawn-out battle to fight, for, in Boston, unlike London, the bearing-rein was worn by cab and omnibus horses and even by the teams pulling coal carts. The secretary of the Massachusetts Board of Agriculture, addressing a meeting of the Boston Music Hall in 1869 said, 'I have many times seen a team overladed with coal tugging up yonder Beacon Hill, straining every nerve, often plied with the lash, and sometimes with the toe of a cowhide boot, while the power of the too-willing horses was crippled by a useless and senseless check-rein.'

In America a third type of bearing-rein was sometimes used. It was called the Kimball Jackson overhead check, and although it was only correctly used on trotting horses it was in fact often seen on carriage horses as well. The overhead check, as its name implies, came down over the top of the horse's head and forced its muzzle up in the air instead of tucking it in to his chest like the ordinary bearing-rein. The Poor Rich Horse, the subject of a pamphlet put out by the American Humane Education Society in 1900,[*] was condemned to wear the overhead check.

> Driven by a tall coachman with high hat and white gloves, he looked very gay as he pranced up to the door of an elegant establishment on the avenue. The breast of the noble creature was covered with foam, and he held his head very high. His mouth was stretched wide open, and he tossed his head up and down and back and forth, and pawed the air with his fore feet. So high were his eyes – almost looking toward the sky – that he scarcely seemed able to see a fat old dray horse that stood near regarding him as belonging to another set than his, entirely.

---

[*] *The Rich Poor Horse and the Poor Rich Horse*, Fairchild, Mrs C.M., American Humane Education Society, 1900.

The Poor Rich Horse told the Rich Poor Horse, whose head was unconfined, how it felt to wear the overdraw check. 'My harness is a – perfect torture to me. My eyes are almost blinded by the glare of the sun, and my neck aches and my head throbs.' On hearing this, the 'compassionate attaché of the dray' decided he was after all the more fortunate of the two, in spite of the fact that he had to haul a heavy load of dirt about the city instead of a 'pretty doll's wagon'.

Yet the overhead check continued to be used. Mr Merwin, the author of a book entitled *Road, Track and Stable*, defended it hotly.

> The check-rein [he protested] as all horsemen know, is often essential to the safety of life and limb. People who write tracts or letters to the newspapers condemning it *in toto* have no knowledge of horseflesh beyond what they derive from an acquaintance with same sedate family nag of mature years. If they had a stableful of young horses to exercise in harness in winter weather, they would change their minds on this point. Many gay horses can be driven in perfect safety provided they wear check-reins, especially if they wear the over-draw check; whereas the same horses without checks would be likely at any moment to put their heads down and run away, or, if they had a touch of deviltry, to kick up behind.

By 1905 the gag bearing-rein had become rare in the United States. ('Only the very newest dollars ... permit this turkey-cock style of harnessing.[*]') But the ordinary bearing-rein continued as popular as ever. It was emphatically recommended by a woman named, unbelievably, Belle Beach.[**] Miss Beach was a New Yorker and a stickler for etiquette. She had no use for people who failed to cover the buckles of their harness when in mourning or who used a loin strap when not accompanied by a servant. For her, the chief use of the bearing-rein was to preserve appearances.

> Bearing-reins are particularly necessary in pair driving, [she wrote] for however well matched two horses may be in appearance, they

---

[*] *Riding and Driving*, Price Collier, New York, 1905.
[**] Beach, Belle, *Riding and Driving for Women*, New York, 1912.

seldom carry their heads naturally at just the same height. In that case the horse who naturally carries his head high should have his bearing-rein quite loose and the other quite tight, so that their heads may be at the same height. Nothing looks worse than to see two horses in a pair carrying their heads one low and one high. Most of the best authorities on driving also say, and I have no doubt that it is true, that bearing-reins keep a tired horse up and make his going easy; they also keep him from nodding.

Miss Beach disapproved of the use of the overdraw check on carriage horses, not because it was cruel but because it was incorrect. In fact it is still in use in at least one American community today. The Amish, a religious sect living in the United States, disapprove of machinery on principle and drive about in buggies. I have seen a line of these buggies drawn up outside a supermarket and in each case the rough-coated nag had its head held up by the overdraw check. I once asked an Amish friend why he did this and he gave exactly the same reason as Mr Merwin did in 1893. It made the horse less likely to run away with you.

Another aspect of cruelty that was greatly alleviated by *Black Beauty* was the traffic in decrepit horses. Anna Sewell was not exaggerating when she described cases of worn-out cripples being sold for a few pounds and worked until they literally dropped between the shafts. It happened all the time on both sides of the Atlantic. Mr Angell described cases of veterans changing hands for as little as thirty-nine cents and being flogged up and down the streets of Brighton, Massachusetts. In England the R.S.P.C.A. fought these abuses with more vigour than they did the bearing-rein (perhaps because they were associated more with the lower than the upper classes) and their historian, Mr Moss, has ascribed a large part of their success to Anna Sewell's book.[*] Probably the last case of cruelty to be directly remedied by *Black Beauty* was in 1924. In that year a Texas cowpuncher, arraigned for ill-treating his pony, was sentenced to gaol for one month during which period he was ordered to read *Black Beauty* at least three times.

---

[*] Moss, A.W., *The Valiant Crusade*, Cassell.

Inevitably at this stage one asks the question, 'Is there still cruelty to horses?' The obvious reply is, 'No, because there aren't any horses.' One is reminded of Mr Angell who, after a European tour, commented that the Venetians treated their horses better than anyone else and then admitted that there were only seven horses in Venice, and these belonged to a riding school. The horses in Britain today, like the horses in Venice a hundred years ago, are kept almost solely for recreation and many of the forms of cruelty which Anna Sewell described have ceased automatically. Of the 825 convictions obtained by the R.S.P.C.A. for cruelty to animals in 1968, only thirty-eight were for cruelty to horses, ponies and donkeys. Figures for the same year in the United States are not easily available but the number of convictions in Massachusetts (with a population of six million) was only two. It is possible, however, that animal societies in that State are less vigilant. It is interesting to note that one of the two cases involved a gun. A man shot two of his neighbour's horses, killing one of them, because they strayed into his garden.

As our society becomes more affluent we can expect a rise in the horse population and possibly a rise in the convictions for cruelty to horses. Already the proliferation of inadequate riding schools designed to cash in on the new craze for riding among teenagers, has caused ears to prick in horsey circles and in 1964 a Conservative M.P., Sir Jocelyn Lucas, won parliamentary time to introduce a Riding Establishments Bill. Animal welfare organisations rallied to his support. The Horses and Ponies Protection Association conducted a survey of 1,200 schools. In well over a quarter the Association found the animals neglected and little or no supervision of riders. Some horses and ponies were in such a terrible condition that they had to be destroyed as soon as they could be bought from the offending riding school. Day-to-day control was often in the hands of teenagers. In one case a girl of fifteen had opened a school in a field without stables or buildings. The ponies, all unbroken two-year-olds, were totally unsuitable for teaching children and were fed on potatoes from a fish and chip shop owned by the girl's father.

Affluence has also led to a rise in private ownership of horses among classes of people who have not kept horses before and cases of cruelty have resulted from their ignorance. One hears of accounts of ponies being kept in suburban toolsheds and fed on household scraps. The practice of buying sets of horseshoes through mail-order houses and tacking them on at home is becoming more common. Several cases of lameness have resulted from a nail being driven into the quick of the hoof by a do-it-yourself blacksmith.

In the United States, where there is more money, it seems to me that there is more cruelty. Many Americans regard a horse as a status symbol, an expensive toy to add to the row of shining automobiles in the garage. They ride him when the weather is good and they are in the mood. Otherwise they leave him in the stable – often for weeks at a time. And that stable is sometimes filthy and devoid of water for many hours in the day. At the barn where I used to rent a horse in Massachusetts a three-year-old did not leave his stall more than six times between August and May (the period I was there). I would often hear him kicking the walls of his box in a frenzy of frustration when he heard my horse leaving the stable. I heard of a case of a neighbour's husband who left his stallion behind when he deserted her. The animal could not legally be sold and had not been out of his stall for three years.

For many Americans in the Middle West and beyond, the horse is tied up with the great American cowboy dream. In Illinois, the only State besides Massachusetts where I have lived for any length of time, the horse-owner is often a manual worker. At five p.m. he stops filling the tanks of cars at a gas station, dons a wide hat and sets off for the city fairground where he keeps his horse. Once there he vaults into his heavy western saddle and sets off at a gallop only to pull up in a cloud of dust fifty yards on. Stopping at speed is one of the feats required by contestants in a sport called 'Western Games'. When expertly performed by a quarter horse of the type used for ranching, these games are wonderful to watch. The horse is so well trained that it can be ridden on a loose rein and guided almost entirely by its rider's legs. Just occasionally, when poorly trained or out of condition, vicious spurs and a savage bit are used to achieve the same result. I have seen a white horse at the end of such a performance with sides stained red. The lot of broncos in small travelling rodeos is not much happier and a society exists to combat this evil in Colorado.

In America too, mutilations are still practised for purposes of the show ring that have been illegal in this country for many decades. A breed of horse known as the saddle-bred (a riding-horse with the exaggerated high action of the hackney) is expected to hold its tail vertically when performing in the ring. By a pcocess called 'tail setting' the tendons at the base of the tail are severed and the tail is held up day and night by an elaborate harness.

Cases of cruelty through real neglect, however, are rare on both sides of the Atlantic and the few ill-used animals dwindle to insignificance beside the number of healthy, well-cared for ones. One likes to suppose that these owe something of their well-being to a book that taught their owners to turn pale at the sight of a stall without water or a groom entering a stable with a lighted cigarette in his mouth.

9

REPRINT AND FILM

Over the years Black Beauty had proved a horse remarkable not only for speed but for stamina. Few of the improving books written a century ago are still to be found on sale. Yet any bookshop on either side of the Atlantic will produce several copies of *Black Beauty*;* probably two paperbacks, a cheap hard-cover version and a couple of 'classics'. Woolworths is rarely without a copy.

Black Beauty has joined the horse immortals. He ranks with Alexander the Great's Bucephalus, Don Quixote's Rosinante, Dick Turpin's Black Bess and Pegasus, the winged horse of the Muses. His book was described in the twenties as 'Unquestionably the most successful animal story ever written' (Vincent Starrett). In 1932 the author of one of its many introductions wrote, 'While animals are loved ... the world will not readily let it die.' In 1958 Roger Lancelyn Green conceded that it was still 'the classic among horse stories even in this age of "pony books"'.

Black Beauty has proved one of the world's bestsellers. Margaret Sewell, a woman as given to accuracy and understatement as her aunt, claimed that it was the sixth most popular book in the English language. The sales to date have been estimated at thirty million, a remarkable figure when you consider that the entire works of Dickens are estimated to have sold little over forty million. Since

---

* It is of interest to note that the book was banned for a short period in South Africa about 1956. The erroneous association of ideas is perhaps understandable if not forgivable. The newest Negro model agency in New York is called Black Beauty.

Jarrold's copyright expired in 1927 almost every famous name in British publishing has been associated with the book and barely a year has passed without a new edition appearing. The only exception was the period of the Second World War when even the Everyman edition, kept in print with enormous difficulty, was out of stock from July 1945 to February 1947 because of the paper famine. To compensate, no less than three new editions appeared later in 1947. In 1954 the book was for sale in thirty-five editions from twenty-five English and American publishers.[*]

Strangely enough, *Black Beauty* had to wait until the First World War for a worthy illustrator. Although it was written in the age of the great illustrators, none of these was invited to embellish it and it was a woman, Lucy Kemp Welsh, who, in 1915, drew the pictures that for me will always be associated with the book. The Dent edition in which they appeared was reissued in 1950 and contains both line drawings and colour pictures, but to my mind the line drawings are superior. Miss Kemp Welsh has a real feeling for horses. Not only could she draw them accurately but, while fitting them into a decorative design, she never allowed them to lose their vitality and movement. There were other illustrated Black Beauties before this. The first was Jarrold's 1894 edition, copiously decorated with ink and wash sketches by the popular illustrator, John Beer. To me these sketches are unattractive and the one depicting the remains of horse after the stable fire is quite repellent. Cecil Aldin's colour plates for the sumptuous Jarrold 1912 edition are certainly superior. In 1932 Wheelwright produced some attractive drawings for Harrap, but modern artists have produced little of note and much that is grossly inaccurate. In a recent American edition Squire Gordon approaches the flooded bridge bereft of John Manly, the empty beer dray that was Captain's undoing is loaded high with barrels, and Farmer Thoroughgood wears dungarees complete with bib and braces. Of modern English illustrators, Lionel Edward is the best known, but he cannot topple Miss Kemp Welsh from her pinnacle.

---

[*] I am indebted to A. A. Dent, the author of an article in the *East Anglian Magazine* entitled 'Miss Sewell of Norfolk', for several facts about the publishing history of *Black Beauty*.

Needless to say the book has been translated into all the major European languages. In Spanish *Black Beauty* has become *Azabache*, in French *Prince Noir* and in Italian *Re Moro*. In the Italian edition, which came out under ecclesiastical auspices, Mr Blomefield the vicar was converted into a doctor to avoid the scandal of a priest with children.

Early in its career *Black Beauty* was also translated into many Asiatic languages, as can be seen from an article which appeared in the *American National Magazine*.

> These include Arabic, printed at Beirut, Syria; Hindustani, Lucknow, 1895; Hindustani, Calcutta, 1900; Telegu, Madras, 1898; Italian, Florence, 1896; Italian, Turin, 1904; Greek (modern), Athens, 1894; French, Lausanne, 1902; and Swedish, Orebro, 1894. Besides these editions, printed abroad, the book has been published in German at Cincinnati, in Spanish at New York, and in Italian at Boston. Only the other day I was told by a traveller to China that she had seen the story printed as a serial in a native magazine at Shanghai. I have no doubt that other translations have been made which have not come to the attention of the American Humane Education Society.

In 1908 Jarrolds were proud to announce that 'it is being done into the Kaffir tongue with a view to its circulation among the native races of South Africa'. The book was also translated into Japanese.

More recently *Black Beauty* has benefited by the modern mass communication media. In England alone the story has been broadcast three times and televised once. Dramatised versions have been put on gramophone records. The most recent, an L.P. brought out by Music for Pleasure, came out as recently as 1965. And it has received that final accolade of success for a book today – it has been filmed; three times to be exact, in 1921, 1933 and 1946. The most recent production was from Twentieth Century Fox under the direction of Nosseck, starring Mona Freeman. Lovers of *Black Beauty* will be interested in the story line. Squire Wendon, attempting to raise his motherless daughter Anne, presents her with a colt Black Beauty, in the hope that by disciplining him, she may learn to discipline herself. Passing through Birtwick Farm, Bill Dixon, a young American, arouses Anne's interest by expressing his hope of finding a very beautiful young colt when he returns to England in two years.

Anne breaks the colt herself, and is just anticipating the fun she will have riding him when her father decides to send her to finishing school. Anne rebels, preferring to stay with Black Beauty. When Bill returns, however, this time with Lady Evelyn Carrington, his attitude brings Anne to realise that she is still considered a child. To 'show them', Anne mounts Ginger, a high-spirited horse, and puts on a reckless display of horsemanship which results in a spill that leaves her unconscious. Bill madly rides Black Beauty miles for a doctor. Anne recovers, but Black Beauty's legs are badly injured. With the romance between Bill and Evelyn seemingly developing, Anne decides to enter finishing school, tearfully bidding Black Beauty goodbye.

When Anne is gone, Squire Wendon orders that Black Beauty be shot to spare the horse further suffering, but a groom spirits him to another farm in the hope that he will recover before Anne's return.

Anne, now radiantly beautiful, returns from finishing school. Bill is bowled over. Discovering that Black Beauty has been sold as a carriage horse, Anne starts a frantic search for him. Bill sets off after her. After investigating one false lead after another, Anne finally learns that Black Beauty has eventually been sold to a coal merchant, but when she reaches the latter's barn she is horrified to find it in flames. She impulsively rushes in to save Black Beauty but is overcome by smoke. Bill arrives and dashes into the building. Finding Anne, he places her across Black Beauty's back and leads them both to safety.

The persistent popularity of *Black Beauty* becomes all the more remarkable when one considers the fate of its contemporaries. When Jarrold brought out the first edition they classed it as an improving book and advertised similar ones at the back of it. *Claims for Kindness to God's Creatures, Emily Milman: Or, the Little Sunbeam of the Farmhouse, The Merryweathers, a Temperance Story for the Young, The Happy Village and How it Became So* (this last was by Anna's aunt, Maria Wright). Where are they now? As dead and forgotten as the works of Mary Sewell herself.

Indeed, of the hundreds of books written with a humanitarian motive in the last century probably only a handful are now read. The titles that spring to mind are Charles Kingsley's *The Water Babies*, a book intended to inculcate kindness to children of all classes, and *Uncle Tom's Cabin* by Harriet Beecher Stowe. And of these two one suspects that the former survived not because of its good intentions but because it belongs to that timeless category, the fairy tale. At this point it is tempting to enquire what Kingsley would have thought of *Black Beauty*. When it appeared his tireless pen had been stilled for three years. It is just possible that the book would have been too sad for him for he was a soft-hearted man. *Uncle Tom's Cabin* he was unable to finish. 'It was too painfully good, as I found before I had read half a volume.' And he preferred horses to negroes.

Black Beauty started a new category of book, the animal story. Of course there had been animal stories before. Anna as a child was familiar with the talking animals of La Fontaine (and indeed *Black Beauty* is a kind of extended fable, for in it animals talk and a moral is drawn). In her own century James Greenwood wrote a series of books about talking South African animals, including *Bear King*, and in 1861 Ballantyne's *The Dog Crusoe* appeared. But these books only amounted to a handful.

There was, however, a book published six years before *Black Beauty* that one feels certain Anna must have read. It was George Macdonald's *At the Back of the North Wind*, the haunting story of little Diamond, the boy who was swept off by the North Wind and, between magical adventures with her, drove his father's cab through the streets of London. The cab-horse, like the boy, was called Diamond, and there is a scene where he is overheard in conversation with his stable-mate which is extraordinarily reminiscent of *Black Beauty*. There are other points of similarity between the two stories, like the scene where the horse Diamond, disfigured by hard work, is recognised by his old groom. The story of George Macdonald's cabman and his son closely resembles that of Anna Sewell's. They also had a favourite regular customer, preferred to risk bronchitis to taking shelter in their own cab, had a rush to catch a train (at King's Cross Station this time) and regarded tea and coffee as superior to hard liquor. At the end of the story they, like Jerry Barker and his family, are whirled off to a happy home in the country.

At the Back of the North Wind, however, was not primarily an animal story and of the predecessors of *Black Beauty* in this genre it is hard to find one that could be definitely said to have influenced it. Its imitators, however, are legion. Within less than twenty years of its publication Jarrold could offer a complete animal book list, including

Uses and Abuses of Domestic Animals (uniform with *Black Beauty*), *To Central Africa on an Iceberg* (the adventures of a white bear), *Shireen and her Friends* (pages from the life of a persian cat), *Sable and White* and *Beautiful Joe*. These last two were autobiographies of dogs.

Sable and White, published in 1894, was the work of the enormously prolific retired naval surgeon, William Gordon Stables. He was an eccentric who was often seen in Fleet Street in full Highland dress and spent the last twenty-five years of his life touring England in a horse-drawn caravan which he preferred to call a land-yacht. He mostly wrote adventure stories for boys which were published in the *Boy's Own Paper* along with his advice column recommending cold baths and hot porridge as cures for almost everything.

The adventures of Luath the Scottish show collie are extraordinarily similar to those of Black Beauty. His first memory also was of a green meadow with a stream at the bottom and he also learnt that the rich are not always happy for as a show dog he endured torments from constant travel. After a fire he got separated from his master and embarked upon a series of adventures which included a spell with a vivisectionist. He even met an equivalent of poor Ginger in the person of a champion mastiff who died of too much showing. 'His coat grew harsh and his body thin, and there was a melancholy in his once bright eye that was painful to witness by anyone who had known him in the heyday of his beauty and glory.' Luath, like Black Beauty, ends his days dreaming under the trees in his first home. Dr Stables did not write well, his humour was laborious, his descriptions of cruelty harrowing and his sentimentality unbearable. On this last point it is sufficient to quote the titles of three of his chapters. They were 'Cold in the Beautiful Sunshine', 'Never, Oh, Never Again' and 'Don't Die and Leave Me Jim'. The book, understandably, went out of print in 1902.

The author of *Beautiful Joe*, Mrs Marshall Saunders of Halifax, Nova Scotia, freely admitted taking *Black Beauty* as her model. Indeed, her book was the winning entry in a competition set by Mr Angell to produce a canine equivalent of *Black Beauty*. Hezekiah Butterworth, one of the judges, explained the aims of the competition in a preface to the book. 'The wonderfully successful book, entitled *Black Beauty* came like a living voice out of the animal kingdom. After the ready welcome that it received, and the good it has accomplished, it followed naturally that someone should write a book to interpret the life of a dog to the humane feeling of the world.' In the first chapter of his book Joe notices his mistress laughing and crying over 'a little book that she says is a story of a horse's life'.

The book in fact bears less relation to *Black Beauty* than does *Sable and White*, for Joe starts in a cruel home (where a milkman cuts off his ears) and graduates to a kind one with a minister's family. It is understandable, however, that Joe won a prize from Mr Angell for he devoted his 266 pages to barking out advice on the care of animals from cows to canaries, much of it culled from Mr Angell's own writings. The book was quite successful and deserved to be, for the advice it gave was accurate and interlarded with entertaining anecdotes about animals obviously based on life. Furthermore, it was blessedly free from sentimentality. A new edition came out in the thirties.

10

CHILDREN'S CLASSIC

We are left with the task of explaining why *Black Beauty* has lasted so well. For me its charm is summed up in its opening sentence. 'The first place that I can well remember was a large pleasant meadow with a pond of clear water in it. Some shady trees leaned over it and water lilies grew at the deep end.' To lovers of the book these lines are deeply evocative. They speak of the doomed English countryside that even in Anna Sewell's day was under threat of demolition. *Black Beauty* is a book that smells of fields after rain and this is one of the reasons why it has lasted.

Strangely enough there are few actual descriptions of landscape. One of them occurs, symbolically, after Reuben Smith's fall. 'It was a calm, sweet April night; there were no sounds but a few low notes of a nightingale, and nothing moved but the white clouds near the moon and a brown owl that flitted over the hedge. It made me think of the summer nights long ago, when I used to lie beside my mother in the green pleasant meadow at Farmer Grey's.' For vividness combined with brevity this could hardly be bettered. And this brings us to the second reason for *Black Beauty*'s excellence; its economy with words. Of its forty-nine chapters few are more than five pages long. The style, no doubt because of the circumstances under which the book was written, is pared to the bone, a great selling-point to juvenile readers. Children also enjoy the opportunity to identify. Anna Sewell spirits them inside the gleaming hide of her horse. They learn what it is to go on four legs, to have ears that prick and a tail to swish off flies. They feel the cold steel of the bit between their teeth, the stiff crupper under their tails and the weight of the carriage that follows them everywhere whether they like it or not.

Not only are they inside the horse but they're *on* his side, for *Black Beauty* is a strongly partisan book. The world is made up of good and bad people and we may know them by their treatment of animals. This attitude is summed up in one of James Howard's sermons (and it is probably what makes the endless sermonising of the grooms at Birtwick bearable to modern children). Cruelty, said Howard, was the devil's own trademark, and if we saw anyone who took pleasure in cruelty we might know who he belonged to, for the devil was a murderer from the beginning, and a tormentor to the end. On the other hand, where we saw people who loved their neighbours, and were kind to man and beast, we might know that was God's mark.

Black Beauty is a cathartic book; it purifies through pity and fear. The first comment of almost everyone who reads the book is, 'It's so sad!' And most children like sad books. 'Go on, I like it,' was the cry of a small boy of my acquaintance when his mother stopped in the middle of a chapter, alarmed by the deluge of tears the story was producing. Between the ages of eight and eleven I read it regularly four times a year for the same reason.

And the book is exciting as well as sad. Many times during the story the reader holds his breath in suspense. Will Black Beauty escape from the burning stable? Will Jerry outbid the loud-voiced brute who wants to buy him at the horse fair? Will he die on Ludgate Hill? The chase after Lady Anne on her runaway horse Lizzie is as vivid as any in children's literature.

> For about a mile and a half the road ran straight, and then bent to the right, after which it divided into two roads. Long before we came to the bend she was out of sight. Which way had she turned? A woman was standing at her garden gate, shading her eyes with her hand, and looking eagerly up the road. Scarcely drawing the rein, Blantyre shouted, 'Which way?' 'To the right!' cried the woman, pointing with her hand, and away we went up the right-hand road. Then for a moment we caught sight of her; another bend and she was hidden again. Several times we caught glimpses, and then lost them. We scarcely seemed to gain ground on them at all. An old road-mender was standing near a heap of stones, his shovel dropped and his hands raised. As we came near he made a sign to speak. Blantyre drew the rein a little. 'To the common, to the common, sir; she has

turned off there.' I knew this common very well;[*] it was for the most part very uneven ground, covered with heather and dark green furze bushes, with here and there a scrubby thorn tree; there were also open spaces of fine short grass, with ant hills and hole-turns everywhere; the worst place I ever knew for a headlong gallop.

We had hardly turned on the common, when we caught sight again of the green habit flying on before us. My lady's hat was gone, and her long brown hair was streaming behind her. Her head and body were thrown back, as if she were pulling with all her remaining strength, and as if that strength were nearly exhausted. It was clear that the roughness of the ground had very much lessened Lizzie's speed, and there seemed a chance that we might overtake her. While we were on the highroad, Blantyre had given me my head; but now, with a light hand and a practised eye, he guided me over the ground in such a masterly manner that my pace was scarcely slackened, and we were decidedly gaining on them.

About halfway across the heath there had been a wide dike recently cut, and the earth from the cutting was cast up roughly on the other side. Surely this would stop them! But no; with scarcely a pause Lizzie took the leap, stumbled among the rough clods and fell. Blantyre groaned, 'Now, Auster, do your best!' He gave me a steady rein, I gathered myself well together and with one determined leap cleared both dike and bank.

Motionless among the heather, with her face to the earth, lay my poor young mistress.

To children the practical nature of the book is attractive. The tips on grooming, care of diseased hooves and correct procedure if a horse falls are eagerly stored away for future use. And they appreciate its lack of sentimentality. Anna Sewell makes no bones about how a horse should end its life. It should be shot. The kindly Jerry puts a 'sure bullet' through Captain's head after the accident rather than sell 'a good old servant into hard work' and there is no talk of horse heavens or ethereal cab-horses. Perhaps the quality one admires most in Anna Sewell was her refusal to allow even one pale-haired little girl

---

[*] The original of this common was probably Buxton Heath, near Dudwick House.

to die of tuberculosis. The temptation was too much for almost all her contemporaries, including Harriet Beecher Stowe, whose child heroine is inevitably borne away by the 'soft insidious killer'.

Sentiments like these have rendered the vast bulk of Victorian children's books unpalatable to the present generation. Perhaps a subsidiary reason for *Black Beauty*'s long life is that it is free of them. It remains to be seen whether the book will survive the next hundred years as well as it has survived the last.

APPENDIX I

OTHER BRANCHES OF THE SEWELL FAMILY

The Norfolk Sewells do not appear to have been connected with other well-known families of the same name. No amount of research can establish a relationship between them and the Anglo-Dutch historian of Quakerism, William Sewel, whose book, published in 1720, made such a deep impression on Charles Lamb. (William was the son of a Kidderminster Brownist who emigrated to Holland to escape persecution.) Neither do they appear to have been connected with the Cumberland Sewells whose records go back to 1549. A branch of this family moved to the Isle of Wight and produced a remarkable group of brothers and a sister who were Anna's contemporaries. They were William Sewell, founder of Radley College, James Edward Sewell, Warden of New College, Robert Clarke Sewell, first Prime Minister of New Zealand, and Elizabeth Missing Sewell, the prolific tractarian novelist, author of *Amy Herbert* and other best-selling rivals to the books of Charlotte M. Yonge. From the Cumberland Sewells also were descended the banking Sewells of Manchester. There were also Sewells (or Shewells) in Gloucestershire from the sixteenth to the eighteenth centuries, and in Bedfordshire, where Sewell is a place-name.

According to the author of *The Sewells in the New World*, the American Sewells (or Sewalls) are descended from a landed family who lived in Warwickshire in the first half of the sixteenth century. Henry Sewell sailed for Boston in 1634 to avoid taxation and religious intolerance under Charles I and settled at Newport. His son Samuel, Chief Justice of Massachusetts, was the first and most distinguished of the many legal men produced by the family. Samuel had some of the characteristics of the Norfolk Sewells for he was a man of high principles and great moral courage. He was the judge in the famous trial of the witches of Salem. After condemning nineteen witches to death, he retired to contemplate and emerged, unrecognisable, to publicly abjure his error in church. He never made another public appearance if he could avoid it and so great was his influence that another witch was never executed in the United States, although the practice continued in England for some years.

All Anna Sewell's close relatives on her father's side were descended from her grandfather William Sewell for, although he had two brothers and three sisters, none of them had children and only one of them, yet another Abraham (more commonly known as Abram) married. His bride was Mary Langley, otherwise known as 'pretty Miss Langley', an heiress. William's younger brother, Philip, and his three sisters 'lived and died in single blessedness'. Philip was a partner in a large water-mill at West Acre, on the River Nar, near Swaffham, and when he retired went to live with his sisters at Wereham. All 'lived to be well advanced in years' (Philip was ninety-one when he died) and left a name behind them that was 'both honoured and respected'.

APPENDIX II

THE SEWELL COAT OF ARMS

The coat of arms born by the Warwickshire Sewells, who go back to 1500, was 'Sable; a chevron between three bees, volant, Argent'.

But as in the archives of the Herald's College this device appears in the name of the Girlingtons who had applied for and received a formal patent before the Sewells did, some branches of the Sewell registered other coats of arms which, however, include the bees.

APPENDIX III

WILL OF ANNA SEWELL

This is the last Will and Testament of me Anna Sewell of Catton near Norwich. I appoint my dear Brother Philip Edward Sewell, my Nephew John Wright Sewell, my Niece Margaret Amie Sewell to be the Executors and Trustees of this my will and I desire that after payment of my just debts and funeral expenses a sum of twenty pounds be provided and to be paid away in small weekly sums to such of those poor people as I now assist as may then require it and that a legacy of nineteen guineas each be paid to my dear friend Margaret Taylor, to my cousin James Hunton and to my friend Mrs. Eyles and that my said Executors hold the remainder of my property or the proceeds of it in trust to pay the income arising from it to my dear Mother during her life should she survive me and after her death that the income be employed as my executors judge best for the comfort of my dear Father should he survive my dear Mother and require it and after the death of my dear Mother and Father that they divide my property or its proceeds in equal shares among those of my dear nieces and nephews the children of my Brother Philip and his dear Wife Sarah Sewell as shall then be living and I hereby revoke all former wills made by me. My property now consists of 15 shares in the London and County Bank and Co., £600 Utica and Ithica Railway Bonds, £100 Toronto Water Works Bond and some money in my Brother Philip's hands.
Anna Sewell

Signed and delivered as the last will of the above named Anna Sewell on the 11th of April 1878 we both being present at the same time with her. Lucy Edith Sewell. Fanny Eliza Mortimer.

INDEX